Contents

Preface   vii

1. I'm the Greatest, Yes Sirree, That's All You'll Ever
   Hear from Me!   3
2. Falsity without Deception: As Possible As the Law
   Says, but Not As Probable   5
3. Puffery: Used Because It Works, Legalized Because
   It Doesn't   12
4. The Roots of Sellerism   27
5. Warranty: How Much Promise Do You Find
   in a Promise?   47
6. Misrepresentation: How Much Lying Do You Find
   in a Falsehood?   62
7. Opinion and Value Statements and Puffery:
   Avoiding Fact and Keeping Sellerism Alive   68
8. The Federal Trade Commission: Accelerating the
   Consumerist Trend   90
9. Reasonable Consumers or Other Consumers?
   How the FTC Decides   113
10. The FTC and Puffery: Some Wins and Some Losses
    in the Fight for Consumerism   124
11. Additional Kinds of Puffery, Beginning with
    Obvious Falsity   139
12. Puffing with Social and Psychological Claims   151
13. Puffing with Literally Misdescriptive Names   158
14. Puffing with Mock-Ups   167
15. Puffery's Immunity Should Be Eliminated   176

Notes   197
Table of Cases   228
Index   235

Preface

       In this second edition, published nineteen years after the first, the most obvious updating comes in the new examples of puffery. That is also the most trivial change, however, since the "new" are merely more of the same old thing. As such, they give continuing support to my earlier argument that advertisers surely believe, whether they care to admit it or not, that puffery works.

       Among changes I find more significant are the characterizations in chapter 3 of several distinct types of puffery, some making stronger claims than others, which I had not the wit to recognize earlier. I use the difference to counter the argument that some puffs are innocuous, a point that advertisers can be counted upon to make in an attempt to deflect discussion from the equally evident point that so many others are quite the opposite.

       By thus observing across the ensuing years the responses that advertisers, regulators, and consumers have made to my criticisms, I have been able to develop what I feel is a stronger critique in this edition. For example, much evidence on how consumers react to puffery is now available from researchers who have done empirical studies on the topic. Some of their work originated, gratifyingly, in response to the first edition of this book. Other support comes from a group of lawyers who, upon rewriting a specific area of the law, are currently questioning puffery much as I have.

       The complete rewriting of this edition's final chapter reflects those and other contributions of information and analysis not available earlier. Thus, while the entire book has been rewritten or reedited at least lightly, the biggest changes occur in chapters 3 and 15, the latter replacing the original last two chapters. I have dropped the original chapter 8, for reasons given at the end of chapter 7, and have incorporated the content of the original chapter 12 into adjoining chapters. The original chapter 15 is now presented in two parts, in chapters 13 and 14.

Since the first edition I have widened my study of questionable ad claims. I examine several types, in addition to puffery, in *The Tangled Web They Weave*, 1994, also from the University of Wisconsin Press. My analysis of those other types, however, shows that they exist through advertiser and regulator attitudes that were developed first to deal with puffery. As puffery goes, so have gone the rest. Thus the analysis offered here remains the key to understanding why so many of today's advertising claims are deceptive at worst and uninformative at best.

THE GREAT AMERICAN BLOW-UP

1

I'm the Greatest, Yes Sirree, That's All You'll Ever Hear from Me!

The book you are about to read is a superior piece of work. It demonstrates the sheerest true excellence in its treatment of one of the outstandingly important topics of our time. You will find every moment informative and entertaining to a degree you have never before encountered in the world of fine literature. This much-applauded volume has earned for its author a rightful place as one of the top writers on the contemporary scene.

The paragraph you have just read is the purest baloney, and it is precisely the topic of this book. It is puffery. It is the pretentious opinion of salesmen and advertisers, exaggerating their wares, magnifying value, quality, and attractiveness to the limits of plausibility, and beyond. It is false, and I know it is false; I do not believe it. If you had believed it, and bought this book because you relied upon the belief, you would have gotten less than you bargained for in the marketplace. You would have been cheated.

And you would have been cheated legally. The law does not acknowledge that such claims lie to you or deceive you. Even though you can't always be sure that Visa is "everywhere you want to be," the law says such statements are permissible. State Farm isn't "all you need to know about insurance," but State Farm may claim so without fear of prosecution. Gillette may not be "the best a man can get," and the Ford Explorer may not be "the best the world has to offer." There's no guarantee that "if it's got to be clean it's got to be Tide," that AT&T is "the best in the business," or that "the Colonel's way is still the best way." Century 21 may not "set the standards for real estate," but that doesn't mean you can "expect the best" from Coldwell Banker, either.

Yet sales pitches of that sort, puffery, which make up a considerable proportion of the claims made in the marketplace, are not against the law. Rather, they are children of the law. Our government regulators conclude that even though such puffs are false, they are not deceptive. They say puffery does not burden consumers with untrue beliefs that affect their purchasing decisions, except for the occasional out-of-step individual who acts unreasonably and therefore deserves no protection. The law assumes most consumers will act reasonably, which means they will automatically distrust puffery, will neither believe it nor rely upon it, and therefore cannot be deceived or hurt by it.

Without a doubt the law just described is as pure a piece of baloney as puffery itself is. This book argues that puffery often deceives, and that the regulations that have made it legal are unjustified. That is because the rules saying these falsities are nondeceptive and therefore legal are based on incorrect assumptions about the facts of human behavior and therefore on incorrect reliance on the legal precedents from which they supposedly derive. This book is about the circumstances that originated and have maintained such strange regulations and have contributed thereby to the unhappiness with which today's consumers view the marketplace. It is the story of legalized lying.

We live in an age when standards in the marketplace need to rise. Outright deceits by sellers were once regarded as acceptable behavior, but today they should not be. Although the consumerism trend has removed most of them, the job is not yet complete. Puffery is the unwelcome residue of the seller behavior that modern law has otherwise replaced; it is the remaining area that has yet to be mopped up. It is soft-core deception, but is deception nonetheless. It is the last outpost for the seller who wishes to tell lies.

The message of this book is that consumer protection regulation should not stop short of a complete elimination of false representations that deceive. The law has allowed puffery to remain without justification and in defiance of the wishes of American consumers who want to deal in the marketplace in peace and in truth. The means exist for reversing the puffery rules, and they should be used. Deceptive claims should be removed entirely, not just partly, from the marketplace.

2

Falsity without Deception: As Possible As the Law Says, but Not As Probable

A long, long time ago the law of the marketplace adopted a rule of thumb to help it decide which seller's claims were legal and which were not. The rule brought some very good results, but it also produced a bad effect we have been paying for ever since. The bad effect was puffery. What produced it was the rule that falsity is not always illegal.

A simple beginning approach to regulation would be to say that what is false should be illegal and what is not false should be legal. The bad would be punished, the good would be spared, and all problems would be solved. But a more sophisticated second look soon showed that such a rule would not accomplish that, after all; instead, it would spare some of the bad and punish some of the good.

Such analysis eventually led to a more proper rule, that the law has most wisely adopted, saying that only a *deceptive* claim is illegal, whether or not it is false. What is not deceptive is not illegal, whether or not it is true.[1] The difference is significant because falsity and deception are not equivalent; deceptiveness is closer than falsity to what harms consumers. Accordingly, words and pictures directed by sellers to the public, even though not false, may now be considered by the law to be deceptive and therefore harmful and illegal. Sometimes, too, they may be considered, even if false, to be nondeceptive and so harmless and legal.

All of that is good simply because it is correct. If our law systematically approved all nonfalsity, we would fail to assist those consumers injured by such content. And if we systematically condemned all falsity, we would be unfair to those sellers and advertisers who affect no one adversely with such messages. An example of falsity that is not deceptive is a recent commercial showing a Jeep traveling beneath the snow, its presence indicated only by the ruffling of the surface and the glow of its lights. The car cannot really do that, but the regulators undoubtedly will never find anyone who expects it can. Thus there can be no disappointment nor harmful deception, even though there clearly is falsity.

On the other hand, the Federal Trade Commission once found the makers of toy racers to be deceptive in some nonfalse television representations showing the cars moving at high speeds along their tracks. They were photographed from a position so close to the track that they zoomed past in what appeared as an exciting blur on the screen. The photography was true; you can match it by moving your hand past your eye at point-blank range. But the FTC believed children who got these toys for Christmas would expect the same effect in their own play, and would be disappointed by what really happened. Despite its technical truth, the claim was found deceptive.[2]

So we find the regulators were correct when they separated deception and falsity and declared that the law's task was to identify deception as a feature independent of falsity in sellers' claims. We also know from the record of many decades, however, that the task has been a most difficult one to carry out. It is one thing to say deceptiveness is the thing to be identified; it is another to do it. Unfortunately, neither the regulators nor anyone else can always satisfactorily distinguish between those sellers' claims that are deceptive and those that are not.

It is far easier to detect falsity than to detect deception. Falsity is objective; we can find it by looking at nonhuman objects. We can check to see whether the product for sale matches the stories told about it. If the toothpaste lacks the ingredient the ad explicitly claims it has, then the ad is false. We must examine the claim carefully and test the toothpaste properly to be sure our decision is accurate, but usually we can confirm that it is.

Deception is different; it is subjective, which produces considerable room for doubt. It is a property of human beings. We look for it within the mind of the consumer, the person who is considering the object. If the sales message makes consumers believe the toothpaste contains something it doesn't, then it deceives them. Maybe the message is actually true, but if its result is a false belief that consumers might reasonably acquire from it, then it is deceptive.

Individual consumers are the sole persons who can tell us about instances of deception or nondeception that occur within their own minds. They are free to report having been deceived or not, whether they were or not, as they see fit. No outside observer can directly identify the alleged deception's existence or nonexistence. Yet the regulators, who need desperately to know, are always outside observers. They can "know" deception only through their own arbitrary judgments about it. They examine all observable matters, including consumers' testimony and any evidence that supports or denies that testimony. Then they make their own inferences independently, and some of them "see" deception and some of them do not. Finally, they total up their various opinions to see who is in the majority, and that is how they determine whether deception exists legally.[3]

The problem of puffery is the same. The question is not whether it is false, which so much of it is,[4] but whether it is deceptive and therefore illegal. To that question the law and this book make opposite findings: the law says puffery is not deceptive,[5] and I say it is. I believe the law's finding is incorrect.

Of course I accept the existence of falsity without deception, and of deception without falsity, as events that reasonably and frequently happen. I am sure the law has properly identified many such instances of both types of occurrence. But with certain types of false claims that I have combined under the name puffery, I believe the law has been systematically wrong in finding no deceptiveness. Just as it would be wrong to make the simpleminded assertion that all falsity is automatically deceptive, I feel it is equally wrong to flip completely to the opposite assertion that certain types of falsity are automatically nondeceptive.

My argument is made in support of the consumer, yet it is ironic to note that advertisers are constantly engaged in a similar protest. They, too, insist that the law has made a systematic mistake in determining deception. While I am concerned that much of the falsity the law calls nondeceptive should properly be called deceptive, advertisers are concerned that much of the nonfalsity the law calls deceptive should be called nondeceptive. In this way industry, too, is unhappy over the law's decisions about deception, including in the 1990s Jenny Craig and a number of other providers of weight-loss pills and programs, Häagen Dazs ice cream, Stouffer Foods, Honda and Toyota cars, Unocal and Seventy-Six gasolines, Revlon skincare products, Hasbro toys, Mr. Coffee, General Electric light bulbs, Hefty and Glad trash bags, Campbell's Soup, Orkin Exterminating, Kraft cheese, Volvo cars, and Mazola Corn Oil.[6]

The Federal Trade Commission decided in the case of Kraft, for example, that its ads deceptively implied that its "Singles" slices contained as much calcium as five ounces of milk and more calcium than most imitation cheese slices. The ads did not state those claims explicitly, and Kraft denied vehemently that they implied any such thing. Despite the opposing claims, neither the government agency nor the manufacturer could directly observe any deceptiveness or nondeceptiveness. Only consumers who viewed the Kraft commercials could do so, and key evidence in the case was obtained by surveying samples of them.[7]

It's obvious that people's disposition to "see" deceptiveness depends upon their preference for having the message either prohibited or retained in use. That is why it would never do for consumers' or sellers' organizations to make the decisions about it. Both of them dislike deceptiveness, of course, although there is no surprise in learning that the advertisers don't see as much of it when they look around. When messages are explicitly false, the advertisers are prone to explain them as only jokes or little white lies so obvious that no one possibly could be deceived by them. When the messages are not explicitly false, advertisers have trouble conceiving of them as being deceptive in any way at all. Thus, while advertisers hate deception when they see it, they tend not to see it very often.

Consumer spokesmen, in fairness, have been known to be equally inventive. When messages are explicitly false, these persons are tempted to be sincerely certain that proof of deceptiveness follows automatically. And when messages are not explicitly false, consumerists can be brilliant in showing how they must nevertheless be deceptive.

Given the possibility of such contradictory views, wouldn't it be helpful if the law's determinations did not need to be based on so slippery a concept as deception? Why don't we just go back to falsity, which is so much easier to determine? Besides, it's a bad thing, isn't it? People should be kept from communicating false messages! Why don't we just slip back to the old idea that anything that's false is illegal, and anything that's not is not?

We cannot do that, unfortunately, because a concentration on falsity ignores what the law is trying to do. The law regulates the seller's messages in order to prevent the harm that can come to consumers, through no fault of their own, when their purchases give them less than what they reasonably believed they were bargaining for. The law is not regulating the message so much as it is regulating consumers' fate. It is not the message sent, but the message received, that determines that fate.

It may be compelling to believe that the message received is equivalent to the message sent, but the regulators know from experience that it's not always so. They have seen many occasions where the buyer was treated unfairly although there was no falsity. And they have seen many situations where all concerned, including the buyer, agree that the buyer was not disadvantaged even though the seller's statements were false. There is no doubt that the troublesome separation of falsity and deception exists precisely because it must.

The regulators have also seen situations where the buyer was disadvantaged and the seller's statements were false, but the buyer's ill luck appeared due to his own carelessness rather than to improper behavior by the seller. Deceptiveness, legally, means not just that the buyer may be fooled but that the seller's message could reasonably be the cause.[8] Buyers may fool themselves all day long and the law will not protect them.[9] Determining whether consumers have reasonable perceptions of what messages say requires another inference, unfortunately, and therefore another bit of arbitrariness.

Consider the fate of Herbert A. Williams, who bought a car in Milwaukee, Wisconsin. The salesman at Rank & Son Buick, Inc., said the car was air-conditioned, and Williams found knobs on the dashboard marked "Air." Several days after purchase he found these knobs produced nothing but ventilation (just what they said: air!). Williams sued, but the Supreme Court of Wisconsin told him that "one cannot justifiably rely upon obviously false statements." The court found he had been given ample opportunity to examine the car on his own, including one and a half hours when he drove it away from the premises unaccompanied. No great search, the court said, was required to discover the absence of an air-conditioning unit.[10]

True, the purchase was made in March in a wintry climate, eliminating any possibility that an air conditioner would be used for its customary function. It is also true that the jury, in the original trial, found that Williams had a right to rely on the salesman's claim, which meant it found he did not know of the supposedly obvious falsity. But on appeal, since Williams had identified air conditioning as the main reason for buying that particular car, the Supreme Court of Wisconsin considered it doubtful that he had not checked to see whether it was there. It was clear to the court, by the logic of law even if not the evidence of fact, that Williams had made the examination and flunked it. His suit was thrown out.

The regulation of sellers' representations, as with all other areas of law, depends on the facts of the individual case. There were additional facts that may have contributed to the seller's victory. Williams testified he had relied not only on the salesman's statements but also upon a Milwaukee Journal ad for the car that claimed "Full power, including FACTORY AIR CONDITIONING." The ad, however, was not proved by Williams's counsel to have appeared any earlier than two days after he signed the purchase contract; thus his alleged reliance upon it was thrown out. No doubt Williams would have been more successful with the court if his testimony had not thus been discredited. Without this mixup, the misrepresentation in the ad might have counted more heavily against the seller. But would Williams have been exonerated? We do not know.

How should a typical consumer feel about this case? How should a seller feel? There was a finding that the salesman had lied, intending to defraud. The decision was clearly a case of ruling that the improper behavior of the buyer rendered inconsequential the improper behavior of the seller. Should the seller be excused in that way?

If you are not entirely pleased with that decision, it may be consoling to know that the Wisconsin court accepted it by the slightest majority, 4–3. The dissenting justices said the misrepresentation couldn't have been all that obvious, since the jury found as a fact that it hadn't been known to Williams. Furthermore, said the dissent, the finding of fact was up to the jury, since it had heard all the testimony. The court had the right to overrule the jury on matters of law but not on matters of fact. Therefore, Williams had a right to rely on the salesman because the misrepresentation wasn't obvious.

The dissenters did not go further, as some might, to argue that the buyer had a right to rely on the misrepresentation even while knowing its falsity, simply because the seller had said it. As long as we are being arbitrary, why not argue that the seller's responsibility renders inconsequential the buyer's, just the opposite of the rule applied! Whether or not society would accept that the solution to one extreme is to switch to the other, the possibility is cited here simply to illustrate that the kind of thinking used arbitrarily to benefit sellers might be used just as readily to benefit buyers.

The rule about obvious falsity is only one of many strange rules you will see in this book. If you disliked that one, you'll detest the rest. The reader who questions whether falsity is necessarily obvious will raise even more questions with what follows, because that rule depicts the clearest separation of falsity and deception that we will see.

To find that the clearest is not clear at all is only to illustrate the problems to be examined as we continue. They are all based on the assumption that some objective falsity is not subjectively deceptive, and that some objective nonfalsity is subjectively deceptive. There is a certain naturalness when a decision finds deception in conjunction with falsity or nondeception in conjunction with nonfalsity. Were all the world's sales messages examined, one of these two results probably would be declared in most cases. But the other possible decisions are terribly troublesome. Falsity is sometimes not deceptive and nonfalsity is sometimes deceptive, which leaves us with much uncertainty as to when deception of consumers truly occurs. We often fail to be satisfied with the answers we get on such issues.

My own dissatisfaction is the basic reason I have written this book. I believe there has been a systematic tendency to answer wrongly the question of whether certain types of falsity are deceptive. The law has decided, inaccurately I believe, that puffery and other falsities are nondeceptive in the face of strong reasons for believing they are actually deceptive. Let's see what those reasons are.

3

Puffery: Used Because It Works, Legalized Because It Doesn't

There are several types of falsity that the law says produce no deception. Along with puffery, they include:

1. obvious falsity,
2. social-psychological misrepresentations,
3. literally misdescriptive names, and
4. mock-ups.

Before I finish I will describe all these categories as "puffery" in the sense that they all involve claims that falsely puff up the product to be greater than can legitimately be claimed. But since the law applies the term technically to only one of the types, I will first stick to that narrow definition and then later expand the idea to include the others. Until we reach chapter 11, then, *puffery* will be restricted to the technical meaning the law has traditionally given it.

That meaning makes it the marketplace term for what elsewhere would simply be called an opinion statement, expressing the seller's evaluation of the advertised item. However, it also involves an added feature that does not apply outside the marketplace. By legal definition, puffery claims praise the advertised item by using subjective terms, stating no fact explicitly, and thus representing no factual content to consumers and so creating no basis for them to believe anything about the item that would affect their purchasing decision.[1] The portion following the last comma is the added feature, and I will eventually show how it makes a big difference to both advertisers and consumers.

For practical purposes puffery's definition should probably also indicate its quintessential form, which it takes not always but very often. That form, which makes the strongest of its claims, consists of superlatives such as "best." Used unqualifiedly, "best" and its synonyms such as "favorite" or "tops" or "last word" describe the advertised item as the overall top-rated brand in its product or service category, reflecting the fact that battles of brand against brand are the most common form of competition to which advertising is addressed. Although the term "better" is discussed later as usually making a weaker claim, it may also mean "best" when consumers see it as meaning better than any or all others (examples follow below).

Calling a brand "best" can also be done in a qualified way, in phrases referring to specific attributes such as "best performing." Other variations include terms such as "most," as in "most durable," or descriptives ending in "-est" such as "fastest acting" or "longest lasting." Also frequent are wordings that imply being best through exclusivity of the cited attribute, which "nobody else" or "only" the advertised brand has. While such phrases may sometimes mean there is no other member of the category, examples cited below typically suggest that competitors exist and the advertised item beats them all.

The best-known examples of puffery are slogans used repeatedly, sometimes for years, on behalf of nationally advertised products and services. Perhaps the oldest is P. T. Barnum's description of the circus as "The Greatest Show on Earth." One might call it the king of them all, which would be puffing about puffing.

The following are among the many examples of such unqualified or qualified superlatives abounding in the advertising of the 1990s. The portion in boldface is the statement's subjective superlative expression, the key to its identification as puffery. Such words or phrases are typically considered under present law to be nonfactual and so immune from consideration as deceptive:

The **best** a man can get (Gillette)
The **best** in the business (AT&T)
The **best** the world has to offer (Ford Explorer)
The **best** small car in America (Ford Escort)
The **best** never rest (Ford)
The **best** part of waking up is Folger's in your cup
The **best** tires in the world have Goodyear written all over them

The very **best** chocolate (Nestlé's)
You get the **best** sound ever (AT&T True Voice)
Get Dad the **best**—for less (Burlington Coat Factory)
Bring out the Hellman's and bring out the **best**
Expect the **best** (Coldwell Banker)
The Original and **Best** (Kellogg's Corn Flakes)
The Colonel's way is still the **best** way (Kentucky Fried Chicken)
We make the world's **best** mattress (Serta)
Best on glass (Windex)
Seattle's **Best** Coffee (retail chain)
Best Foods (among other brand names using "best")
The **next best** thing to a dental cleaning at home (thus, **best** you
    can do at home) (Colgate Tartar Control)
The **most** fluffy softness (Downy)
The **most** trusted name in nails (Hard-As-Nails)
The **most** reliable snow thrower ever made (Troy-Bilt)
The **most** popular cruise in the world (Carnival)
The **finest** 200-speed film (Kodak)
Only the **finest** rums come from Puerto Rico (Rums of Puerto Rico)
America's **Finest** (cookies)
Some of the **greatest** values in America (J. C. Penney)
Now holding Wisconsin's **greatest** closeout sale in history (one
    car dealer, but typical of many)
The **biggest** news in cleaning since the sponge (Comet: showing
    product, but no other news)
The **biggest** meal deal America has ever seen (KFC Mega Meal)
The **biggest** combo for the money on the planet (Hardee's)
Colgate leaves teeth the **cleanest** they can feel
The **richest** coffee in the world—100% Columbian Coffee
If you want your family to wear the **whitest** whites, don't forget
    the Clorox bleach
If you want the **softest** tissue you can get for your family,
    Charmin's the only one
America's **favorite** neighborhood (Applebees restaurants)
The **last word** in shavers (Braun)
Champion (spark plugs)
Ziploc has the **lock** on freshness (Dow)
They **set the standards** for real estate (Century 21)
The **height** of fashion (Armstrong floors)
Comfort **King** (mattress)
Gold Medal (Flour)

Blue Ribbon (beer and other product categories)

Secret will keep you **dryer than any other** kind out there

A **better value than its leading competition**, and that's more than an empty promise (Ford Escort)

Nobody does breakfast like IHOP does breakfast

Nobody gets the dirt out like Hoover. Nobody

Nothing helps strengthen and protect problem nails like the original, unsurpassed Hard-As-Nails clear formula

It's like **nothing** you've ever used before (Caress Moisturizing Body Wash)

Nothing energizes your day like a Beautyrest night (Simmons)

Nothing succeeds like Nestlé's Sweet Success

Nothing looks like L. A. Looks

Nothing takes care of a mouth like Listerine

Nothing's got the power of Gold (Visa Gold Card)

Nothing else comes close (Learjet)

Why trust those moments to **anything else** than Kodak film

There's **no formula like** Head & Shoulders dry scalp shampoo

Fast food will **never be the same** (Taco Bell)

The **only** fitness apparel that looks as good as it performs (Speedo)

Quality like this comes **only** from Pella

Without Lorraine, it's just not a sandwich (Stella Foods' cheese)

You don't get your home totally clean **until** you use Lysol

Dole 100% juices—the taste you **can't get anywhere but here**

Today's engines **need** Castrol GTX

Painful gas **needs** Gas-X

Every cut **needs** the protection of Neosporin (antibiotic)

Getting teeth really clean **takes** Colgate tartar control

If it's got to be clean it's **got to be** Tide

Here are some of the same kind of puffs from the 1970s or earlier, featured in the first edition of this book. They could be called historical classics:

Get the **best**—get Sealtest

Blatz is Milwaukee's **finest** beer

The **greatest** show on earth (Barnum & Bailey)

The world's **greatest** newspaper (Chicago Tribune)[2]

Andeker—America's **greatest**

The **biggest** little treat in all the land (Wrigley)

The world's **most** experienced airline (Pan Am)

King of beers (Budweiser)

When you say Budweiser, you've **said it all**
Breakfast of **Champions** (Wheaties)
Instrument of the **immortals** (Steinway)
GM—always a step **ahead**
When you're out of Schlitz you're **out of** beer

The superlative puff thus says a scale of superiority exists, from best to worst, top to bottom, and the advertised item stands alone at the top step or rank of that scale. That is the principal reason I feel the law is wrong in describing puffery as stating no fact and so giving the consumer no basis for making a purchasing decision. It may not do so explicitly, yet it cannot be solely an opinion to say that a product is top ranked. It must be so for a reason, and that reason is a fact. Before engaging in the details of that argument, however, let's look at the additional forms apart from superlatives that puffery takes.

A slightly weaker form states, not that the advertised item is the best of its category, but the subtly different point that it is the best possible, meaning technically that others could be equally good. Among the ways of saying this is to claim perfect or top performance, or to claim that nobody is better:

Perfect rice everytime (Minute Rice)
The **perfect** balance of luxury and technology (Lincoln)
Who says nothing's **perfect**? (Amstel beer)
Perfect Sleeper (mattress)
The **ultimate** driving machine (BMW)
The **ultimate** fresh breath (Breath Savers, Peppermint)
Ultimate Finish (makeup)
Top Flite (golf balls)
Premium, Premier, Peerless (many brands of many products)
A-1 (steak sauce)
State Farm is **all you need** to know about insurance
Ziploc is **all you need**
Visa—it's **everywhere** you want to be
As smooth as they come, **as pure as** it gets (Miller Genuine Draft)
Nothing's been proven to last longer than Advil
Nothing's stronger (Ultra Strength Ben Gay)
Nothing's more effective when you've got a big thirst (Gatorade)
Nothing comes closer to home (Stouffer frozen foods)
Nothing cleans stains better than Clorox bleach
Nothing soothes away heartburn faster than Mylanta

Nothing tops ice cream better than Hershey's chocolate syrup
Nothing works better than Midol PMS
There's **nothing** this can can't do (Lysol disinfectant spray)
There's **no better** guard against colors that run (Cheer)
You can trust Gerber. There simply is **no better** [baby] formula
There's **no softer** way to shave (Skintimate)
You **can't imagine a better** snack (Handi-Snacks)
Pure natural aloe—is there **anything better** that soothes summer
  dry skin? (Vaseline Intensive Care)
You **can't buy a more impressive** car for less (Toyota Corolla)

Although such wordings do not explicitly claim the advertised item is best, consumers can, and probably often do, see them as claiming to be the best.[3]

Another weaker form of puffery is the claim that the advertised item is not best but better. Examples from the 1990s (and some earlier) include:

For my tough headaches, Advil just works **better**
Velveeta cooks **better**
New Ultra Biz—the **better** stain getter
Things go **better** with Coke
Gas gives you a **better** deal (American Gas Association)
Live **better** electrically (Edison Electric Institute)
Ford gives you **better** ideas
The **better** stain getter (Ultra Biz)
Better care makes **better** cats (Cat Chow Special Care)
The one that tastes **better** (Fiber One cereal)
It simply slides, rolls, folds, protects, unfolds and drives **better**
  (Plymouth Grand Voyager)
Keep mildew stains away **longer** (Vanish Mildew Stain Remover)
We try **harder** (Avis)
Stronger in the bottle; **stronger** in the bucket (Lysol cleaner)
Lestoil (Cleaner) (a negative approach to a positive claim)
It's **cleaner;** it's **dryer;** it's Always
Sure Ultra Dry keeps you **dryer**
For dazzling, **whiter** teeth (Aquafresh Whitening toothpaste)
Heal cuts **faster** with Neosporin
When **others can't** cut it, Comet can (does not say all others)

These claims indicate a comparison to at least one competitor, and consumers may recognize in some cases that only one serious competitor exists: for Coke, Pepsi; for Avis, Hertz; and for gas and electricity, each other. But even when there are multiple competitors, consumers might see the comparison as referring to all and thus implying best.

A still weaker type of puffery states subjectively that the advertised item is not best or better but merely great or very good. As the grammarians would say, we are descending the descriptive scale for adjectives, from superlative to comparative to positive. But even these are comparison terms, implying positions on a scale ranking the various brands. And given the strength of expression, consumers could see them as implying superiority over some, or many, or even all of the competition:

> If you want **great** taste that'll never let you down (Bud Light)
> It's what all **great** sandwiches have in common (Lorraine cheese)
> **Great** hair (Pert Plus)
> If it's Weber, it's **great** outdoors (barbecue grill)
> A new fragrance of **extraordinary** elegance (Coty)
> Items of **exceptional** quality and fashion, at an **extraordinary** price (J. C. Penney)
> **Incredible** lather and **incredible** skin (Oil of Olay)
> An **amazing** new micro cleansing formula (Colgate Tartar Control Toothpaste)
> **Miracle** Gro (plant food)
> **Miracle** Whip (salad dressing)
> **Uncommonly good** (Keebler)
> If it tastes **too good** to be fat free, it's Kraft Free (salad dressing)
> The Vidal Sassoon Academy—the **world-famous** center for haircare
> **Famous** Footwear (shoe chain)
> Bayer works **wonders**
> The **wonderful** world of Disney
> **Wonder** Bread
> **Gourmet** (cat food)
> **Professional** care for your hair (Vidal Sassoon)
> To clean like a **pro** get Pro 409
> **Cracker Jack** (candy)
> **Deluxe, Excel** (each involving several brands)
> For an **extra degree** of protection (Degree antiperspirant)
> **Extra** Quality, **Extra High** Quality, HQ **High** Quality, HGX **High** Grade, **Super** HG (High Grade), **Super High** Quality, **Professional** Quality, **Professional** Recording Quality, **Premium**

Grade, **High** Output—**High** Resolution, **High** Chroma—**High** Quality, **High** Grade Dynamicon (various VCR tapes)

Super Paint (Sherwin Williams)

Super Suds (soap powder)

Kodak **Royal Gold** (film)

We treat you **right** (Dairy Queen)

Doing it **right** (J. C. Penney)

The **right** fit for clean teeth—Crest **Complete**

You can be **sure** if it's Westinghouse (appliances)

You can **trust** your car to the man who wears the star (Texaco)

Trust Preparation H

Trust is Tampax

Recommended by doctors. **Trusted** by women (Preparation H)

Advanced medicine for pain (Advil)

You'll **love** the stuff we're made of (Pizza Hut)

You'll **love** the way we fly (Delta)

Every kid in America **loves** Jello brand gelatin

I **love** what you do for me (Toyota Previa)

Some things are **worth** the price (Acura)

Get your burger's **worth** (Burger King)

Pay Less (drug stores)

Big taste for a small town (Johnsonville brats)

It's a **lot** of sandwich (Wendy's)

Good and **Plenty** (candy)

Twice the hotel (Embassy Suites)

Clorox 2—**tough** on stains, **easy** on colors

Easy Off (oven cleaner), **Easy** On (starch), **Easy** Wave (hair product), **Easy** Wipes (Cloths), **Easy** Wash (stain remover), **Easy** Bake (toy)

easy opening (various packaged items)

Assembles in **minutes** (things that usually don't)

As we near the lower end of the puffery scale, consumers are probably less likely to see a top-scale ranking claimed, but nonetheless may see "high" or "higher" claimed. Two more categories remain, including statements that the product is merely good (not exceptionally good as before):

You're in **good** hands with Allstate

If it's Borden's it's got to be **good**

With a name like Smucker's, it has to be **good**

M'm M'm **good** (Campbell's soup)

It's just naturally **good** (Nabisco Shredded Wheat)
We bring **good** things to life (General Electric)
Good and Plenty (candy)
Good News (razors)
Cookin' **Good** (chicken)

These claims are relatively modest, although there is no reason to believe their creators are any less modest in purpose than other advertisers. They no doubt expect a high ranking to be perceived.

Finally, we come to terms that could be interpreted as at least good, and possibly better or best, although they do not say so explicitly. Instead they describe specific features, all highly subjective and sometimes perhaps fanciful or fantasylike:

Fly the **friendly** skies of United
Something **special** in the air (American Airlines)
There's a **smile** in every Hershey Bar
We're there when you need us (Ryder rental trucks)
The **smart** money is on Budget (rental cars)
Maytag—the **dependability** people
Tabasco brings out the **unexpected** in food
You're not fully clean until you're **Zestfully** clean (Zest soap)
It's the **real** thing (Coke)
Cope (pain reliever)
Complete (toothpaste, bran flakes)
Classic (brands in various product categories)
Cover Girl (cosmetics)
Designer . . . (several products)
We are driving **excitement** (Pontiac Grand Am)
Prudential has the **strength** of Gibraltar
The taste that **never gets old** (Orchard's Best juices)
Cover the earth (Sherwin Williams)
Come to where the **flavor** is (Marlboro)
Off **Skintastic** (bug repellent)
Decadence, Obsession, and others (fragrances)
Fantasy Fudge (recipe with Kraft Marshmallow Creme)
Computer **Revolution** Headquarters (Best Buy)
The next **revolution** in shaving closeness (Gillette)
The **future** of eye makeup (Maybelline)
Taste the **future** (Budweiser Ice Draft)

Although these terms are intended no less than "best" or "better" to create perceptions of specialness and high rank, they are less direct in doing so. Thus the entire set of listings is ordered from the strongest to the weakest claims. All of them represent the type of subjective opinion claims in selling that are popularly known as puffery.

Now to mention the puzzling thing about these many examples. Although all of them are likely to be excused as puffery under the legal definition given above,[4] I believe many of them really do not properly reflect the explanation claimed by both advertisers and regulators that because they are subjective opinions they cannot amount to objective facts. Many of them, I suggest, using the analysis of chapter 2, are simultaneously both.

Of course there is no question they are subjective, stating opinions that vary from person to person. We as individuals will not necessarily agree, and we have the right not to, about the extent of beauty, deliciousness, attractiveness, popularity, or many other qualities of an advertised item. My opening statement about the superiority of this book qualifies as such puffery, and I am certain it will find agreement with some people, if only my relatives. There will always be someone who thinks Barnum's circus was the greatest or Goodyear tires are the best, while others think otherwise. In other words, subjective claims are a legitimate form of thinking and speech, and of consumer reaction to things advertised.

However, the legal definition also says that puffery states no specific facts. That is a conclusion I think is often not legitimate, because I think many or most consumers who see a claim that a product is the greatest or finest will often also see claimed that it is greatest or finest in some factual way. When Goodyear claims to have "the best tires in the world," does it not imply that certain standards of tire making exist, and that the brand has the physical features that meet those standards? The features are not explicitly mentioned, but the fact that they exist is surely implied to consumers. What else, really, can "best" mean?

We have already seen that the law's purpose is to regulate subjective deception rather than objective falsity, and the key to the subjectivity of a message is not what it says to consumers but what it means to them. It is a part of our nature to draw implications from messages, and to treat them as being just as much present as if they had been explicitly stated. When I see blinking lights at a train crossing I stop immediately, treating the lights as implying a train no less certainly than if I were seeing the train itself. When I am told that Nestlé's makes the very best chocolate, why would

I not with equal certainty take the statement to mean that Nestlé's is judged superior by specific standards existing in the chocolate business?

Perhaps we shouldn't draw such implications, but we do. Experts in semantics[5] have tried valiantly to teach the public the difference between implication and actual statement, arguing that implications are acceptable as no more than tentative guesses about what something means. The blinking lights are not the train, the semanticists tell us, and they make a useful point in doing so. I have seen crossing lights blinking when there was no train. I have seen left turn signals blinking on cars that did not turn left. And in the marketplace, I have seen products called "best" that were not.

That is why I am puzzled over the definition of puffery. Those instances of it that imply facts should not legally be puffery at all. Yet they remain because the law chooses to ignore any consideration of what they imply. Advertisers insist on defining puffery only by what it literally states. And the law, for reasons I find inexplicable, goes along with their wish. While the law says no person acting reasonably relies on such claims as meaning any specific thing, I say people do that very often.

We might concede as a matter strictly of language structure that puffery states nothing, but as a matter of human behavior we can't state that at all. Can we ever believe that something means nothing? "Nothing never happens" is what an anthropologist once said in dismissing such a possibility.[6] Even if we assume more conservatively that some opinion claims will be recognized by some consumers as having no factual content, the possibility can remain that many do have factual content. The difference between the law's position and mine is that while the law says puffs never mean anything factual, I say that most of them may and that many do.

Further, I say that the facts implied by a piece of puffery are frequently false—or at least not known by their speakers to be true, which amounts to falsity in the sense that they know they have no basis for the claim. Only in a minority of cases will a puff imply true facts. Certainly some items for sale are truly the best in objective ways, and a puff that says so must be called accurate. Polaroid may say it gives you pictures faster than any other camera, and that is factually true. Other types of true puffs consist of subjective judgments that happen to be agreed upon by all who have judged the matter. Everyone, for example, would say that rubber automobile tires give a more comfortable ride than tires of wood or metal, which would allow advertisers to puff rubber as the greatest without fear of implying anything false.

But true puffs are scarce. Notice that the tire example involved a product category, rubber tires; it did not involve the various brands of tires. And while the Polaroid example was about a brand, only one brand exists in its category of producing pictures on the spot. Thus neither example involved competing brands, which is the most typical market situation in which heavy advertising and selling are used. Where there are competing brands, only one can be superior and the puffs of the others must be false. All, in fact, could be false in cases where there is no established objective basis or consensus of subjective judgment available to prove that any single brand is superior.

So there aren't many situations where a puff *can* be true, and when it's true there aren't many situations where the seller wants to use it. A true puff is usually obviously so or widely known to be so, and the seller therefore has no need to make the point. Polaroid wouldn't bother today to tell us its pictures appear sooner than do those of other cameras. It told us that at first, of course, but the fact has long since been deemphasized in its ads. No rubber company would bother telling us that rubber is superior to metal for making tires. What they want to tell us is that their own brand is best, which everybody doesn't know and which often isn't true.

Any advertiser that knows its product to be factually superior will surely state the factual basis rather than the puff. Did Procter & Gamble settle for describing Crest as the "best" once they were able to say it was the first toothpaste to earn the endorsement of the American Dental Association? Puffery is what you say when you can't say something like that, which is why I feel justified in stating that the puffs we see are very likely to have no actual basis and thus to be false.

Paging through an issue of *Smithsonian* in 1995, I saw a claim for Kodak that "There are times when only the finest 200 speed film will do." A typical puff, I thought, but then the next line referred to the "finest grain 200 speed film money can buy." That made a difference, because while "finest" unaccompanied would typically mean "best," "finest grain" means smallest, which makes a fact claim. One might quibble over whether having the finest grain means being finest overall, but at least the advertiser turned the subjective feature into an objective one, offering the consumer a real physical feature as support for its persuasive effort.

Another 1995 ad was similar: "Only the finest rums come from Puerto Rico. That's because only in Puerto Rico is aging guaranteed by law. And aging is what gives our rums a smoothness that has made them preferred over all others." In this case the finest competitor was the one aged the longest, and again a factual basis for the claim was given. Meanwhile, what happens when ads much more typically use unaccompanied puffery, which implies such a factual foundation but fails to identify it? Isn't it likely that such claims actually have no factual basis, and isn't it likely that consumers who reasonably think they do will be deceived?

Such a prospect notwithstanding, much opposing opinion says puffery deceives no substantial numbers at all.[7] The law takes this position, and the advertisers are only too willing to agree. "How far down the road toward idiocy," queried the chairman of *Advertising Age*, "do we go to 'protect' the person who would consider such a phrase a guarantee of superiority?"[8]

That is precisely the viewpoint that must be countered in order to drive legalized falsity out of the market. I know of a big, whopping, absolutely conclusive reason for arguing that puffery is believed by a substantial portion of the public, and in my opinion it proves the point beyond any doubt. The reason is that advertisers and salesmen use it all the time. Puffery is endemic in American salesmanship, practically the soul and substance of the American way of selling. It is an established contributor to a decades-long success story achieved by professionals far too skilled to retain a practice the public would see instantly as false. Selling goods is one of the most expert acts ever developed on our continent, and experts don't continue using methods that fail!

Why would the salesman have told Herbert Williams[9] the car was air-conditioned if he had not expected Williams might believe it? The court called the claim obviously false, but if buyers always noticed the falsity then why would the salesman have relied on it? Why would Kellogg advertise its corn flakes as the best if the consumer always noticed the "obvious" facts that the company offers no proof for the claim, and that other cereal makers make claims that contradict it? While advertising's elder spokesmen pontificate from the boardrooms that reliance on puffery is restricted to a few idiots, the industry's toilers in the vineyards, the copywriters, keep turning out the puffs on the obvious assumption that they have a wide-ranging effect. The true industry position is indicated by the ads rather than by the speeches. The line would not be used if Kellogg felt it had no effect.

When law and advertiser disagree over whether these messages work, one should ask who is the greater expert at determining what sells products. The industry's conviction that puffery works is proof enough for me that it does, because I have a great admiration for the expertise of the advertising profession. When experienced professionals commit themselves to the continuing use of such themes, it can only be from the knowledge that they will sell.

Of course there are few admissions of that by industry people. Witness the attempt by FTC Commissioner Mary Gardiner Jones to draw such an acknowledgment from an industry spokesman at commission hearings on the nature of the advertising process.[10] Commissioner Jones suggested that every advertising claim is surely made with the purpose of influencing the consumer's decision. She then added, in the manner of a chess player's gambit, hoping the opponent will bite, the comment "This would mean there is no such thing as puffery."

In chess the player may safely refuse the gambit, but the advertising executive was in trouble whether he bit or not. Choosing to protest, he cited the "metaphor" (as he called it) of the washing machine growing ten feet tall in the detergent ad, and argued that such representations were not intended to be believed. Commissioner Jones persisted, asking, "How would you expect it to function if not to be believed?" The reluctant concession, finally, was "I'm sure they intended that metaphor to be translated into some beneficial attribute."

A rare voluntary admission of the same was made by an advertising agency president, Peter Geer, in a speech titled "Those Fourteen Words."[11] The words were the slogan of one of his agency's clients, Eli Lilly: "For four generations we've been making medicines as if people's lives depended on it." Geer's analysis of the claim's effectiveness was to call it

> a naked boast. A simple unproved assertion . . . of the sort that those of us who pride ourselves on being skilled practitioners and accomplished critics of advertising would normally . . . dismiss out of hand as unsubstantiated assertions of superiority, without documentation and without support. . . . Lilly isn't saying anything in these ads that is buttressed by evidence, and yet, these ads attain levels of conviction and believability that the most reasoned persuasion often fails to achieve in advertising.

He was saying that puffery works and he's glad he uses it. Such candor is not frequent in advertising, but one easily imagines that other purveyors of puffery use it only for the same reason. If the advertisers are convinced, by whatever proofs they find acceptable, surely the regulators should seriously consider the same conviction. Contrary to what the law assumes, there seems little reason to deny that puffery actually is believed and relied upon to a substantial extent.

There is also research evidence of puffery's impact, presented in chapter 15, which shows further that we are dealing with an effective means of communication. Advertisers do not develop techniques to persuade only a few people; that's not how mass communication works. Techniques must be successful with vast audiences or be discarded. Puffery's continued existence in sales messages addressed to vast audiences shows that its makers find it effective with a substantial portion of the public in obtaining reliance and altering purchase decisions.

Why does the law disagree? Why does it ignore such evidence and rule arbitrarily that people who act with reasonable sense and care in the marketplace will not be deceived by puffery's falsity? In what follows, I will describe the long history of why that has happened.

4

The Roots of Sellerism

The key to puffery's legal acceptability is that its roots lie in yesterday's sellerism, not in today's consumerism. I use the term *sellerism* to indicate the law's former tendency to favor the seller considerably more than the buyer in the rules governing sales transactions. *Consumerism*, then, indicates the law's tendency to favor the buyer relatively more in those rules today than it did under sellerism.

We will see in this chapter that favoring sellers was culturally desirable in the early United States and that the law reflected that desire. We will also see that the balance of power more recently has trended to favor consumer interests and that many of the sellerist laws have been revised accordingly. It is conceivable that the consumerism trend eventually will turn the tables to favor buyers more than sellers, or at least will achieve equality of the two in the eyes of the law. That's not guaranteed, of course, but there's no doubt that the trend has already eliminated the gross favoritism once shown toward sellers.

Many forces oppose consumerism and will work to see it eliminated. In the 1990s the consumerist trend that was evident at the time of this book's first edition has long since faded, and the next turn back in that direction has not appeared. Still, as the events described in this chapter show, our society has moved overall in a consumerist direction for decades, indeed for centuries, despite reverses during some periods. The best guess, therefore, is that the future will maintain the consumerist thrust.

Given this assumption, it is natural to expect the old sellerist laws to be eliminated from the marketplace and replaced by rules more consistent with today's standards. In numerous instances this has already happened, yet many laws remain unchanged today as remnants of sellerist times. Because they do, the vast movement of sellerism that began so long ago is not yet over. Consumerism predominates, but sellerism is not yet dead. What we have might be called an incomplete consumerism flavored heavily by a stubborn sellerism that refuses to be pushed off the scene. For the time being these features are immovable objects, while consumerism is a resistible force.

The decisions that favor sellers by finding falsity without deception are among those immovable objects. They were central developments of the era of sellerism, and they remain today as loopholes thwarting the move to consumerism. They obstinately reflect ancient rather than modern assumptions about how people should and do conduct themselves in the marketplace. The obstinacy is no accident; it reflects a movement that dominated the first century of the life of the United States and is still deeply rooted in our thoughts and customs. To see why sellerism clings to us today, let us move back in time to the year it was founded. It is 1534, an ancient era in which nothing like the modern marketplace exists. Nothing, that is, but a two-word phrase set down in Latin that points the way to the twentieth century.

Many things that shaped our lives happened in busy 1534. The Protestant Reformation emerged in England with the Act of Supremacy, by which Henry VIII made himself head of the English church. Anne Boleyn maneuvered through the second of four years that led her from Henry's altar to his chopping block. Thomas More was imprisoned, awaiting his own headsman. Francis I burned Protestants, while Calvin fled his French homeland to write his *Institutes* in Switzerland. Charles V, emperor of Germany, hounded by Luther, still reigned. Ivan IV, the Terrible, later czar, was grand duke of Moscow at the age of four. Gustavus I was consolidating the Swedish Reformation with a beneficent autocracy, while the sultan of the Ottomans, Sulieman I, the Magnificent, widened his holdings of European soil. Clement VII died and Paul III was crowned pope; the Jesuits were founded by Ignatius Loyola. Michelangelo abandoned the Medici tombs and departed Florence forever for Rome. Titian was fifty-seven, Palestrina eight. Copernicus had composed his revelation on revolution but would not yet consent to its publication. Rabelais was publishing, but anonymously, his best-known work. In the New World the Incas and Peru were being subdued by Pizarro, while other explorers and conquerors turned their attention to North America.

And in 1534 a compiler of English law named Fitzherbert wrote about buying a horse, "If he be tame and have ben rydden upon, then caveat emptor."[1] These famous Latin words, translated as "Let the buyer beware," stated the essence of sellerism in law: buyers must look out for themselves. If they look at their purchase carefully, they will not need the law. If they don't look, or don't look carefully, the law will not protect them. Buyers must accept full responsibility for a sales transaction; the seller accepts none. They must rely upon and trust nothing but their own personal inspection of their purchase, ignoring any representations of the seller that they do not confirm for themselves. Any buyer who does otherwise must suffer all consequences of a decision that turns out badly.

Thus we discover the beginning of protected lying, of legally nondeceptive falsity. Puffery and other falsehoods are permitted today primarily because caveat emptor introduced such legalized lying many centuries ago. Puffery of course goes back farther than 1534, no doubt occurring in the conversations of Adam and Eve ("I've found the nicest apple, Adam dear . . ."). But we are concerned with the way it became established in American law as legal even when false (while now outlawed, incidentally, in some other countries).[2] In its heyday caveat emptor permitted enormous amounts of outright deliberate lying, the most blatant kinds of which are now prohibited. But the lesser ones that remain, and are the topic of this book, got their immunity from the same source. In this sense we can place the beginning of puffery in the year 1534, with the advent of caveat emptor in the law and sellerism in the marketplace.

How and why caveat emptor emerged involve mysteries never fully answered. Throughout the Middle Ages the law of the market leaned severely toward favoring consumer rather than seller.[3] Some writers have stated that caveat emptor prevailed throughout the Middle Ages as a heritage derived from ancient Rome, but the Romans, coiners of Latin phrases though they were, did not give it birth. The impression that they did remains widespread despite the efforts of a legal historian, Walton H. Hamilton, to destroy the myth.[4] His luck is indicated in an advertisement by the publisher Grolier: "Remember the Roman who said 'Caveat emptor'? We don't. But we remember that he said it. . . ."[5]

Despite that advertiser's acknowledged encyclopedic grasp of history, no Roman said that at all. People have mistakenly thought so, Hamilton discovered, because the Romans indeed had no remedy to protect buyers who bought goods and later found them defective. Yet that reflected only that they traded little and so had no appreciation for the protection needed in such transactions.[6] The Romans simply had no law on the matter, whereas caveat emptor was not the lack of a law but rather a law that provided specifically for a lack of protection.

As Europe progressed into the Middle Ages, trade grew and laws to control it were fully developed. Life was regulated strictly, and bad bargains did not go unpunished; there was no place for such a thing as caveat emptor.[7] St. Thomas Aquinas, speaking for the principal lawmaker of his time, the church, made clear that sellers were responsible for defects.[8] When a seller made false statements about his wares, even if innocently, he must make good the loss. When he knew of a defect, he must reveal it to the buyer. Buyers, too, had responsibilities; if after purchase they found they had received more than they anticipated, they must compensate the seller for the hidden gain. Only in one respect did Aquinas reflect what later became sellerism; he felt, in keeping with an apparently ancient adage, that the seller need not reveal any obvious defects (although, he said, it would be virtuous to do so). That exception was no great concession to the seller, however, because "obvious" in Aquinas' day meant really obvious.

Aquinas was the great rationalizer in the church's reluctant acceptance of the values of trade.[9] As trade began to appear in the early Middle Ages, the church made clear its condemnation of it, but later was compelled toward greater indulgence by perceiving the advantages, indeed necessities, of dealing with merchants. But how could it do so without upsetting its own clearly stated standards? Aquinas saved the day by stating a distinction between rightful and wrongful trade, the one serving the community generally while the other served only the worldly profit motives of the trader. At first only a minor portion of trade was rightful, but the concept gradually grew until most trade eventually was found to serve God as well as man. Well beyond 1534, however, the church controlled trade strictly and had no room for caveat emptor. "In ecclesiastical polity," Hamilton writes, "there was no place for the notion that the seller was not responsible for the goodness of his wares."[10]

Secular justice in the Middle Ages was equally authoritarian, keeping sellerism at bay.[11] The craft guilds and market towns controlled craftsmen and sellers tightly, treating them virtually as licensed public officials. The guilds obtained monopoly powers as their reward, and contributed a high level of workmanship and honesty as justification for it. They drew up standards of size and quality, and craftsmen who produced articles otherwise were fined, and for multiple violations were thrown out of the trade.[12] The result was equivalent to consumerism, though the aim was not to serve buyers as such but to serve the entire community.[13] The cheater was held to transgress against everyone, including his follow workers as well as his customers, a far cry from the later "dog-eat-dog" competitive marketplace of early America. Apart from the market towns, the traders in the Middle Ages had their own courts as well, which developed a body of principles called the Law Merchant. Here, too, trust rather than distrust was the basis of commercial dealings.[14]

At the height of the Middle Ages, then, there was no development of the sellerism idea from the multiple sources of law that might have produced it, including the civil law with its Roman heritage, the law of the guild communities, and the Law Merchant of the traders. Apparently the only place the caveat emptor tradition could have come from was the trade conducted outside the law.[15] Lawful trade was gaining in acceptance by the church and in general respectability with the public, but there remained a fringe area of wandering traders, "persons without rank or of mean estate,"[16] who appeared today and were gone tomorrow, and from whom no redress could be had when defects were found only tomorrow. Among them were the multitudinous horse traders of whom Fitzherbert spoke. In this outlaw market, that had no formal legal structures yet developed customs of behavior nonetheless, the rule of action readily evolved that you must look out for yourself because no one else will.[17] As with the Romans, that was not law but a folkway reflecting the lack of a law. Yet it was apparently from such a source that the notion of caveat emptor eventually grew into actual law.

How could a folk custom that disagreed with the law of the land eventually be made part of that law? It happened because the king and his courts decided to formulate a national law, rejecting various existing regulations and drawing substitute rules from whatever sources they pleased. Church (canon) law, civil law, and the laws of the guilds and the merchants had been dominant for a long time, but as the Middle Ages waned the growing power of the king grad-ually "nationalized" their jurisdictions. It was not without protest among Englishmen, Hamilton wrote: "The towns were constantly apprehensive over the prospect of His Majesty's encroachment upon their liberties."[18] But inevitably the legal dominance of the church and of the local and regional secular powers was blotted out by nationalization. None of the laws subordinated in this way included the concept of caveat emptor; only the lawless element of trade was "ruled" by that principle. Yet the king's courts, wanting to do everything possible to encourage growth of trade, ignored the precedents of the lawful markets and chose instead a precedent from the lawless ones. In that way caveat emptor gained official English recognition.[19]

The king's courts did not accomplish the change in the days of Fitzherbert, but they used Fitzherbert as support when they did. They also used other sixteenth- and seventeenth-century writings and events which, as did Fitzherbert, reflected no particular support in previous law for caveat emptor, but could later be interpreted as precedents when such interpretation was desired.[20] Primary in doing so was the celebrated case of the seller who lied about something called a bezar-stone.

A bezar-stone was a funny thing indeed, but before identifying it we must describe what steps an astute seller might take, as one did in the bezar-stone case, to invoke the principle of caveat emptor. We have said that under that rule buyers had to rely solely on their own inspection of the item they bought, and otherwise had no protection against eventual discovery of a defect in its quality. Technically, however, the caveat emptor rule never pronounced such a responsibility unqualifiedly. Certainly it could not apply where inspection by the buyer was impossible, as when the goods were in a ship at sea or if the seller intervened deliberately to keep the buyer away from them, as in refusing to reveal their location.[21] A buyer truly unable to inspect had no trouble getting legal support for relying on a seller's claim that turned out to be false.

Nor did caveat emptor always apply for buyers who *could* inspect prior to purchase; it applied only where a pair of stated conditions both were absent. If the seller made a misrepresentation about the goods that constituted (1) warranty, and/or (2) fraudulent misrepresentation (fraud), then caveat emptor would not be recognized.[22]

A *warranty*[23] was a seller's factual statement treated by the law as a promise that must be kept. To be such, a statement needed wording such as "I promise" or "I warrant," and if worded that way it was a warranty whether or not it was false and whether or not the seller knew the truth. The seller might be entirely innocent, yet was responsible if it was a warranty.

A *fraudulent misrepresentation*[24] was a false statement consciously known to be so by its speaker (usually the seller, although buyers can make false claims in trade, also). When that conscious knowledge existed and could be proved, the seller was responsible for the falsity.

Thus buyers had two methods under caveat emptor by which they could take sellers to court for a false claim: they could show the seller worded it as a warranty and/or stated it fraudulently, knowing it to be false.

Those two possibilities appeared superficially to supply ways for consumers to protect themselves. But in reality they came to operate in the king's common law as aspects of sellerism by becoming easy for sellers to avoid. Sellers were entitled legally to lie so long as they escaped warranty and fraud charges. Consequently, the cases such as the bezar-stone incident that made such escapes relatively easy became the main events that established caveat emptor and the era of extreme sellerism.

Rules that are on the books but can rarely be applied give only the appearance and not the real substance of regulation. Warranty and fraud were of that sort, being strictly burdens to buyers compared with the previous provisions that had outlawed false claims in no uncertain terms. Sellers in the early Middle Ages were wholly responsible for the goods, whether they manufactured them or obtained them from someone else. To Aquinas conscious falsity was sin as well as fraud, but even innocent falsity (which was neither) obligated the seller to make good the buyer's loss.[25] The same held true in the civil law (the heritage of Rome) and the law of the merchants; sellers were responsible for their claims, and were responsible beyond such claims for all qualities that buyers might reasonably expect in the goods. The idea was nonexistent that buyers had to prove fraud or warranty in order to confer liability on sellers for misrepresentations.

Yet eventually the rules developed that those steps must be taken. Existing records do not show exactly when and how it happened. English common law's earliest recorded treatment of fraudulent misrepresentation in sales (then called deceit) appears in a case from the year 1367 in which a person took some "beeves" from their owner and sold them "as if they had been his own." He did not say the cattle were his, but was found to know he was not the owner, and the act of selling was itself the representation held deceitful.[26] The record of that case is very slim, and allows the conjecture that the court did not mean to rule that a misrepresentation must be known false by its speaker to be illegal. Perhaps the court meant merely that the falsity of the seller's act was sufficient to make it illegal.

By happenstance the falsity was about ownership, and we might imagine that persons who possessed something but had not purchased it could hardly help but know consciously that they did not own it. They might be innocently ignorant of defects in its quality, but could not be ignorant as to whether they owned it. Accordingly, and I am speculating, the court might well have found that the seller knew he was not the owner only because it seemed obvious and added to the case against him, without necessarily meaning that conscious falsity was required generally for making sellers responsible.

Whether or not that speculation is correct, the fraud requirement crept into the king's common law at some date by some sort of event, very possibly accidentally because it was not present in the laws preceding it. And it favored sellers considerably because there were many cases in which sellers' falsity was evident but the buyer could not prove it in court.

Dale's Case[27] from 1585 shows how effectively this inability could work against unfortunate buyers. The seller had sold "certain goods" to the buyer, not owning them and not saying he owned them. The true owner showed up and forced the buyer to return the goods to him. The seller's falsity was just as evident as in the 1367 case, and the buyer brought suit accordingly. But his case failed because his counsel made the technical error of failing to *allege* in court that the seller *knew* of his falsity. By procedure, the court was not empowered to investigate charges not specifically alleged.

One of the three justices, Anderson, argued on the grounds of the 1367 case that conscious falsity should be assumed by the court whether alleged or not, because it was obvious. He therefore favored a decision for the aggrieved buyer who would otherwise lose both the goods and the money paid for them. Anderson's viewpoint produced a divided court on the question of what the seller had known to be true, but all three justices agreed that conscious knowledge of falsity needed to be shown to find legal misrepresentation. That appears to have been the earliest case to make that point clearly.[28]

Readers perhaps should imagine cases of their own to appreciate the strong degree of sellerism that the fraud requirement produced. Suppose a seller falsely describes a product to you, and you make the purchase on that basis. You discover the defects later, but the seller refuses to return your money or replace the product. You sue, and the judge asks you whether you can prove the seller knew the falsehoods were false. You state you are certain of it, but you acknowledge there is no way you can prove that. The judge concludes that the seller has committed only innocent and not fraudulent misrepresentation. The seller goes free and you are stuck. Today there are ways by which you may charge nonfraudulent misrepresentation with liability,[29] but in the sixteenth century it was fraud or warranty or nothing at all.

As misrepresentation became a seller's tool, so did warranty. We do not know precisely when the notion developed that an object sold would be held legally guaranteed by sellers who warranted. The laws in England prior to the king's common law had bound sellers to guarantee outrightly what they sold. Warranties might be demanded and supplied to clarify the terms of a sale, but were not needed to hold a seller liable.

Nonetheless, an English court found a man liable in 1383 for falsely warranting the quality of a horse.[30] This first-recorded mention of warranty apparently signaled a new custom in which sellers' explicit warranties would be the only means to create their guarantees. Other cases that undoubtedly contributed to the change are lost in the obscurity that veils ancient events. Eventually we find Fitzherbert, in the same year he mentioned caveat emptor, writing that "It behooveth that he [the seller] warrant it [the wine] to be good, and the horse to be sound, otherwise the action will not lie. For if he sell the wine or horse without such warranty, it is at the other's peril, and his [the buyer's] eyes and his taste ought to be his judges in that case."[31]

To say a warranty was *necessary* for the buyer to avoid "peril" was a big move to sellerism. And the next development, in which only certain types of sellers' statements would constitute warranties, was even more so. Preceding laws had hold no special wording necessary to make a seller's claim a warranty. "Between a simple word and an oath God draws no distinction," Aquinas had said.[32] But now the "simple word" turned out to be no warranty unless indicating by its wording that the seller intended it so.

This extremely sellerist point, which practically eliminated the buyer's access to warranty protection, was developed primarily in the bezar-stone case. As we look at that famous case of 1603, known in the records as *Chandelor v. Lopus*,[33] we will consider fraud as well as warranty, because the case had the coincidental effect of showing how the luckless buyer under caveat emptor could be denied both of those supposed protections at once.

The issue in *Chandelor v. Lopus* was whether Chandelor, a jeweler, should be liable for selling to Lopus an object described inaccurately as a bezar-stone. Since that ancient curiosity is not for sale in our modern stores, we should describe it. The *Oxford Dictionary*[34] identifies the bezar-stone as a "calculus or concretion" formed of concentric layers and found in the stomachs of animals, chiefly ruminants (cud chewers), including in particular the "wild goat of Persia." "Bezar" comes from a Persian word meaning "counterpoison" or "antidote."

Whatever freed the body of a particular ailment was the "bezar of that ailment." The owner applied it to the diseased part of the body to obtain the cure.[35]

Lopus apparently tried that without success. We know, at any rate, that he discovered his prize to be no bezar-stone. We also know he subsequently was told in court that Chandelor had not *warranted* the object to be such. Chandelor had only *said* it was, and that was not enough. The court declared that "the bare affirmation that it was a bezar-stone, without warranting it to be so, is no cause of action."

What a wondrous decision, to say a statement of fact has no legal status as such. Sellers may make statements with utter disregard for their truth, because they are only claims and not warranties. Sellers may have their cake and eat it, too; they offer the statement as true, and the buyers are responsible if it is false. The buyers are persuaded because they receive a promise, then find that the promise unfulfilled was never a promise at all—only a claim.

The difference between affirmation and warranty gave caveat emptor a force it could not otherwise have had. If every selling claim were a warranty, caveat emptor would have had a much narrower scope. It would have applied only to the extent that sellers kept quiet about the particular features of an object. Sellers, of course, could easily remain silent where the features were hidden aspects that buyers would not know about nor think to inquire about, or when buyers were reluctant to press a point. But once asked for information, sellers would hardly want to decline, since such action could warn buyers of trouble.

To separate affirmation and warranty, however, granted sellers a far greater immunity from responsibility. Rather than be trapped by requests for information, they could issue all sorts of statements in the guise of being informative, the while carefully avoiding phrases such as "I warrant," "I promise," or "I guarantee" that were the only actions that could compel them to be really informative. Buyers of course could always ask sellers to warrant their claims, but as with the unfortunate Lopus they often did not.

Some buyers probably were reluctant to ask, with a formal request seeming socially improper because it implies that one does not trust the seller. One may not, indeed, but it is embarrassing to confront openly a person who has just "affirmed" that something is so. Undoubtedly many buyers had strong tendencies to trust, or at least to avoid showing distrust, despite the law's assumption that all persons engaging in trade were automatically distrustful. Sellers, knowing full well that the presumed distrust was merely a theory, turned the situation swiftly to profit.

Other buyers may have failed to realize an affirmation was not a warranty. We can hear Lopus protesting, "But he said it was a bezar-stone. He didn't say, 'I think it's one, but I'm not sure.' He said it absolutely was one. What more could he say?" Despite that, the court decided Chandelor did not specifically word the statement as a promise he was willing to back up. And that was that!

In this way the concept of warranty evolved from a principle of action for buyers to a principle of action for sellers. In original form it was intended to give buyers a way to hold sellers responsible for claims. In brief logical form the rule stated, "If warranty, then protection." Sellers, however, were not slow in grasping the significance of the corollary proposition, "If no warranty, then no protection." Although the second was not logically required by the first, it was made law as well. And in the way it aided sellers rather than buyers, it stated the true essence of caveat emptor as that principle came to be famous. There's no surprise, then, in finding a modern dictionary defining caveat emptor by its negative rather than positive form: "the principle that the seller cannot be held responsible for the quality of his product unless guaranteed in a warranty."[36]

With the seller-favoring nature of the rule due greatly to *Chandelor v. Lopus*, we should wonder why such a questionable decision was made by the English court. Possibly it went as it did because of the peculiar nature of bezar-stones. Could the judges perhaps have meant only that an affirmation should not in fairness be regarded as a warranty about something so subjective as that, without intending to rule more broadly that affirmations about most things shall never be warranties? This possibility, posed by a legal writer named Grant Gilmore,[37] is based on the reasoning that, while most objects of trade have solidly tangible physical features, the characteristics of the bezar-stone depended more on the user's state of mind.

We might think of the matter as an early example of the placebos doctors use today, pills that contain no medicine but work because patients think they do. The bezar-stone was apparently accepted by substantial numbers of people so we might wonder whether Lopus gave it a good try. Did he apply his stone to the right place and rub, press, or scratch hard enough, and exhibit sufficient faith in his cure to make it work? We shall never know whether he did, nor what disease he had, nor whether his stone might have been the bezar, after all, of some different ailment.

And if it was difficult for Lopus to determine all this, it must have been even more difficult for Chandelor to know with certainty that it was actually a bezar-stone. Perhaps the judges, though they might have been stern in punishing Chandelor had he misrepresented something simpler to assess, such as a horse, were less willing to condemn him for a wrong assertion about something that might really have been a bezar-stone had Lopus only thought so strongly enough! Perhaps under such conditions Chandelor could not reasonably have warranted the stone, so the court protected him by declaring that such affirmation was not a warranty. If Gilmore's speculation is correct, then the intended meaning was obscured in the reporting of the case in the permanent court records. We do not know, of course, but court reporting in 1603 is known not to have been very reliable.

There were other accidents, too, with *Chandelor v. Lopus*, that altered the case's outcome. Perhaps before describing them I should say I will be identifying other accidental happenings in this book, enough to suggest that the law of the marketplace developed as it did almost entirely by chance. I interpret these accidents as significant, because a principal purpose of this look at history is to determine whether sellerism is as strongly rooted in law as advertisers tend to believe, or whether it has a relatively weak foundation that would tend to justify the efforts of those who would replace it with consumerism. The many accidents contributing to the development of sellerism of course encourage the latter belief.

That does not mean, however, that the circumstances producing particular cases are the sole events that determine the law. Probably more critical than what the precedents are, or how solidly they are established, is the matter of *how a court wants to rule*. Precedents are often available to support either side of a case, which gives a court the opportunity to choose those that suit its predilections. A law text such as Prosser and Keeton's treatise on torts[38] reveals topic after topic where a long list of decisions made in one direction is followed by another list made oppositely. In United States law this occurs often because there are fifty independent states, with many accepting a certain rule while many others reject it. The only time it cannot happen is when the Supreme Court resolves an issue and imposes its ruling on all lower jurisdictions. But in the law of the marketplace there are many issues never taken to the Supreme Court and therefore never decided conclusively.

The critical thing about *Chandelor v. Lopus*, therefore, was not just that it happened accidentally but also that the English courts *wanted* to rule in favor of sellers.[39] They therefore found *Chandelor* convenient to cite. Had it never existed the task would have been harder, but the courts would still have based their decisions on whatever precedents or arguments they could scrape up in favor of sellers. That explains why many of the cases we will see below cited precedents that seem scarcely appropriate for the role, or offered arguments whose logic seems severely strained in reaching the decisions they supposedly compel. Had the courts wanted instead to favor buyers they would merely have ignored the sellerist cases and used other cases that in fact became the ones ignored all those years. So in emphasizing the accidentalness of many decisions I am not implying that sellerism wouldn't have happened if the accidents hadn't.

But the accidents have another sort of significance because of the current trend toward replacing sellerism with consumerism (remember, these terms indicate that the law primarily favors one party over the other). As the switchover from favoring sellers occurs in recent times, the old precedents of sellerism have been gradually swept away. And they can be swept away much more readily when found to have been questionably established in the first place. Advocates of sellerism may argue today that caveat emptor cannot be rejected because the heritage that produced it has been consecrated for all time as a creed of human conduct. Many cases examined in this book, however, suggest that such argument is foolish in light of what actually happened.

So let's return to see what accidents befell the infamous case of *Chandelor v. Lopus*. Absent inadvertent misfortune, the court probably would have found Chandelor liable for fraudulent misrepresentation. The misfortune came in the original court case brought by Lopus. The case called *Chandelor v. Lopus* that we have already described was an appeal of that first case by Chandelor before the Court of the Exchequer. The original case was held before the King's Bench,[40] which awarded Lopus a judgment on the grounds that Chandelor was deceitful in representing the bezar-stone. But the case contained a lucky charm for Chandelor, not a bezar but a charm to cure legal ailments. It was the fact that Lopus' suit failed to *allege* that Chandelor's deceit was fraudulent (conscious, deliberate). Misrepresentation, as established in the earlier *Dale's Case*, was not illegal otherwise, yet poor Lopus did not charge fraud specifically.

Perhaps he had the same lawyer as did the buyer-plaintiff in *Dale's Case*, it being the same mistake that enabled the defendant there to escape.

In his Exchequer appeal (*Chandelor v. Lopus*), Chandelor successfully urged that technicality. All the judges but one refused to consider a matter called to the court's attention improperly. The dissenter was Anderson, the same who had dissented on the similar point in *Dale's Case*. Both times Anderson thought a fraudulent misrepresentation existed and so should be held liable even if not alleged. But he was outvoted, and Chandelor escaped action on the misrepresentation charge. That done, the court then considered warranty. There would have been no need to find Chandelor liable on both fraud and warranty counts, so if the fraud charge had stuck, the court would have ignored whether Chandelor warranted and would never have explained why it though he hadn't. But luck brought the warranty issue to bear, and Chandelor escaped action on it, too.

He escaped for the moment only, because Lopus initiated the third court case in the series, this time charging fraud specifically. Again ill fortune played a role, as this suit was omitted entirely from the customary publication of court records. In 1618 a casual mention was recorded in another case to the effect that Lopus had won.[41] In 1894 the missing case was discovered in manuscript and finally printed. But it did not resolve the doubt, as the apparently incomplete report ended with the judges adjourning while still divided.[42]

The result of all these events was to immortalize Chandelor's apparent victory in *Chandelor v. Lopus* rather than the final decision, which may have been different. Without all of these accidents there would have been no legitimizing of the difference between warranty and affirmation. Had Lopus alleged deliberate misrepresentation in the original King's Bench case, or had the final case been adequately reported, the warranty aspect of the sale would have been little noted. And had the object of sale not been a bezar-stone, perhaps Chandelor's affirmation would have been a warranty after all.

But the accidents happened, and caveat emptor was on its way. The buyer's loss of warranty protection because affirmations were not warranties was the key to the subsequent fantastic growth of sellerism. Such developments did not produce a full-blown caveat emptor in the seventeenth century but served to enable its eventual acceptance. Fitzherbert's rule was in contrast to typical market operations of his day, and the judgment against Lopus occurred similarly in a context of no general inclinations toward sellerism.

But, as Hamilton states, "The words were there, ready to bear the ideas of a later age."[43]

The later age brought many events alien to the Middle Ages.[44] Power in human affairs was transferred in great quantity to industrialists and traders who used it to escape the authoritarian rule of church and king. In the lands of the Reformation, religion had become less authoritarian anyway, and in fact developed the helpful dogma that business and trade were God's work rather than the devil's. From Protestantism and the philosophers came the notion of individualism, stating that individual human beings could reason and look out for themselves. From the economists came the notion of laissez-faire, holding that merchants and their customers would arrive at fair and proper bargains through the automatic process of competition, without need for regulation. All of these developments led during the seventeenth and eighteenth centuries to the significant notions that sellers and buyers were equal and therefore none of their interactions need be guaranteed.

How anyone could claim seller and buyer truly were equal seems amazing in light of other events of the time! The growth of trade exposed buyers to much reduction in their trading competence at the exact time the theory arguing the opposite was developing. In earlier days buyers were often as competent as sellers in assessing goods; there was less need to ask sellers to describe them. Sellers had little chance to engage actively in "selling" (that is, "persuading"). They could only present the item for sale and hope it would withstand the examination it would surely get. Nor could they escape examination of their own reputations as well; sellers in early times were well known personally in the communities where they dealt.

But times changed. Now objects appeared, from strange places, offered by strange sellers. Old objects appeared from a greater variety of outlets, bearing new and unfamiliar distinctions in features and quality. Goods began to be manufactured, using technical processes not generally understood by the public. The chance that buyers could match sellers' understanding dwindled as they became less able even to identify goods, much less assess their quality. The idea of true equality of seller and buyer in an age of professional selling seems thoroughly unnatural.

The very name of the rule, caveat emptor, suggests that society realized no true equality was involved. Why not call it, given equality, caveat venditor as much as caveat emptor? Under equality buyers would gain the better bargain as often as sellers, and the rule might properly be worded, "Let *both* parties to the bargain beware." I cannot imagine a judge or anyone else pronouncing sellers and buyers equal and then asserting as the logical outcome that it was the buyer who was to be wary.

But it's what happened! Those who benefited from the new alignments of power decreed that equality existed and caveat emptor applied. Particularly in America did it happen, in the new lands with the vast frontiers where growth and development were valued above all else. "All purchasers, in presumption of law, are deemed competent judges of what they are about to buy," argued counsel for a seller defendant in a New York case of 1804. "If they will purchase without attention to circumstances," he added, "the maxim of caveat emptor ought to apply." The court agreed; case dismissed. The decision sermonized that caveat emptor was a rule of fine moral standing, having the useful social function of causing buyers to be at their best: "I see no injustice or inconvenience resulting from this doctrine, but on the contrary, think it best calculated to excite that caution and attention which all prudent men ought to observe in making their contracts."[45]

This stressing of the opportunity for moral disciplining was a rationalization thrown in by a court anxious to bolster the affairs of business. It was, as Hamilton suggests, a notion new and American in origin: "Not until the nineteenth century, did judges discover that caveat emptor sharpened wits, taught self-reliance, made a man—an economic man—out of the buyer, and served well its two masters, business and justice."[46]

No one said anything about its applying to the seller, too. The case was *Seixas and Seixas v. Woods*,[47] in which Woods had sold to the plaintiffs a shipment of "peachum wood" identified falsely as "brazilletto," "the former worth hardly anything, the latter of considerable value." Woods, as agent for a distant merchant, was as uninformed as buyers often are. Knowing only that the invoice described the cargo as brazilletto, he advertised it as such, and when the Seixases bought it he showed them the invoice and made out the bill for brazilletto. Upon discovery of the inaccuracy he refused to take back the wood or return the payment. The resulting suit brought judgment against him, but review by the New York Supreme Court brought reversal on the grounds that no warranty existed and that the misrepresentation was not fraudulent because Woods was fooled just as the Seixases were fooled, or at least there was no proof otherwise.

The court was firm in holding that caveat emptor, although not caveat venditor, should be applied in the absence of warranty and fraud. Justice James Kent cited the precedent of *Chandelor v. Lopus*, and noted that "there is no instance in the English law of a contrary rule being laid down." He acknowledged that he might alternately have followed the civil law of Roman heritage, which had preceded the king's common law and was much different: "The civil law . . . is more rigorous towards the seller, and makes him responsible in every case for a latent defect. . . . By the civil law, says Lord Coke, every man is bound to warrant the thing that he selleth, albeit there be no express warranty; but the common law bindeth him not, unless there be a warranty in deed, or law."[48]

Note the chance for the newly developing American law to reject the king's law that embraced caveat emptor and adopt another heritage that had no place for such rule. The American nation had recently relieved itself of the yoke of English control and was free to follow its own lights as it had in many other areas. But Kent thought the English in this instance had made the correct decision: "The rule of the common law has been well and elegantly vindicated by Fonblanque, as most happily reconciling the claims of convenience with the duties of good faith. It requires the purchaser to apply his attention to those particulars which may be supposed within the reach of his observation and judgment."

Was the identification of "brazilletto" really within the reach of the Seixases' observation and judgment? Were all purchasers, as Woods's counsel claimed, truly "competent judges of what they were about to buy"? Surely they were not, and the law's automatic presumption that they were seems enormously unreasonable. It seems particularly so when the buyer's usual level of competence is reduced by the distraction caused by the seller's false claim. Yet the New York court was firm on the point, just as was Herbert Williams' court much later (see chapter 2), that the Seixases' opportunity to examine the goods made it incumbent upon them to be responsible for what they bought.

Charging a buyer with responsibility might seem more palatable if the seller were held equally responsible. One might draw a contrast with twentieth-century negligence cases in which the law of some states permits a finding of a certain percentage of negligence by each party. The arrangement seems appropriate for *Seixas*, since both sides were ignorant of the error being made. But the law controlling their transaction gave all or nothing, and when both were negligent the buyer got the nothing.

Caveat emptor rolled on to a high point in 1870 when Justice Davis stated for the Supreme Court that "no principle of the common law has been better established, or more often affirmed. . . ."[49] Well established it was, yet the arbitrariness reeks. Events were not fitted to the law; rather, the law was fitted to the events desired by those who felt any trade was better than none at all: "Trade is beginning to grow, and beginning to appear desirable. Actions against sellers will embarrass trade, and be bad policy. They would increase the risks of trading to an unforeseeable extent, and so discourage enterprise in trade."[50]

The solution, therefore, was to adopt standards in the market that would never be accepted in other areas of human endeavor. The difference was never so well illustrated as by a court case in which a defendant tried to excuse his shabby deeds by holding the rule of caveat emptor against the plaintiff, only to be told that the events of the case occurred away from the marketplace and so caveat emptor did not apply.[51] The year was 1885, and the court's opinion was given by Oliver Wendell Holmes, who we will see later was instrumental in establishing puffery's legal status.

In this case before the Supreme Judicial Court of Massachusetts, Holmes considered the situation of some persons who, due to legal obligations they had failed to meet, had some property including eight fishing traps "attached" by a deputy sheriff. Or so the deputy said, though it later turned out his statement was false. "Attaching" means taking under control, and the owners of the traps, who had left them spread in a field for drying, were told by the deputy that if they "meddled with them it would be at their peril." The traps were perishable, subject to destruction by freezing to the ground in winter ice and snow. The owners, therefore, periodically begged the deputy to take proper care of them. They were never touched, however, and subsequently suffered damage that ruined them entirely.

It later developed that to attach the traps validly, the deputy would have had to take them into his actual physical possession. On these grounds he denied responsibility for the damage done, claiming he had not legally made the attachment and so could not be held liable. The owners, nonetheless, went to court on the grounds of the deputy's statement to them prior to the time of damage that he had in fact attached the traps. The owners declared they were justified in relying on the claim of attachment and were not obliged to check further with legal authorities to verify its truth.

The deputy's defense was to rely on caveat emptor, by which the owners were obligated to check the truth for themselves and not rely on his claim. Had the owners ascertained the legal requirements for attaching goods, they would have realized there was no legal attachment. The deputy had not warranted his statement, nor was it fraudulent misrepresentation because the falsity was "obvious" (meaning the owners would have discovered it had they examined the law). Given this, the deputy argued, the owners were fully responsible through failure to exercise the ordinary care expected of them.

Not so, decided Holmes. The deputy's defense, he said, was based on cases "concerning the manifest quality of goods offered for sale." But this was not a matter of the marketplace, not a transaction between buyer and seller, nor a transaction that the owners of the traps undertook voluntarily. Beyond the marketplace, one cannot require persons to distrust claims simply because they themselves may have the ability and opportunity to obtain independent verification: "The standard of good faith required in sales is somewhat low, not only out of allowance for the weakness of human nature, but because it is not desirable to interfere too much for the purpose of helping men in their voluntary transactions more than they help themselves."

Aside from sales, however, the rule was different. The deputy sheriff was held responsible and required to pay the owners $3,298.07 in damages. Thus do we see the difference it makes in law to be dealing in the marketplace. If the deputy had told his lies in a selling transaction, he would have gone free. *The standard of good faith required in sales is somewhat low*! Indeed it was, and in America has always been.

Yet in the twentieth century caveat emptor has lost its original strength, as we will see in subsequent chapters that discuss what elements of it are now eliminated and what still remain. Chapter 5 will examine the warranty rule, detailing its rise from the seeds of *Chandelor v. Lopus* as a tool of sellerism, and its later change as sellerism gave way to consumerism. Chapter 6 will describe the parallel story of misrepresentation, which also in modern times has had a long slide from the heights of sellerism. In these chapters we will see the trend toward rejection of caveat emptor and toward imposition of liability upon sellers and manufacturers for the claims they make and the goods they sell. Chapters 8 and 9 will show how the Federal Trade Commission has further replaced sellerism with consumerism.

In the remaining chapters, however, beginning with Chapter 7, we will see the story of those remnants of caveat emptor and sellerism that persist in the law today. They are, of course, the several varieties of puffery, of false claims that may deceive the consumer but which the law by its sellerist traditions still describes as being nondeceptive. It has often been written in this century that caveat emptor is dead.[52] The intention of this book is to show that it is not. The standard of faith required in sales may be considerably improved by consumerism's many developments, but it is still much lower than we would like it to be.

5

Warranty: How Much Promise Do You Find in a Promise?

In describing caveat emptor we saw how the warranty concept, potentially a powerful tool of consumerism, was created but quickly defined so that it would hardly ever apply. In this chapter we follow those sellerist interpretations from English into American law, and see how they eventually changed so that the advantages warranty gave consumers in theory were finally realized in practice. There is still some trouble today in getting warranty law to help consumers, but the trend away from sellerism has been distinct and will probably continue. The methods used to keep sellers' claims from being warranties will die hard, though, and while they remain the ghost of the bezar-stone will yet haunt the land.

The trail of warranty is strewn with ironies and accidents, only the first of which occurred with Lopus' magic cud. Some further zany events helped keep *Chandelor v. Lopus*[1] alive as what jurists call a "leading case." One occurred after England's Lord Holt made consumerist rulings in 1689 and 1700. He rejected the development seen in chapter 4 that kept affirmations from being warranties, but by untimely luck his words were distorted so that they appeared to support the *Chandelor* doctrine rather than oppose it.

A seller sold two oxen belonging to another that he affirmed were his own. Contrary to *Chandelor*, Holt ruled that the bare statement of ownership warranted that the seller had legal title to the oxen. Since the warranty was breached, the buyer could recover from the seller for the loss when the oxen had to be returned to the real owner. Holt's reasoning was the essence of simplicity: the buyer had no way to know the real owner, and thus he deserved warranty protection.[2]

That was what the dissenter Anderson had said in *Dale's Case* in 1585,[3] but it took a century for the viewpoint to win a court majority.[4]

Holt didn't directly reject *Chandelor*, because the latter was concerned with the quality of goods rather than with their ownership. While buyers couldn't determine ownership by examining the oxen, they could check their quality. Therefore Holt's reasoning about lack of opportunity to know the truth was not necessarily applicable to sellers' affirmations about quality. His cases were significant, nonetheless, because they established that "mere" affirmations *sometimes* amounted to warranties, rebutting the implication from *Chandelor* that they never could. That small exception paved the way for the eventual discrediting of the bezar-stone case in favor of deciding that affirmations typically *do* amount to warranties.[5]

A funny thing happened to Holt's idea, however, upon being quoted in *Pasley v. Freeman*.[6] Justice Buller ruled therein that "It was rightly held by Holt, C.J., in [*Crosse* and *Medina*] that an affirmation at the time of a sale is a warranty, provided it appear on evidence to have been so intended." The latter phrase of Buller's statement was wrong; Holt had wanted affirmations (of ownership, at least) to be regarded legally as warranties whether the seller intended them to be so or not. But when *Pasley* emerged as a leading case in the law of misrepresentation, Buller's mistaken interpretation became much quoted in critical later cases, turning the treatment of warranty away from Holt's consumerist reasoning and back toward that of *Chandelor*.[7]

The error's consequences were especially felt in 1804, when Buller's mistake was incorporated into *Seixas and Seixas v. Woods*,[8] which became the leading case for establishing caveat emptor and the warranty rule in American law. The seller Woods, as we saw in chapter 4, called the wood brazilletto when it was not, and was sued on the ground that he therefore had warranted it so. "If the facts in the case do not amount to a warranty," the Seixases' lawyer argued, "it will hardly be possible to create one." But the court disagreed, Justice Kent deciding that "The mentioning of the wood as brazilletto wood, in the bill of parcels, and in the advertisements some days previous to the sale, did not amount to a warranty to the plaintiffs. To make an affirmation at the time of the sale, a warranty, it must appear by evidence to be so intended (Buller, J. . . .)."

Seixas was decided in New York, a major industrial state whose legal pronouncements weighed heavily on the courts of other states, many of whom welcomed the principle that not all affirmations were warranties. When the Massachusetts court disagreed, however, *Brad-ford v. Manly*[9] emerged in 1816 as the first American case to condemn *Chandelor* and rule that something less than a specifically worded promise about the nature of goods should legally be a warranty. The buyer Bradford had examined a sample before purchasing two casks of cloves from Manly, but found what he later received to be inferior. A jury upheld his suit because "the purchase was made upon the confidence that the whole quantity was represented by the sample." On appeal Manly argued that he should be liable only for an express statement of warranty and he had made none, citing *Chandelor* and *Seixas* among his authorities.

This brought a direct confrontation in which the old cases lost. Chief Justice Parker of Massachusetts held that "a sale by sample is tantamount to an express warranty." He expressed a viewpoint of plain fairness, asking, "For what purpose is a sample exhibited, unless it is intended as a representation of the thing sold?" No one, he said, would expect a seller to give an explicit statement of warranty along with his sample, because "What would an honorable merchant say, if, when he took from a mass of sugar or coffee a small parcel, and offered to sell by it, the man who was dealing with him should ask him if it was a fair sample, and call upon him to warrant it so?" Rather than ask such an embarrassing question, Parker thought, most buyers would take the sample itself as an express warranty that what was sold would be similar.

Parker appears to have grasped the true state of a typical buyer's mind, one reluctant to accuse sellers openly of speaking falsely. *Chandelor* required doubting buyers to say to the seller, in effect, "You stated such-and-such, but are you willing to state it again in a way that will make you legally liable for it?" Such statements tend to imply distrust, which most people don't want to charge routinely. Parker's solution, making the seller's original statement stand legally as the appropriate guarantee, eliminated any need to ask for more.

Parker also said *Chandelor* "would not now be received as law in England," and, he added, "certainly not in our country," a pointed rejection of *Seixas*. He added that in a case of "two or three years ago" he had ruled in favor of a buyer who purchased a commodity on the basis of a newspaper advertisement offering "Carraccas cocoa." Parker had interpreted that ad, too, as an express warranty.

Elsewhere the shadow of the bezar-stone remained for some time on both sides of the ocean. A classic English illustration of its effects came when a seller gave a buyer the following receipt: "Received of Mr. Budd 10£ for a grey four year old colt, warranted sound in every respect." Finding the horse to be only three, the buyer sued for breach of warranty, but the court found it significant that part of the statement came before and part came after the word "warranted." The judge concluded: "I should say that . . . the intention of the parties was to confine the warranty to soundness, and that the preceding statement was matter of description only. And the difference is most essential. . . ."[10] One wonders whether both parties really meant to confine the warranty to soundness, and whether they agreed that mere "matter of description only" need not be subject to standards of truth. The age of the colt was important to the buyer for breeding reasons, and while he may not have told this to the seller, we can scarcely imagine that he openly disclaimed its importance either. Probably he thought he was adequately covered by the wording, and was furious on finding that he wasn't.

The Supreme Court of Pennsylvania, meanwhile, repudiated *Chandelor* in 1831, then reversed itself in 1839 and retained the bezarstone principle. In the first case[11] the court agreed with *Bradford v. Manly* that "a sample, or description in a sale note, advertisement, bill of parcels, or invoice, is equivalent to an express warranty that the goods are what they are described." Chief Justice Gibson dissented strongly, however, and with a change in the court's make-up his Chandelorian viewpoint prevailed in the later case, *McFarland v. Newman*.[12]

A jury found that McFarland made a "positive averment" that the horse he was selling was sound except for a temporary display of ordinary distemper. The disease being actually permanent, the jury returned a verdict for the buyer. On appeal, Gibson obtained the majority he lacked earlier and reversed the rule with the ringing declaration that "the naked averment of a fact is neither a warranty itself nor evidence of it." His view, despite being what one writer called "a singular atrophy of legal development,"[13] became so dominant in Pennsylvania law that it remained long after the position was revoked everywhere else. The difference was so great that Samuel Williston, in his famous treatise on sales law, found it necessary to discuss Pennsylvania in a separate section, apart from all other state laws.[14]

Typical of the trend elsewhere were cases repudiating *Seixas* right in its home state of New York. James Kent's influential *Commentaries on American Law* observed in 1867 that there was doubt that *Seixas* had been properly decided.[15] Kent himself was no longer alive, but ironically the expression of doubt written into his fifth edition by a later editor was published under the name of the original author. Although Kent had decided with the majority in *Seixas*, vigorously defending *Chandelor* and similar precedents, the writer in charge of updating his work now had second thoughts upon reading cases such as *Bradford v. Manly*.

This revised judgment became law in New York in *Hawkins v. Pemberton* of 1872.[16] The record established the problem in this now-familiar way: "Did the plaintiff [seller] warrant the article to be blue vitriol? It is unquestioned that . . . he represented it to be blue vitriol." The old rule lost when the court decided: "It is not true, as sometimes stated, that the representation, in order to constitute a warranty, must have been intended by the vendor as a warranty. . . . The vendor will not be permitted to say that he did not intend what his language clearly and explicitly declares. . . . He is responsible for the language he uses, and cannot escape liability by claiming that he did not intend to convey the impression which his language was calculated to produce. . . ."

From a modern viewpoint one cannot help feeling that common sense at last prevailed. Of course sellers shouldn't be allowed to claim they didn't mean to imply what their language clearly was calculated to imply—what could be more fair! As in *Bradford*, and harking back to *Dale's Case*, the decision was made precisely on the grounds of sheer fairness, with the comment added that the doctrine of *Chandelor* had been exploded. As for *Seixas*, the *Hawkins* court declared that old case "thoroughly overturned" and said it "can no longer be regarded as authority for the precise point decided" because "the law was not properly applied to the facts. . . ."[17]

Except for independent Pennsylvania, *Hawkins* typified the turnabout of United States law in the late 1800s to make affirmations of fact equivalent to warranties. The trend was solidified by the drafting of the Uniform Sales Act early in the next century. Until that time, warranty law had been a matter of common law, developed through the opinions of judges in court cases. In contrast, statute law is enacted by legislatures in response to general needs. The Uniform Sales Act[18] was a model statute drawn with the hope of standardizing sales law in all the states. The success of any model statute depends upon the number of adoptions, and during the period 1907–42 versions of the act were passed by thirty-four states, plus Alaska, Hawaii, and the District of Columbia. It said:

§12 Definition of Express Warranty.—Any affirmation of fact or any promise by the seller relating to the goods is an express warranty if the natural tendency of such affirmation or promise is to induce the buyer to purchase the goods, and if the buyer purchases the goods relying thereon. . . .

Passage of the act, and a corresponding Sale of Goods Act that preceded it in England,[19] assured that warranty law would enhance consumerism in the twentieth century. Cases continued, however, that harked back through ignorance or stubbornness to the old sellerist interpretation. In 1913 England's House of Lords dredged up Buller's quotation of Holt to the effect that any warranty must be so intended by the seller.[20] It was so obvious a mistake that it might have been easily corrected but for the nasty complication that Lords was forbidden to overrule its own decisions.

In Pennsylvania, the court managed several times to ignore the Uniform Sales Act and rely upon Gibson's decision about the "naked averment of a fact."[21] In 1965, fifty long years after the state's passage of the act, a court of appeals had to remind a Pennsylvania judge that he went against his own state's law in instructing a jury to find no express warranty unless the seller actually intended to be bound by his statement.[22]

Too, a number of states never adopted the Uniform Sales Act. But the act was eventually succeeded by the Uniform Commercial Code, which by 1968 was adopted in every state but Louisiana. The code's section 2–313, defining warranties much as had section 12 of the Uniform Sales Act, finally brought the ancient bezar-stone interpretation to an end.[23]

Defining all factual affirmations as warranties, however, was not the end of the ways that warranty developments have aided modern consumerism. To see the rest we must describe *implied* warranties, entirely distinct from those discussed so far. While warranties consisting of statements made literally by the seller are called *express* warranties, implied warranties are those held to exist legally without being expressed. They apply automatically, whether or not the seller consents, whenever a sale of goods is transacted.

Implied warranties are the utter opposite of caveat emptor. At its sellerist height the Latin phrase not only excused sellers from responsibility for misrepresentations that were neither warranty nor fraud, but also excused them from responsibility for any features of the goods about which they made no representations at all. Buyers were obligated to inspect all nonrepresented matters themselves, and to rely wholly upon that inspection, with no legal recourse. Sellers had zero accountability with respect to their silence.

The implied warranty reversed that situation, making the seller wholly accountable. The more implied warranties there are, the less buyers need check the goods themselves to fulfill their legal obligation. Should there eventually be implied warranties covering every characteristic of the goods sold, and every aspect of the selling transaction, there would be no more caveat emptor. That point has not yet been approached, but the trend over time has resulted in the firm establishment of the general concept and a small number of applications.[24]

In the days of sellerism the implied warranty concept was largely nonexistent. One exception, deriving from ancient statute, amounted to an implied warranty of the pureness of food and drink imposed on persons selling those articles in public places ("common vict-ualers").[25] That rule reflected the tendency of the early Middle Ages, as we saw in chapter 4, to make sellers wholly responsible for the quality of their wares. It was one of few such rules to be retained when the king's common law was established. The law of owner-ship (title) also moved quickly at an early time toward an implied warranty. We have already examined how sellers' statements of own-ership came to be regarded as *express* warranties even though they indicated no intent to warrant.[26] The *implied* warranty of ownership went a step further, holding ownership warranted by the act of the sale even if the seller said nothing.

Such an implied warranty had not existed in the 1367 case in which a man sold "beeves" as his own,[27] nor in *Dale's Case* of 1585 although the dissenting judge favored such a concept.[28] "It shall be intended," Justice Anderson stated, "that he that sold had knowledge whether they were his goods or not." About two hundred years later Sir William Blackstone agreed that "In contracts for sales, it is under-stood that the seller undertakes that the thing sold is his own."[29] Such conclusion seems far more reasonable than the lame excuse given by the majority in *Dale's Case* that "it may be, the defendant [seller] did know no otherwise but that they were his own goods." Admittedly no proof was offered that the seller knew the truth about ownership, but the implied warranty concept eventually adopted assumed that sellers *ought* to know and therefore were responsible for knowing even in rare cases when they might not. In America this implied warranty of ownership (title) was made standard by the Uniform Sales Act[30] and the Uniform Commercial Code.[31]

Early English law, meanwhile, resisted any implied warranties beyond pure food and ownership. The American states followed suit, particularly New York and Pennsylvania, which supported continuance of the *Chandelor* and *Seixas* doctrines about express warranties. Pennsylvania's Chief Justice Gibson admitted in *McFarland v. Newman* that the implied warranty of title existed, but declared haughtily that "caveat emptor disposes of all beside." In the long run he was proved wrong as the development of other implied warranties moved the law instead toward disposing of caveat emptor.

There emerged two implied warranties of the quality of goods, one guaranteeing their "merchantability" and the other their "fitness for a particular purpose." Merchantability means a product shall be fit for the uses to which it is ordinarily put, which are not all the uses to which buyers may put it. Buyers of dress shoes may benefit from the warranty if wanting them for ordinary walking or social purposes, but not if wanting them for mountain climbing. For the latter intention, however, today they may invoke the implied warranty of fitness for a particular purpose, which means a thing will be fit for a purpose they specify to the seller.

The merchantability warranty, where enacted, applies automatically to all transactions of sellers established in the community as merchants of that item (which excludes people selling used cars and other items on their own). The fitness warranty is not similarly automatic but applies when buyers make the particular purpose known to the sellers and the sellers understand that the buyers rely on their judgment. Generally that understanding requires an explicit request by the buyer, although sometimes sellers are presumed to know it through their knowledge of usage in the community.

These two implied warranties do not guarantee all aspects of quality that may be disputed, including what buyers may regard as "good" quality. They guarantee only the minimum goodness needed for the object to carry out its ordinary or particular purpose.

Merchantability was poorly treated when first proposed in England.[32] In *Parkinson v. Lee* of 1802,[33] grain was purchased from an agent of a grower who had watered it to increase weight and enhance price. As in *Seixas*, Parkinson brought the suit against an agent who knew nothing of the deed. But unlike the peachum wood in *Seixas*, which was detectable on the spot by anyone with proper expertise, the grain had a hidden defect leading to rot that was impossible to detect at time of sale. Also, while *Seixas* involved an express claim, no representation was made that the grain was unwatered.

Parkinson's dilemma was precisely that which seems most unfair under caveat emptor. The seller made no representations and therefore had zero responsibility, yet Parkinson had no conceivable opportunity to discover the defect no matter how hard and long he examined it. To remedy this unfairness his counsel argued for "an implied warranty . . . that the commodity should be in a merchantable condition at the time of the sale." What makes sense in the twentieth century, however, made something less than that before. One justice agreed there had been some legal thinking about implied warranties, although no acceptance of them.[34] Parkinson's suit therefore was doomed because "He exercised his own judgment upon it; and knowing, as he must have known, as a dealer in the commodity, that it was subject to the latent defect which afterwards appeared, he bought it at his own risk. . . . If he doubt the goodness, or do not choose to incur any risk of a latent defect, he may refuse to purchase without [express] warranty."

Suppose a merchant today says a similar thing after you buy a television only to have the picture tube blow out on the first day. "You should have known," says the dealer later, "that it was subject to the latent defect which afterwards appeared." Picture tubes, after all, are going to go bad *sometime*! Ordinary purchasers can't determine the date any better than Parkinson could tell the hops were watered, but they know it could happen and so should know enough to demand an express warranty against the event. Otherwise they must take the television at their own risk, or else not buy it.

That won't happen today, because the law has long since taken the big step further that implied warranties represent. In 1815 the seeds of merchantability were established in England in *Gardiner v. Gray*.[35] The object of sale was described as "12 bags of waste silk" in a sale note written when the bargain was made, before delivery. On delivery the goods were found to be "of a quality not saleable under the denomination of 'waste silk.'" The seller contended that the goods were customarily described by that name, but the buyer charged that the circumstances implied a guarantee that the goods would be merchantable, rather than merely describable, as "waste silk." Lord Ellenborough's opinion found that "The intention of both parties must be taken to be that it shall be saleable in the market under the denomination mentioned in the contract between them. The purchaser cannot be supposed to buy goods to lay them on a dunghill." Lord Ellenborough had been one of the justices in *Parkinson*, and he noted that Gardiner had bought his silk on the basis of the description only, whereas Parkinson had examined some of his hops before purchase. It is hard to imagine what difference a chance to examine could make for a defect impossible to see, but the court thought it had made Parkinson negligent in a way Gardiner was not. Those who examined their purchases were to be held responsible at law for knowing everything there was to know about them, whether it was possible to know or not![36]

There is apparently no leading case in which merchantability was introduced to America,[37] but the concept was established here in the nineteenth century and has been enshrined in the Uniform Sales Act[38] and the Uniform Commercial Code.[39]

The implied warranty of fitness for a particular purpose began in the 1800s with several English cases[40] and was established in American law by *Kellogg Bridge Company v. Hamilton* of 1884.[41] Hamilton was a subcontractor to Kellogg Bridge, which had driven foundation piles in the early phases of a bridge-building job. When Hamilton came to erect the bridge he found the piles insufficient, suffered losses through delays and extra work, and sued for damages. Kellogg Bridge obviously knew the specific purpose for which the piles were intended, and the trial judge instructed the jury that an implied warranty existed that the work was suitable and proper for that purpose. Kellogg Bridge appealed to the Supreme Court that no such warranty existed, but the Court found there was and confirmed the judgment for Hamilton.

Although *Parkinson* involved merchantability and *Kellogg Bridge* the fitness warranty, both involved latent defects. The latter decision shows what a remarkably different attitude had developed toward such defects over the eighty-two-year span: "While Hamilton must be charged with knowledge of all defects apparent or discernible upon inspection, he could not justly be charged with knowledge of latent defects which no inspection or examination, at or before the sale, could possibly have disclosed. . . . The buyer did not, because in the nature of things he could not, rely on his own judgment. . . . He must be deemed to have relied on the judgment of the company. . . ."

Kellogg differed from *Parkinson* by involving direct dealing with the manufacturer, who should have known of the piles' unfitness for their purpose, whereas *Parkinson* had involved an agent who had no chance of knowing. Still, it's hard to believe that the *Kellogg* result stemmed solely from that fact. The wording of the two cases suggests that a much greater sympathy for the buyer had developed by 1884. Hamilton was not told brusquely to go get an express warranty if he was worried about hidden defects. He was told his reliance on the piles' fitness was justified because the fitness qualities were hidden and he was left with no reasonable choice but to rely.

The implied warranty of fitness for a particular purpose eventually was codified into the Uniform Sales Act[42] and the Uniform Commercial Code.[43] There is no question under the now-applicable UCC that both implied warranties of quality apply for defects that inspection could not reasonably be expected to reveal, whether the buyer has the "opportunity" to inspect or not.[44]

For features of the goods an inspection might reasonably reveal, application of the two implied warranties cannot always be assumed. The Uniform Sales Act was interpreted in courts to mean that when buyers could examine, whether they did or not, they were responsible for whatever the inspection ought to have revealed.[45] This seriously crimped the help given buyers by implied warranties, but the point was changed when the UCC superseded the USA. Buyers who inspect the goods today are responsible for what the inspection ought to reveal, and the implied warranties are negated for those features. But if they have the opportunity to inspect but do not use it, they are now held to forfeit the implied warranties only where they specifically refuse a demand by the seller that they inspect. If the seller does not insist, it is not considered that the buyer has refused. In this way it is relatively less likely today that the once-formidable inspection obligation will interfere with the chance to employ the implied warranties.[46]

The UCC also provides that the buyer's unsuccessful inspection or refusal to inspect will not negate the implied warranties if the seller has stated the content of such warranties expressly and the buyer has indicated reliance on those words rather than on examination. In such case the seller's words are said to transform the implied warranties into express warranties, which will not today be overruled by the buyer's inspection obligation.[47] That is a real breakthrough for buyers who use the opportunity, because sellers will scarcely deny upon express request that their goods are merchantable.

The availability of implied warranties and the liberalization of the definition of express warranties have made major contributions in converting sellerism to consumerism. But we cannot leave the topic before considering two related matters also given strong consumerist interpretations in this century. One of them concerns the reach of a warranty, meaning whether a manufacturer's warranty is given only to the retailer or whether it extends to those to whom the retailer sells. Early sellerist interpretations held that the warranty stopped with the retailer, and the ultimate customer enjoyed only those warranties given by the latter. The theory was that two separate sales occurred, and the conditions of one transaction could not be imposed on another (there must be "privity of contract," in legal parlance).[48]

Today the law says that claims made by the manufacturer directly to the public, as in mass media advertisements, amount to express warranties directly to the buyers. The new theory is that when sales messages are aimed beyond the dealer, it is only fair that the warranty protection be extended as well. This consumerist interpretation is owing largely to *Baxter v. Ford Motor* of 1932,[49] in which Baxter purchased a car from a local dealer from whom he had received promotional materials distributed by Ford to aid dealers in making sales. The materials said Ford's Triplex Shatter-Proof Glass Windshield was "so made that it will not fly or shatter under the hardest impact. . . . It eliminates the dangers of flying glass." That proved false when a pebble from a passing car broke Baxter's windshield, blinding his left eye and damaging his right. Sued, Ford did not deny its representations were express warranties, but argued from established precedent that they extended no further than the dealer. The Washington state court decided that the old understandings must be revised:

> Radio, billboards, and the products of the printing press have become the means of creating a large part of the demand. . . . It would be unjust to recognize a rule that would permit manufacturers of goods to create a demand for their products by representing that they possess qualities which they, in fact, do not possess, and then, because there is no privity of contract existing between the consumer and the manufacturer, deny the consumer the right to recover if damages result from the absence of those qualities, when such absence is not readily noticeable.

That reasoning was widely adopted in other states, and decisions to the contrary since then have been rare.[50] In addition, since 1960 the implied warranty of merchantability has been held to pass from manufacturer directly to ultimate purchaser. In *Henningsen v. Bloomfield Motors*[51] the court held that "under modern marketing conditions, when a manufacturer puts a new automobile into the stream of trade and promotes its purchase to the public, an implied warranty that it is reasonably suitable for use as such accompanies it into the hands of the ultimate purchaser. . . ." *Henningsen* even extended the coverage of the warranty beyond the buyer to his wife, who was the one injured: "It is our opinion that an implied warranty of merchantability . . . extends to the purchaser of the car, members of his family, and to other persons occupying it or using it with his consent. It would be wholly opposed to reality to say that use by such persons is not within the anticipation of such a warranty. . . ." With cases such as these,[52] there is no longer much threat to warranty protection from the fact that manufacturers do not sell directly to consumers.

A more serious threat to protection comes when makers and sellers disclaim warranties by indicating "not warranted" or by using such statements as "all warranties express or implied are hereby disclaimed" (or by selling "as is," which means the same). Or they indicate warranties but then say they are offered "in lieu of all other warranties express or implied." Remember, this means all warranties as the UCC defines them, meaning all factual claims. Such treatments threaten to eliminate the warranty status of advertising or any other claims made to buyers prior to presentation of the written contract, reducing the claims to mean no more than did Chandelor's or Woods' "affirmations" about bezar-stones and brazilletto. Such practices threaten implied warranties as well, which could throw consumer protection back to the way the unfortunate Parkinson knew it.

Although consumers can hope a disclaimer will be invalidated if later challenged, there isn't much they can do about its sheer presence. In theory buyers can dicker with sellers over such wording, but in practice they probably can't negotiate successfully to have it removed. Here is what a Federal Trade Commission report stated about such chances: "Automobile sales normally involve the unilateral imposition of terms by the seller. It is unrealistic to view an automobile warranty as a voluntary contract between two bargaining parties. The purchaser of an automobile has no true bargaining power beyond the power to haggle over price."[53]

Disclaiming, for all of that, is not entirely bad. It helps society because many transactions can be made on no other reasonable basis. That is particularly true in the secondhand market; for example, auto dealers might decline trade-ins if they had to repair them and sell them with warranties. They would give up their profit if they felt there might be no profit. The person who exchanges the car is also benefited, because it has trade-in value only if the dealer can sell it "as is." Finally, buyers are benefited who can afford cars only at the low prices that such practices make possible.

But disclaiming may be unconscionable where sellers do not reasonably require it, and especially where buyers may reasonably expect warranties to exist. That occurs when items are presumed to be new or when buyers are not aware of the disclaimer in advance, as when they see it only at the contract-signing moment that invariably comes after the buying decision is made. When the disclaimer becomes part of the bargain although not part of the decision, it may be regarded as an unreasonable attempt to defeat the effects of a warranty. As the court in *Henningsen* said, the manufacturer's disclaimer amounted to a "studied effort to frustrate the protection afforded by an implied warranty of merchantability."

Too often disclaimers of warranty have remained in force, under provisions of the Uniform Sales Act and the Uniform Commercial Code, and their widespread use could reverse consumerist developments in warranty law.[54] At least, though, the trend favors the buyer, with the UCC imposing tighter regulations than the USA did. The UCC describes wording attempting to disclaim express warranties as contrary to the essence of the bargain between buyer and seller,[55] and sanctions disclaimers of implied warranties only when buyers are not unduly surprised by their presence.[56] In addition, wrote an expert on warranty law, "The courts have displayed no very favorable attitude toward disclaimers, construing them away, or finding that they were not adequately brought home to the plaintiff."[57] A problem remaining is that consumers may accept disclaimers at face value rather than bring the challenges that might defeat them, but at least they are susceptible to defeat.

The warranty law we have examined is used primarily in suits brought by individual consumers. As such it is not directly relevant to the operation of the primary legal vehicle today for consumer protection, the Federal Trade Commission. Since a warranty is unlawful only in being breached, not merely in being communicated, it cannot be prosecuted if never challenged by a consumer. The Federal Trade Commission, in contrast, using procedures we will see in chapter 8, prohibits sales claims on their mere potential to deceive, without having to show that any consumers used them and were subsequently harmed.

That does not rule the FTC out of acting against warranties, because it can rule against them as deceptive or unfair claims.[58] The commission's capabilities, however, are limited because it cannot act on behalf of individual consumers, its legal role being only preventive and not remedial. Suits to obtain personal remedies such as damages must be brought by the individuals themselves, and that is the special value of warranty law.

Nor do modern developments in misrepresentation law, which we will see in chapter 6, eliminate the importance of warranty regulations. Charges of misrepresentation may also be brought by individuals, but it is often easier to win under warranty. A statement can be judged a warranty on the basis of its wording alone, while the liability of a misrepresentation depends on various complicated assessments of the seller's culpability in making it and the buyer's right to rely on it.

In summary, consumerist developments in warranty law have been most useful in easing the burden of caveat emptor for twentieth-century consumers. We have seen the trend from low to high probability that a seller's statement will be deemed a warranty. In the extreme sellerist era claims were not express warranties except when sellers intended them to be so, and implied warranties did not exist. Today, in contrast, warranties are far more likely to exist and to compel sellers to observe their responsibilities to consumers.

6

Misrepresentation: How Much Lying Do You Find in a Falsehood?

As with warranty law, the probability that misrepresentation law will benefit consumers has increased dramatically since the early English cases. While misrepresentation at the time of *Chandelor v. Lopus*[1] was most difficult to prove, today it is relatively easy, principally because of no longer having to prove fraud.

Chapter 4 described the sellerist idea that buyers had to show that sellers were consciously aware of their falsity and used it with deliberate intent to deceive. Misrepresentations not fraudulent were not unlawful, and the consequences to buyers were severe. Misrepresentations made in true innocence might damage them, but the sellers would escape responsibility. Further, falsities made consciously and deliberately were called fraud only when buyers proved it, which they often could not do. Such rules were virtually an invitation to sellers to commit legalized lying.

The first breaching of the fraud barrier came in a 1663 case most uncharacteristic of its time in generosity to a buyer. Ekins bought a building because the seller told him the rent paid by the tenants was £42. When after purchase the rent turned out to be only £32, he claimed fraud and won in *Ekins v. Tresham*,[2] even though he was unable to prove that the seller knew of the falsity. The court chose to assume by sheer logic that Tresham must have known the true amount. It was similar to the decisions of Lord Holt[3] that a person could not help knowing whether he held legal ownership to goods.

Such reasoning, however, failed to impress most courts in the seventeenth and eighteenth centuries.[4] The fraud requirement for misstatements other than ownership and rent claims was solidly affirmed, particularly in the influential case of *Pasley v. Freeman* of 1789 in which Justice Buller declared: "The fraud must be proved. . . . The assertion alone will not maintain the action; but the plaintiff must go on to prove that it was false, and that the defendant knew it to be so."[5] That position was adopted in American law in *Seixas and Seixas v. Woods* in 1804.[6]

An English case in 1801, meanwhile, led to more weakening of the fraud barrier. In *Haycraft v. Creasey,*[7] Creasey falsely represented to Haycraft that a Miss Robertson might safely be extended credit. In truth the lady was a poor risk; she defaulted to Haycraft's loss, and it became known after the fact that various persons had reason to think she might do that. But Creasey had not known those facts; he was duped and did not know his statements were false. It seemed like one more case where the person who spread the falsity would go free by doing so innocently, and the sole liability would fall on the claim's unfortunate recipient.

Haycraft, however, pursued what seemed a likely angle. He showed that Creasey had been most definite in his assertion, saying, "I can positively assure you of my own knowledge that you may credit Miss Robertson to any amount with perfect safety." To this Haycraft's brother had responded, "I hope you do not inform me this upon bare hearsay; but you do know the fact yourself." To which Creasey answered, "Friend Haycraft, I know that your brother may trust Miss Robertson with perfect safety, to any amount."

Haycraft established that Creasey had no reason to know that, and knew he did not. That is, while Creasey didn't know the statement about Miss Robertson was false, he also didn't know it was true. Thus Creasey stated two falsehoods, the first being that Miss Robertson was a good credit risk and the second that he knew such to be a fact. He may not have known of the first falsity, but Haycraft argued to the court that Creasey surely knew the second and so had misrepresented fraudulently.

The court's ruling went against Haycraft on a point irrelevant to that argument. But all the court members said they were sympathetic to having proof of fraud shown by a speaker's insincerity of belief as well as by the narrower, and harder to prove, ground of conscious knowledge of falsity.[8] Their declaration technically was dictum, an aside rather than a binding legal ruling, since the case was decided on another basis. But the point at least appeared in the record, which led to its being made law in 1843 in *Taylor v. Ashton.*[9] From then on it was clear in England, and recognized as well in America,[10] that fraudulent behavior included making a claim insincerely, knowing you did not know it to be true, as well as making it while knowing it to be false.

That was a strong consumerist interpretation, but from today's perspective it still had limitations. No matter how damaging a falsity might be, it would not be fraudulent unless made with knowledge of falsity or with knowledge of lack of knowledge of truth—in either case, lacking an honest belief. Some statements occasionally were so ridiculously or obviously false that a court would not accept the speaker's assertion that they were made honestly.[11] But if a defense of honest belief could not be rejected, a misrepresentation was not fraudulent and thus not unlawful.

As the nineteenth century progressed, however, some legal experts considered ways to change the rule even more. They were toying with the idea that speakers could be *negligent* even if not fraudulent, meaning that even though they had an honest belief, not knowing the truth nor knowing they didn't know it, still they *ought* to have known of the falsity. Technical experts, for example, by dint of training should be expected to fit that category. Laypersons who commented with honest falsity should not be faulted, but those who represented themselves as experts should be called negligent if their presumed expertise failed them, even though they were completely honest in what they falsely claimed. An 1867 case, *Western Bank of Scotland v. Addie*,[12] reflected that view when the judge told the jury it might find fraud (deceit) if the defendants made statements they did not believe *or statements they had no reasonable ground to believe*. It was a strongly consumerist ruling, greatly increasing the probability of finding sellers legally responsible for misrepresentations that harmed buyers.

Negligent misrepresentation received a sharp setback, however, in a landmark English case that became infamous for failing to accept the principle. In *Derry v. Peek* of 1889,[13] the court found the directors of a tramway corporation had honestly and sincerely, though falsely, claimed in a business prospectus that their company had the right to operate its trams with steam. The General Tramway Act of 1870 had provided that tramway carriages be run only by animal power unless their operators obtained a special act of Parliament authorizing alternate power. The company duly obtained an act authorizing steam power, though under condition that the Board of Trade must consent. On publishing the prospectus the company had not received that consent, though getting it was universally regarded as a "rubber-stamping" procedure. Therefore the court found the directors honestly believed they had obtained the right to steam, and were honestly shocked when the Board of Trade declined consent.[14] The charge of fraud against them was ruled not established.

In announcing the decision Lord Herschell acknowledged but rejected the precedent from *Western Bank* for finding fraud when persons state what they ought not to believe (he called it fraudulent misrepresentation, though it eventually came to be known as negligent misrepresentation). No previous case, Herschell said, had given grounds for so defining fraud. All the valid precedents declared that fraud could not exist where there was honest belief, no matter how foolish it might be: "A man who forms his belief carelessly, or is unreasonably credulous, may be blameworthy when he makes a representation on which another is to act, but he is not, in my opinion, fraudulent in the sense in which that word was used in all the [prior] cases. . . ."[15]

The climate of opinion following *Derry* leaned toward feeling that the persons damaged had deserved relief. The legal writer Williston wrote much later that decisions in which conscious dishonesty had to be proved in order to find unlawful misrepresentation "represented a distinctly lower standard of morality and justice than the contrary decisions."[16] Prosser, another well-known legal interpreter, called *Derry* a "storm center" which in the twentieth century has been "condemned as a backward step in the law," to the extent that a substantial minority of American courts now refused to follow it.[17]

The problem Lord Herschell grappled with in *Derry* was whether to incorporate negligence into the meaning of fraud. Fraud meant conscious awareness of falsity or insincere belief, whereas negligent behavior, even when "blameworthy," didn't amount to that in his opinion. Herschell felt the judge in *Western Bank* was incorrect in trying to assimilate negligence into fraud, even though justice apparently had been well served in doing so and would have been in *Derry* as well. Perhaps Herschell would have ruled differently if the case had been tried for negligence, but it was brought for fraud and had to be judged on that basis. In England his position remained firm until 1963, but eventually negligence was defined as a legal action separate from fraud.[18]

American courts have shown a strong tendency to observe English rulings, and quite a few accepted *Derry v. Peek,* originally at least, as the model for their own decisions.[19] That is the reason for citing so many English cases in a story about American law. In the field of sales regulation American law derived from British law almost as though there was no separation. Other legal areas had differences so vast that the English stance was a major factor in prompting the colonies to revolt. But for misrepresentation and other topics relating to sales messages, early American jurists cited English precedents as though there were no revolution at all.

Derry was controversial, however, and not all American courts agreed to it; some broke away. Negligent misrepresentation was recognized as liable here as early as 1898, and other American courts from the same early date ruled that fraud existed for misrepresentations that were not strictly fraudulent but could be called negligent.[20] Today American law has separated negligent from fraudulent conduct and has found that either may be grounds for finding misrepresentations unlawful.

Can the law go even further and declare misrepresentations liable that are neither of those but entirely innocent? That would be the most extreme consumerist ruling possible, marking a complete reversal of earlier attitudes by transferring to the seller all responsibility for misrepresentation. Buyers would have to prove only that a misrepresentation was made and that they relied upon it to their detriment. Would the law be willing to take that step? The reader who thinks back to the previous chapter will realize that many innocent misrepresentations by sellers are indeed liable today—as *warranties*! We have already seen, in other words, the story of how the law came to hold sellers responsible for their innocent misrepresentations.

If so, however, why should consumers bring suit against fraudulent or negligent misrepresentations, which are more difficult to prove? There often now is no reason for them to employ misrepresentation law because warranty law can be applied with greater ease and often where misrepresentation law cannot.

Despite that, the story of misrepresentation law is told here because it contributed greatly to consumerism in the days before warranty law was adopted universally in the United States. With the Uniform Sales Act never adopted by all states, and the Uniform Commercial Code adopted by all but one state only in 1968,[21] warranties have been available to all U.S. citizens for only a short time. In fact, there are still conditions today under which warranties do not aid buyers. One occurs in the minority of cases where privity of contract still assists sellers.[22] Another is where disclaimers of warranty are used successfully.[23] Still another occurs because warranties apply only to the sale of "goods"—that is, to what the law calls tangible chattels.[24] Automobiles and houses are examples of goods, being physical objects, while stock certificates or building leases are not. False claims concerning such intangibles must still be charged under misrepresentation law, where developments have now moved in some cases to allowing a buyer to recover for entirely innocent misrepresentation (called "strict liability").[25] In this way misrepresentation law still plays a role in consumer protection where warranty law cannot.

Another reason for continuing to value misrepresentation law today is that warranty law has not moved as far in a consumerist direction to protect against opinion (puffery) statements that imply false facts. We will take up such claims in the next chapter, and say here only that misrepresentation law today may guard the consumer against false opinions in certain instances where warranty law will not.[26]

The misrepresentation concept is not technically relevant to the operations of the Federal Trade Commission, which offers (along with the state agencies modeled after it) the most significant degree of consumer protection in America today. To prohibit sales messages the commission need show only their potential to deceive,[27] whereas individuals charging misrepresentation must show that they were deceived, by relying justifiably on the falsity, and incurred specific damage as a direct result.[28] However, the FTC's concept of deceptiveness certainly was founded in the earlier common law concept of misrepresentation. It seems fair to say, too, that FTC's consumer-favoring interpretations of what is deceptive owe their existence to the trends we have described here in misrepresentation law, which have evolved to give consumers considerably more legal protection than they once had.

7

Opinion and Value Statements and Puffery: Avoiding Fact and Keeping Sellerism Alive

This chapter's purpose is to explain that the consumer gains achieved by the changes in warranty and misrepresentation law, however solid they may be, are severely blunted by an important qualification not yet examined. I am sorry that so many such details are necessary to this story, but they cannot be avoided. Many legal rules can be stated easily enough as general principles, but the more you put them into practice the more details you find you must cope with: rule A applies except in situation B although not where aspect C exists, and only for D type of people, and so forth.

Such qualifications often involve obscure points, but the one in this chapter can scarcely be more central in defining the nature of selling claims made in today's advertising and other promotional messages. It is that the rules we have seen on warranty and misrepresentation apply to *factual* representations only.[1] They do not apply to statements of *opinion* or *value*, typically known in the marketplace as puffery. For those supposedly nonfactual statements there are different rules, restricting sellers less and so protecting consumers less. They have lagged in following the trend away from sellerism traced in the previous two chapters, and are the principal reason why the elimination of caveat emptor is far from complete.

How Opinion Statements Gained Special Treatment

The traditional reason for treating opinion statements differently is that by being nonfactual they cannot be true or false and so presumably cannot harm a person who relies on them. I have already explained that I think many such statements *are* factual in the sense that they imply facts, and that many of those implied facts are false, and that such claims therefore are indeed harmful to consumers.[2]

To see why the factual nature of opinions should ever have been denied, let's return again to the early days of English common law. We will see that it considered only the literal content of representations, attributing no importance to what they implied. The literal content of an opinion statement is of course not factual—I have no intention of arguing that it is. But recognition of the process of implication is so well established today that it is difficult to see why the law has clung to the old assumption that sellers' opinions have nothing to do with facts. The early sellerist rulings apparently have such strength that they continue to survive in the face of opposing evidence. We will take a long look at those precedents to see why they have such great staying power.

The exemption of opinion and value statements, thus of puffery, began almost four centuries ago.[3] In *Harvey v. Young*, an English case of 1602,[4] a seller stated that a "term for years" (an archaic phrase meaning an estate held for a specified number of years) "was worth 150 pounds to be sold." The buyer paid that much for it, but later could not get even one hundred pounds. He sought recovery, but failed because the claim "did not prove any fraud; for it was but the defendant's bare assertion that the term was worth so much, and it was the plaintiff's folly to give credit to such assertion." The court did not say it approved the seller's conduct, but only that it found no illegal behavior therein. It was a straight case of caveat emptor, calling the buyer negligent in the absence of warranty or fraudulent misrepresentation for relying on the seller's claim rather than examining the quality of the "term" for himself.

Why was fraud not found? The scanty report[5] added only that if the seller had warranted the value the result would have been otherwise, "for the warranty given by the defendant is a matter to induce confidence and trust in the plaintiff." Apparently, then, a "bare assertion" without warranty was *not* sufficient to induce confidence and trust (in modern terms, to permit justifiable reliance by the buyer). But the point was not elaborated, and we cannot know for certain whether the court intended to say that the bare assertion was not to be relied upon because it was a statement of value and not of fact. We do know that courts in later decisions chose to interpret *Harvey v. Young* in that way.

Another early English precedent was *Baily v. Merrell* of 1615.[6] Baily agreed to transport Merrell's load of wood for a payment of 2s. 8d. per hundred pounds. Lacking scales, he accepted Merrell's statement that the wood weighed eight hundred pounds. The true weight was two thousand pounds, as Baily discovered only when the burden made two of his horses collapse and die. The court told this feckless unfortunate it was his own folly to overload the horses when he could have avoided the disaster by his own initiative. The case was similar to *Harvey* in rejecting reliance on a "bare assertion." But it made fully clear, as *Harvey* did not, that the recipient of the misrepresentation was capable of checking its truth for himself. It also made clear that the rule applied even though the seller committed fraud, the fraud being innocuous because the buyer might readily have perceived it.[7]

The next important precedent was *Ekins v. Tresham* of 1663, already seen in discussing misrepresentation law.[8] The defendant falsely claimed the rent paid by tenants of the building he was selling was £42 rather than the true figure of £32. Hauled into court, he cited *Harvey v. Young* in arguing there was no fraud (deceit) in saying so. The court approved the principle of *Harvey*, giving it support that led to its eventual widespread acceptance, and explaining it as follows: "An action will not lie for saying, that a thing is of greater value than it is . . . because value consists in judgment and estimation, wherein men many times differ."

The court then interpreted *Harvey* further by telling why it could not be applied to the rent statement. Rent could not be confirmed independently by the buyer, the decision said, thereby implying that a statement of value could be. A companion report of the same case stated the distinction similarly, saying that rent involved "certain" rather than "uncertain" amounts of money.[9] The term *fact* was not used in contrast to the term *value*, but the implication in modern terms was that the rent figure was an actual fact while the value figure was not. Therefore the seller could be found liable for misrepresenting rent even though not for value. The case also implied that a person's evaluation of a thing can be made by no one else; indeed, reliance on another to make such judgment was negligence, through which buyers brought full responsibility upon themselves.

The three cases we have examined may have been mere straws in the wind before 1789. The law of fraud was a liquid thing, undergoing the zigs and zags of tentative development. But in 1789 several of the strands were pulled together by the scholarship and authority of the court in *Pasley v. Freeman*,[10] which became the leading English case on fraud and the model for its treatment in the new American republic. It also became the first case to use the term "opinion." The plaintiffs, planning to do business with a Mr. Falch, relied to their detriment on misrepresentations by Freeman commending Falch's credit rating. The court found Freeman's statements fraudulent, and also found the plaintiffs had "no means of knowing the state of Falch's credit but by an application to his neighbors." Since it was one of those neighbors who misled them, the ruling was made as in the rent case (*Ekins*) that the plaintiffs lacked the means to investigate the truth independently. They could not have known the truth about the fraudulent statement and therefore were entitled to recover for the damages caused by their reliance on it.

One of the four justices, Grose, dissented. He agreed the statements about Falch's credit were false, but thought they were not fraudulent and the plaintiffs had the means to know the truth. To illustrate, he cited *Harvey*, *Leakins*, and *Baily* as typical of cases "where the affirmation is (what is called in some of the books) a nude assertion; such as the party deceived may exercise his own judgment upon; as where it is a matter of opinion, where he might make inquiries into the truth of the assertion, and it becomes his own fault from laches [an old legal term for negligence] that he is deceived."

Another justice, Buller, although holding with the majority that Freeman's statements did not fit the category, agreed that the type of assertion Grose had described was not fraudulent. Such an assertion, Buller said, "was of mere matter of judgment and opinion; of a matter of which the defendant had no particular knowledge, but of which men will be of many minds, and which is often governed by whim and caprice. Judgment or opinion, in such cases, implies no knowledge."

Evaluation requires knowledge, of course, but Buller apparently meant there was nothing the seller could know that the buyer could not. The temper of the times ruled out any acknowledgment that sellers might have "particular knowledge" that buyers did not, or that any chance was lacking that the buyer "might make inquiries." The difficulty buyers might have in obtaining equivalent knowledge was not recognized. Stressed was possibility, not probability; the possibility of obtaining equivalent knowledge satisfied the law, while the low probability of actually doing so was ignored.

From the description so far, it appears that the justices in *Pasley* believed opinion or value statements would not typically be spoken fraudulently. The court in *Harvey* had said the false claim proved no fraud, and the *Ekins* decision supported it by defining value as a subjective rather than objective element. Justice Grose's statement, however, added a new dimension when he said that opinion statements would be legally nonfraudulent *even when spoken with conscious intent to deceive*. In other words, they wouldn't be charged with fraud even when they *were* fraud.

That was a startling development. Opinion statements were already less liable than factual ones to charges of fraud because conscious knowledge of falsity was difficult to charge against the maker of statements that presumably were neither true nor false. But a speaker would certainly *sometimes* be aware of the falsity of his opinions, as when he exaggerated them grossly, and so the chance of charging fraud undoubtedly made sellers up to that time wary of using opinion or value claims recklessly.

To take the extra step, however, of entirely removing the possibility of charging fraud was a wildly sellerist action, placing opinion statements far apart from factual statements in degree of liability. With fraud no longer a factor, the seller would be permitted, as long as the buyer could examine the object of sale independently, to make opinion and value claims with utter abandon. Come to think of it, doesn't that sound like today's advertising? A major reason why modern selling claims are the way they are is the release of opinion statements from the fraud rule, owing largely to the authority of *Pasley v. Freeman*. It was only natural that the ratio of now-immune opinion claims to still-liable factual claims would increase significantly and would become the primary type of selling claim we see today.

How did it happen? If conscious intent to deceive would normally produce a finding of fraud, how could Justice Grose hint otherwise? He did so by citing as a precedent *Baily v. Merrell*, a case that expressly condoned fraudulent misrepresentations. *Baily's* finding had been that someone who could check a "readily apparent" truth was obligated to do so even in the face of receiving a fraudulent claim about it.

We will never know why Grose thought *Baily* was relevant to the question of opinion statements. The misrepresentation that harmed Baily was a claim that a load of wood weighed a certain amount—a statement of fact, not value. It seems to have been inappropriately lumped together with the other cases that Grose used to illustrate "nude assertions." While claims concerning monetary value, as in

Harvey, may vary among people and represent subjective judgment and no particular knowledge, the weight of wood is an objective amount that cannot vary from person to person. An *estimation* of weight may vary among people, but a false claim of weight clearly is factual and involves particular knowledge.

Yet Grose lumped such claims together with "nude assertions," a mistake inviting later observers to see him as implying that opinion statements can be spoken with fraudulent intent and yet not amount to fraud. Justice Buller must have grasped that unlikely suggestion from Grose's words, since the record shows his strong objection to it. He pointed out that *Harvey* did not condone fraud; neither did *Ekins*. If a statement was spoken fraudulently it could not possibly be a mere "bare naked lie," Buller said. But Buller did not choose specifically to refute the use of *Baily* as a precedent; he didn't mention the case. The other two justices mentioned *Baily* approvingly without commenting on the point in question. Thus the set of statements by the four justices in *Pasley* tended to leave the impression that *Baily* was a good precedent for determining the law of opinion statements.

Exaggerating this accident was the fact that Grose, interpreting the opinion rule, cited not just one but two precedents dealing with facts rather than opinions. Along with *Baily* he cited a rule from *Rolle's Abridgement*[11] that sellers do not legally commit fraud in claiming falsely the amount of money they have been offered for goods. The amount some previous party offered the seller is certainly related to the value a potential buyer might perceive, but is itself an objective figure. And a claim that the offer was made is a statement of fact, involving particular knowledge. A rule covering such statements appears inappropriate as a precedent for the handling of opinion and value statements. Yet with Grose's help the *Rolle's Abridgement* rule joined *Baily* in lending weight to the idea that opinion and value statements should be treated more loosely than factual statements. In the future those two accidental precedents, and *Pasley* itself, were to be cited in several crucial cases. Without their help, the most extreme sellerist interpretations of the opinion rule, which make legal a great deal of lying today, may never have been established.

Typical of the ideas that passed from *Pasley* into later English law was a statement of the misrepresentation rule in 1810 by Lord Ellenborough: "A seller is unquestionably liable to an action of deceit, if he fraudulently misrepresent the quality of the thing sold to be other than it is in some particulars, which the buyer has not equal means with himself of knowing; or if he do so, in such a manner as to induce the buyer to forbear making the inquiries which . . . he would otherwise have made."[12]

To see what this rule meant for opinion statements, turn it around: A seller is *not* liable to an action of deceit if he fraudulently misrepresent the quality of the thing sold to be other than it is in some particulars that the buyer has equal means of knowing. With opinion statements, of course, buyers will always have equal means of knowing, provided they are able to examine the object of purchase. They will be permitted to rely on such statements *only* when such examination is not possible.

The Ellenborough pronouncement shows the great influence of *Pasley* in handling opinion and value statements. Sellers could be as fraudulent as they pleased in making them, provided they made the object available for buyers to see, and the law would not object. In America *Pasley*'s shadow fell on the first case to mention the opinion rule, Justice Kent citing Justice Buller as authority on the topic: "To make an affirmation at the time of sale a warranty, it must appear by evidence to be so intended; (Buller, J., 3 D. & E. 57; Carth. 90; Salk. 210) and not to have been a mere matter of judgment and opinion, and of which the defendant had no particular knowledge."[13]

Other early American cases also mentioned the matter peripherally,[14] but the first case to establish the opinion exemption specifically here was *Davis v. Meeker* of 1810.[15] Davis bought a wagon from Meeker but later accused him of falsely and fraudulently claiming "he had been frequently offered, by different persons, 50 dollars for the wagon." Davis won a jury verdict, suggesting the jury felt Meeker was aware of his falsity. But in reversing, the appellate court appears to have ruled the deception exempt from liability even though consciously false. It did not say so explicitly,[16] but later rulings quite directly stated that opinion statements should be excused even when consciously false.

The first of these strongly sellerist rulings was in Massachusetts in 1843, beginning a long and liberal interpretation that made that state the great American hotbed of the great American blow-up. In *Medbury v. Watson*[17] Justice Hubbard called *Pasley* "the leading case, in modern times, on the subject of false affirmations made with intent to deceive," and then used the *Pasley* authority to declare: "But in actions on the case for deceit, founded upon false affirmations, there has always existed the exception, that naked assertions, though known to be false, are not the ground of action, as between vendor and vendee. . . . [S]uch assertions, though known by him to be false, and though uttered with a view to deceive, are not actionable. They are the mere affirmations of the vendor, on which the vendee cannot safely place confidence, and will not excuse his neglect in not examining for himself."[18]

In interpreting *Pasley*, Justice Hubbard obviously relied on the dissenting opinion of Grose more than on the majority opinions. Buller had objected to conscious falsity, while Grose relied heavily on cases explicitly condoning such behavior. Hubbard made it clear that an American court now condoned conscious falsity, too. He seemed to recognize in doing so none of the confusion inherent in *Pasley*, and his untroubled vision was accepted wholeheartedly in later cases, including one that blithely reinterpreted *Harvey v. Young* to suit modern needs. In *Veasey v. Doton* of 1862, another Massachusetts case, the jury found the defendant to have known his representation was false, yet the appeals court reversed the finding of liability and said the case was "not distinguishable from Harvey. . . ."[19] We recall that in *Harvey* fraud would have brought liability, whereas in *Veasey* it did not. If that didn't make *Harvey* "distinguishable," nothing could. Massachusetts apparently was most reluctant to let history interfere with its widening of the opinion rule.

As to why these decisions were made, the principal reason probably was the prevailing social atmosphere rather than the quality of the precedents. There are times when precedents provide merely the excuse, feebly if necessary, for doing what a court thinks society wants done. And what the controlling elements of society seemed to demand in early America was sellerism, as best summed up in Hamilton's statement that caveat emptor served well its two masters, business and justice.[20] That is a barbed statement, possibly unfair if interpreted to imply a lack of ethics on the part of the law in nineteenth-century America. What Hamilton meant, however, was that the law was faithfully supporting the prevailing social ethic of the time, by which business could do no wrong.

After *Medbury v. Watson* the rules for opinion and value statements might seem to have been stretched as far as possible to favor sellers. But the philosophy of "anything goes" remained impeded by the requirement that buyers must be capable of checking sellers' opinion claims themselves. Falsity in nonfactual claims, even when fraudulent, was acceptable up to that point, but not beyond. If the buyer could not check, then the seller would be as responsible for statements of evaluation as for fact claims. Do you think the full-blooded sellerists felt hampered by that? Not much, because it wasn't long before another Massachusetts case got rid of that "impediment" and settled everybody down to an even greater degree of good old-fashioned lying.

In *Brown v. Castles* of 1853 the court added the following twist to the rule that deliberate misrepresentations beyond the observation of the recipient amounted to fraud. "This rule," it said, "is not applied to statements made by sellers, concerning the value of the thing sold, former offers for it, &c., it always having been understood, the world over, that such statements are to be distrusted. Multa fidem promissa levant [Many promises lessen confidence]."[21]

Let's analyze the meaning of that. It no longer mattered, after 1853, whether opinion or value claims could be checked independently. Until then buyers had recourse if such claims could not be checked, but now the claims were automatically immune from prosecution whether they could be checked or not. It was a significant change in the law for those buyers who could not make the examination, and the reason given was that buyers should never *want* to check opinion claims anyway because they were supposed to know automatically to distrust them and reject them under all conditions.

Why did the judge make that change? We simply do not know. But we know that the change remained, especially when cited by the Supreme Judicial Court of Massachusetts, ever a friend to the seller, in *Deming v. Darling* of 1889.[22] The case involved a railroad bond represented falsely in typical puffing terms as the very best and safest, an "A No. 1" bond. Oliver Wendell Holmes, later to be famed as a Supreme Court justice, wrote for the court that: "The language of some cases certainly seems to suggest that bad faith might make a seller liable for what are known as 'seller's statements.' . . . But this is a mistake. It is settled that the law does not exact good faith from a seller in those vague commendations of his wares which manifestly are open to differences of opinion . . . and as to which 'it has always been understood, the world over, that such statements are to be distrusted,' (*Brown v. Castles* . . .). . . ."

Those words of Holmes, who thus became the most famous of puffery's judicial godfathers, have been oft quoted for their emphasis and eloquence. And his reference to the 1853 case cemented its status as a precedent. Holmes added some explanation for why he thought the rule was a good one: "The rule of law is hardly to be regretted, when it is considered how easily and insensibly words of hope or expectation are converted by an interested memory into statements of quality and value, when the expectation has been disappointed." He showed no recognition, however, of the big change involved in saying the rule should be applied even when sellers gave buyers no opportunity to examine the object of purchase for themselves.

In examining the *Brown v. Castles* statement, I have pondered whether it might mean not just that people *should* know to distrust all opinion claims, but also that they *do* engage automatically in such distrust. It depends on whether we can interpret the phrase "it has always been understood" to mean that judges have always understood the law as giving consumers no legal recourse if they fail to distrust, or else that consumers have always understood the law as giving them no legal recourse if they fail to distrust, and that consequently they do always distrust.

While some readers of the record may disagree, I choose to interpret *Brown v. Castles* as conveying the latter meaning because later cases gave precisely that interpretation. The first of these came in this pronouncement in 1887 in the same state: "We are of opinion that all the representations alleged in the declaration which are material fall within what is known as 'dealer's talk,' and are not sufficient foundation for an action of deceit. The law recognizes the fact that men will naturally overstate the value and qualities of the articles which they have to sell. All men know this, and a buyer has no right to rely on such statements."[23]

A similar eloquent statement was later made by the famous Judge Learned Hand of the Second Circuit Court of Appeals in 1918: "There are some kinds of talk which no man takes seriously, and if he does he suffers from his credulity. . . . Neither party usually believes what the seller says about his opinions, and each knows it. Such statements, like the claims of campaign managers before election, are rather designed to allay the suspicion which would attend their absence than to be understood as having any relationship to objective truth."[24]

With these statements there was no further doubt that the rule for puffery now was that the law would offer no recourse for it even when sellers spoke it with conscious knowledge of their own falsity and buyers bought while relying on it without having equal means of examining, all for the reason that people knew to distrust it and reject it, and always did so, and so were not harmed by it.

Can you accept the factual assumption that all buyers acted that way? I certainly cannot. I believe a large proportion of the public has always been inclined to trust or at least not to automatically distrust such statements. I don't think that many people, in the last century or now, have automatically distrusted such claims. Nor should they—some of them are true, after all. Why should people accustom themselves to automatic distrust when many sellers they deal with are honest? The judges in *Brown v. Castles* and the later cases simply had no basis for asserting such a fact about human behavior. Prior to that time the law had said no such thing; it had said, rather, that when buyers couldn't check personally they were entitled to trust sellers and to have legal protection against any fraudulent speech.

The result is a rationale for puffery today that actually evades the original reason for excusing false opinions. When the exemption from liability originated it was based on the premise that people could examine for themselves. Yet the rule today ignores whether they can do that, and is based on their supposedly natural tendency to disbelieve automatically. The latter is a significantly different type of proposition. Rather than being based on a norm, on something people *should* do, it is based upon a fact about what they presumably *do* do. Any such rule stands in a precarious position to the extent that what it claims about human behavior may be incorrect. There may very well be numerous consumers who do rely on opinion claims, and indeed why would the advertisers use them if that were not so!

The rule has its absurdities. Where reasonable people rely upon puffery and are deceived by it, as I am certain often happens, it would be absurd to call their action unjustified on the reasoning that they wouldn't have done that in the first place. Furthermore, the rule calls for consumers to distrust automatically all instances of puffery, which could include ones that are true. Investigation, when possible, would enable us to separate the true puffs from the false ones, but automatic distrust prevents us from ever making such a reasonable discrimination.

However, we have seen what happened, whether sensible or not. Returning to our historical survey, the matter of opinion statements had reached the U.S. Supreme Court in 1881,[25] and it duly supported the opinion rule: "The law does not fasten responsibility upon one for expressions of opinion as to matters in their nature contingent and uncertain. Such opinions will probably be as variant as the individuals who give them utterance." The case did not involve the extreme sellerist interpretation from *Brown v. Castles*, nor even the issue of conscious falsity. But the ruling put the Supreme Court's seal on the general idea of the immunity of opinion claims.[26]

In 1902 the topic again reached the Supreme Court.[27] Postmaster McAnnulty of Nevada, Missouri, had stopped delivering mail to an organization called the American School of Magnetic Healing. The school had been turning a good profit until McAnnulty ordered that its mail, including a large volume of money orders, be stamped "fraudulent." It was returned to senders under a statute forbidding "obtaining money through the mails by means of false or fraudulent pretenses, representations or promises." However, the Supreme Court restored delivery, saying: "We may not believe in the efficacy of the treatment to the extent claimed by complainants, and we may have no sympathy with them in such claims, and yet their effectiveness is but matter of opinion in any court. . . . Unless the question may be reduced to one of fact as distinguished from mere opinion, we think these statutes cannot be invoked. . . ."

In 1916 in *U.S. v. New South Farm*[28] the Supreme Court again considered the mail statute after a district court held that "mere puffing or exaggeration" of qualities or value should not be restricted by that law. The Court agreed that "Mere puffing, indeed, might not be within its meaning." But the particular case went beyond puffing, the Court said, because when the seller "assigns to the article qualities which it does not possess, does not simply magnify in opinion the advantages it has but invents advantages and falsely asserts their existence, he transcends the limits of 'puffing' and engages in false representations and pretenses." In thus making clear what puffery was not, the Court recognized its status as a type of claim not subject to charges of fraud. In later years the Federal Trade Commission used the *New South Farm* definition in its own determinations about puffery.

We have now described how opinion, value, and puffery statements became established in American common law. More cases might be cited, but those making the principal points have been chronicled. Warranty law runs parallel; the cases seen in chapter 5 providing that affirmations shall be warranties never deviated from the distinction that they should be affirmations of fact. The Uniform Commercial Code specifies today, "An affirmation merely of the value of the goods or a statement purporting to be merely the seller's opinion or commendation of the goods does not create a warranty."[29]

In chapter 10 we will describe the rulings made on opinion statements by the Federal Trade Commission. Although the commission, enacted by statute, need not follow the rules developed in the common law, its decisions parallel them.

How Opinion Statements Have Been Restricted

To continue this chapter's description, we look at the restrictions imposed by the common law on opinion statements. Despite the impression given thus far of a rampant sellerism, the immunity of opinion statements from liability has been curtailed in certain ways that reflect the modern consumerist trend. In the end, however, we will see that such developments have had less impact on the marketplace than may appear at first glance.

The principal method by which opinion statements have been made liable has been by asserting what the early cases denied—that they amount to misrepresentations of fact. The old cases said opinion statements literally stated no facts, and that was that. The newer cases recognize that opinion statements imply facts and therefore may be liable on that basis. If sellers can be held to have misrepresented facts by what their opinion statements imply, they can be held liable even though the opinions per se may be superficially innocent of falsity. This analysis involves misrepresentation law only; there is little or no provision for designating statements of opinion or value as warranties on the ground that they imply facts.[30]

Although the question of what particular facts an opinion may imply is difficult to answer, the conviction developed rather early that any opinion statement implies at least one. It implies—what could be simpler!—that speakers believe their opinions. As an American case said as early as 1827, "The affirmation of belief is an affirmation of fact, that is, of the fact of belief."[31] Other courts did not leap to accept such reasoning so early, but recognition came when England's Lord Bowen stated in 1885 that "the state of a man's mind is as much a fact as the state of his digestion. It is true that it is very difficult to prove what the state of a man's mind at a particular time is, but if it can be ascertained it is as much a fact as anything else."[32]

The viewpoint that opinions can never be related facts was accordingly disposed of.[33] Furthermore, via another statement of Lord Bowen, it became accepted that there could be implied facts about the *object* of one's opinion. In *Smith v. Land and House* of 1884,[34] the sellers of a property asserted they had a desirable tenant, whereas in truth the tenant paid his rent late, irregularly, and often only under pressure. When the buyers sued against the falsehood, the defense argued it was just "one of the flourishing descriptions which auctioneers insert and which do not amount to a statement of any specific fact." Replied Bowen, "It is often fallaciously assumed that a statement of opinion cannot involve the statement of a fact. . . . But if the facts are not equally known to both sides, then a statement of opinion by the one who knows the facts best involves very often a statement of a material fact, for he impliedly states that he knows facts which justify his opinion."

To say the tenant was desirable, Bowen concluded, "amounts at least to an assertion that nothing has occurred in the relations between the landlords and the tenant which can be considered to make the tenant an unsatisfactory one. That is an assertion of a specific fact." This type of ruling entered American law in a number of cases beginning in 1886.[35] Their impact has been distilled in a summarization of the law called the *Restatement of Torts*, authored by legal experts under sponsorship of the American Law Institute:

> §539 A statement of opinion as to facts not disclosed and not otherwise known to the recipient may, where it is reasonable to do so, be interpreted by him as an implied statement (a) that the facts known to the maker are not incompatible with his opinion; or (b) that he knows facts sufficient to justify him in forming it.[36]

Further restrictions on opinion statements are described in another section of the *Restatement*:

> §542 The recipient of a fraudulent misrepresentation which is one only as to the maker's opinion is not justified in relying upon it in a transaction with the maker, unless the fact to which the opinion relates is material, and the maker
> (a) purports to have special knowledge of the matter which the recipient does not have, or
> (b) stands in a fiduciary or other similar relation of trust and confidence to the recipient, or
> (c) has successfully endeavored to secure the confidence of the recipient, or
> (d) has some other special reason to expect that the recipient will rely on his opinion.[37]

The rule in clause (a) that a presumed expert may not throw his opinions around as carelessly as other people is due principally to *Picard v. McCormick* of 1862,[38] which incidentally contains the earliest legal reference to sellers' opinion statements as "puffs." ("Puffing" had been used earlier in legal parlance to refer to bids entered at auctions for the purpose of driving up prices artificially.) *Picard* involved false statements "by a jeweler to an unskilled purchaser of the value of articles which none but an expert could reasonably be supposed to understand." The court found the jeweler deliberately took advantage of the buyer by claiming that watches and other jewelry were worth far more than what a knowledgeable person would believe.

Contrary to other cases we have seen, the court did not worry about whether the buyer might have inspected for himself. Rather, it emphasized that reliance on the claims was reasonable due to the seller's position. If false claims of value were usually deemed innocent, the court said, it was "only because [they] can rarely be supposed to have induced a purchase without negligence. . . . It is undoubtedly true that value is usually a mere matter of opinion, and that a purchaser must expect that a vendor will seek to enhance his wares, and must disregard statements of their value."

But this case was different, the court stated, because:

> Frauds are easily committed by dishonest dealers . . . and can not be detected in many cases except by persons of experience. . . . We are aware of no rule which determines arbitrarily that any class of fraudulent misrepresentations can be exempted from the consequences attached to others. Where a purchaser, without negligence, has been induced by the arts of a cheating seller to rely upon material statements which are knowingly false . . . it can make no difference in what respect he has been deceived, if the deceit was material and relied on. . . . We think it can not be laid down as a matter of law that value is never a material fact. . . .

We can see what a difference *Picard* made by comparing it to the case of that other nasty jeweler, Chandelor. The court in 1603 never considered that Chandelor was more expert than Lopus in assessing bezar-stones. In those days everyone was presumed an expert on all commodities; the concept of special knowledge didn't exist. The law was concerned that buyers should have equal means to know, but access to the sale object was considered sufficient for that. It took until 1862, 259 years, for the law to decide there might be more to expertise than simply having the jewel in front of your eyes.[39]

The other clauses of section 542 represent similar legal situations in which the modern view is to restrain people from using opinions loosely. Clause (b) also involves special knowledge, with the added factor of a close personal relationship. It refers to the actions of trustees, bank officials, real estate agents, attorneys, priests, physicians, and family members who might take advantage of our trust to persuade us against making inquiries that could reveal falsities.[40] Most trade transactions today, of course, are not conducted between buyers and sellers who have a close personal relationship.

Clause (c) is for miscellaneous conditions where sellers stress rapport with a person due to common membership in a church or other organization, or the fact that they come from the same area.[41] It's based on a case in which a seller gained a buyer's willingness to forgo checking a purchase and rely solely on his claims by stating he was an Irish Catholic like herself and she could therefore trust him.[42]

Clause (d) is for miscellaneous conditions where people might be induced to forbear inquiry through lack of intelligence, illiteracy, or unusual gullibility.[43] It is aimed at sellers trying deliberately to take advantage of such characteristics. Much selling, of course, is done by mass methods aimed at more than one person simultaneously, and most sellers, when they meet individual buyers, would not be likely to know them well enough personally to know of cases of unusual gullibility. But where sellers do learn of such things and deliberately take advantage of them by stating false opinions, they may be held responsible for a fraudulent opinion.

In these ways, the indiscriminate use of opinion statements has been curtailed, and we may easily get the impression from the rules just examined that opinion statements are quite readily associated with facts today and thereby have no freer rein than factual statements.

Reconciling These Contrasting Rules

Let's think a bit about what we've just seen in the two preceding sections. Aren't the cases we saw in the first section, giving sellers the right to a wild-eyed and reckless use of opinion statements, contradicted by the rules in the second section that appear to curtail use of such claims? We saw in the first section, for example, that all buyers realize they have no right to rely on the overstatements of value and quality that sellers will make quite naturally. How can that be reconciled with the rule in the second section that says we may rely when sellers have special expertise? Most sellers have expertise, after all, so wouldn't that largely eliminate the other rule? Or if the first one were insisted upon, wouldn't it obliterate the expertise rule? They can hardly exist together, because application of one tends to squash the meaningfulness of the other. What's going on here?

The answer is that *puffery* is going on. An important characteristic not yet mentioned about the rules in the second section is that they do not apply to puffery! That's a highly significant qualification, because most opinion statements made by sellers constitute puffery. Outside the marketplace puffery is not recognized, and the restrictions specified in the second section apply generally in those other areas. But in the marketplace they apply only to that small proportion of sellers' opinion statements that are not called puffery.

Certain sellers' opinion statements are properly called *opinions-as-to-fact* rather than opinions about subjective value or quality.[44] Such an opinion is not puffery because it involves the uncertain representation of an objective fact (as in "I think this table is made of pine wood") rather than a representation of a subjective feeling (as in "I think this table is worth $100"). Any opinion-as-to-fact, made by a seller or anyone else, is equivalent to a factual statement in that it can be prohibited if it misrepresents.

Most sellers' opinion statements, however, are not opinions-as-to-fact. Don't expect to see an ad saying "We believe this table is made of pine wood." Most sellers' opinions are puffs about value or quality, which means the restrictions the law places on opinion statements simply do not apply very often to the claims sellers make. The marketplace, as we've seen earlier, has a set of rules essentially different from those applied to other human affairs. Thus we resolve the conflict between the two above sections by seeing that opinion statements in the marketplace are handled mostly by the rules of the first and allowed to ignore the rules of the second.

The following shows how the law creates a separate standard for the marketplace, keeping substantial vestiges of caveat emptor alive. It is what the authors of the *Restatement of Torts* have added as "official comment" in explanation of section 542, clause (a):

> Comment on Clause (a): f. . . . The ordinary purchaser of jewelry cannot be expected to know the quality or value of the gems shown him by a jeweler. He must rely and is therefore justified in relying upon the jeweler's statement that a diamond is of the first water and, after making allowance for the natural tendency of a vendor to puff his wares, he is justified in relying upon the jeweler's statement of the value of the gem.[45]

Consider the difference that qualification makes. If your lawyer offers her opinion that one way of writing your will is better than another, you have a right to rely because of her special knowledge.

But if a jeweler tells you a diamond is worth so much or has certain superior qualities, you may rely on his opinion only to the extent of assuming it will not go beyond the "natural tendency" to puff. Don't be misled, therefore, by what *Picard v. McCormick* said about relying on the jeweler because he's an expert. You may do that only to a restricted degree.

Imagine you go to a jeweler and listen to his opinion about a diamond. Recalling the rule, you remind yourself that you must ignore that part of his opinion which is the puff, but you may rely on that part which is not the puff. How can you be expected to do that? Suppose, for example, that the diamond was known in the jewelry industry, by a consensus of experts, to be worth $1,000. Suppose, too, that the jeweler tells you it is worth $1,500. How are you to determine how much of that opinion is acceptable puffing and how much is not? Would it be only puffing if the jeweler said it was worth $1,250, but more than puffing to state any higher price?

What sort of protection is offered to buyers by a rule that outlaws not exaggeration but merely too much exaggeration? Doesn't section 542 amount, really, to a great big sellout to puffery? Notice how it places legal puffing ahead of illegal fraud—that is, the first part of the exaggeration is the puffing part that buyers are told they must accept as legal. To get any protection, they must show that the exaggeration has gone further than that, which will be very difficult to do.

Here is more of the "official comment" on section 542 that the authors of the *Restatement of Torts* have supplied:

d. . . . Thus the purchaser of an ordinary commodity is not justified in relying upon the vendor's opinion of its quality or worth. . . .

e. This is true particularly of loose general statements made by sellers in commending their wares, which are commonly known as "puffing," or "sales talk." It is common knowledge, and may always be assumed, that any seller will express a favorable opinion concerning what he has to sell; and when he praises it in general terms, without specific content or reference to facts, buyers are expected to and do understand that they are not entitled to rely literally upon the words. . . .

Comment on Clause (c): . . . the rule does not apply to one who has by ordinary marketing methods or by the propriety of his past dealings secured the confidence of a prospective purchaser.

No question remains that the handling of opinion statements gives little comfort to consumers. Though the law reflected in section

542 is instrumental in controlling misrepresentations elsewhere, for consumers it is nothing more than a concession to the traditional sellerist use of false opinions and puffs. It mirrors perfectly the Massachusetts cases of the nineteenth century. Caveat emptor may be dead in some senses, but in the land of opinions it thrives today as strongly as ever.

The same status quo attitude is evident in the interpretation of section 539 of the *Restatement*, stating that opinions may be held fraudulent by their associations with incompatible facts. Again, it is illusory to believe that this means what it seems to mean with respect to marketplace transactions. We recall that in *Smith v. Land and House* the seller was not allowed to get away with "one of the flourishing descriptions which auctioneers insert" because he knew something contradicting it. But before we assume that buyers are protected from all such flourishes, let us consider the "official comment" to section 539:

> c. . . . The habit of vendors to exaggerate the advantages of the bargain which they are seeking to make is a well recognized fact. An intending purchaser may not be justified in relying upon his vendor's statement of the value, quality, or other advantages of a thing which he is intending to sell as carrying with it any assurance that the thing is such as to justify a reasonable man in praising it so highly. However, a purchaser is justified in assuming that even his vendor's opinion has some basis in fact, and therefore in believing that the vendor knows of nothing which makes his opinion fantastic.

So! In the marketplace buyers are not justified, as they would be elsewhere, in believing the facts known by the seller are compatible with the opinion. Buyers must understand they may be incompatible, and that the only prohibition is that they may not be *fantastically* incompatible. Apparently the flourish in *Land and House* was fantastically incompatible, but that doesn't mean all such flourishes are. The uncertainty created is similar to saying that the puffery may exaggerate some, but not too much. The jeweler's claim that a $1,000 diamond is worth $1,250 is incompatible with the facts, but perhaps not unreasonably so. Possibly a claim that the diamond is worth $1,500 would be fantastically incompatible. Again, how do we determine such things?

What about the point that every opinion statement implies the fact that the speaker sincerely believes it? No doubt a true-blue sellerist would say it wouldn't be fantastically incompatible for a seller to say his product was worth so much, or was the best or most popular, when he didn't believe it. That would be incompatible only to an ordinary degree. So much for sincere belief in the marketplace.

All of these developments sadly recall the comment of Oliver Wendell Holmes that "The standard of good faith required in sales is somewhat low."[46] No better commentary can be made on the state of good faith in buying and selling than to compare the light touch of sections 539 and 542 on the marketplace with the more solid impact these rules have on other dealings. Why should not the correct rules for the market be the same as those applied elsewhere— being, in other words, what is literally cited in sections 539 and 542, omitting the added comments. Most puffery, after all, comes to us from manufacturers or sellers who purport to (1) have special knowledge that we do not (see clause [a] of section 542), (2) stand in a relationship of trust and confidence to us (clause [b]); (3) have successfully endeavored to secure our confidence (clause [c]); and (4) have a special reason, since their continued use of puffery indicates they think it has been relied upon by a gullible public in the past, to expect we will rely on it again (clause [d]).

Certainly all of these specified circumstances might reasonably be applied to the marketplace. I would like to emphasize especially the condition cited in clause (a) about the representor's having special knowledge. The ancient assumption of caveat emptor, exemplified in *Seixas & Seixas v. Woods*,[47] was that buyers and sellers had equal knowledge. Can anyone imagine today that the manufacturer of a television set or headache remedy or detergent knows no more about its product than the typical citizen who may use it? Under today's market conditions the very notion of making or selling a product implies special knowledge because it *requires* special knowledge. There is no reason why a double standard should exist to excuse misrepresentations just because they are made in commerce.

Similar remarks apply to the rule stated in section 539. There is no reason why knowledge of incompatible facts should be excusable for sellers when not excusable for other people who misrepresent opinions. I once said as much in the *New York Times*,[48] and got a complaint from an advertiser I mentioned. John Galbreath & Co., Realtors, couldn't believe its ad could be associated in any way with incompatible false facts. The headline quoted an official of a tenant company as saying, "Moving to the U.S. Steel Building has really helped us attract and hold good people." I observed that substantiation for the claim was not provided in the ad and would be difficult to obtain because attracting and retaining employees depends on so many factors that the effects of any one may be impossible to isolate.

I acknowledged in the article my acceptance of the claim that the tenant had a lower employee turnover in its new location, and also the supposition that a new modern office building could contribute to such success. But I also pointed out that the move to the new building in Pittsburgh had been made from Philadelphia, which meant that many other changes could have affected employee turnover. My conclusion was that there was no way the advertiser could have known the U.S. Steel Building itself was responsible for the difference. Furthermore, the advertiser must have known it didn't really know, which would be a fact incompatible with the claim.

A letter protesting my comments came from a Galbreath official,[49] protesting that the ad was not in any way false puffery. The ad and similar ones, he said, were "in no way intended to be anything other than statements of truth expressed by the particular parties in reflection of their personal experiences, attitudes and feelings." But he added the following illuminating statement: "We did not ask that the parties interviewed substantiate their comments and we would certainly not question the integrity of anyone of them with respect to observations freely offered."[50] In other words, he had no idea whether the claims were true, which is exactly what I had said in my article. The gentleman precisely verified that a fact incompatible with the puff existed.

What his letter really reflected, of course, was his utter amazement that the puffing claim could be called false on the basis of what he considered a trivial fact. I appreciate fully that commercial operations have been conducted for years under the assumption that such things don't matter. Thus I accept his protest as a genuine objection to my criticism of habits that have been traditional in industry. It's not the only such protest that advertisers have lodged. The over-the-counter drug advertisers were reported to have "bristled with indignation" over FTC's proposed guidelines that would require them to identify a product's "miracle ingredient."[51] What could be more appropriate than having to identify the ingredients in the products they were trying to sell! But such companies have been hiding the facts for so long that they simply won't find it fair to be asked to stop.

Why shouldn't they be asked to stop? Why should the standard of honesty required in sales remain so low? Sellers with their puffery statements should show the same accountability for incompatible facts required in transactions elsewhere. This would not really be a new rule, but merely removal of questionable immunity from an existing rule.

It was 1885 when Justice Holmes made his comparison of market dealings with other human affairs. Unless changes are made, we can be sure that in the area of opinion statements, at least, it still applies.

Factual Puffery: Fiercely Sellerist, but Now Extinct

This subheading was the title in this book's first edition of a separate chapter describing two kinds of puffery that were unusual in being fact rather than opinion claims. They have long since been abolished, and the chapter is omitted in this edition.

8

The Federal Trade Commission: Accelerating the Consumerist Trend

We have already seen great accomplishment in changing the law to favor consumers, but it's all easily exceeded by the actions of the Federal Trade Commission. Its role has been so significant in modern times that observers might be excused for thinking the trend began in that agency. What it did, from its creation in 1914,[1] was to extend the movement to lengths probably not achievable by any other type of regulatory method.

The FTC's first action in that direction was to make sellers' deceptive claims part of its business.[2] The conclusion was not foregone, because the commission's original mandate was to enforce more adequately the nation's faltering antitrust laws. In the FTC Act's original wording: "Unfair methods of competition in commerce are hereby declared unlawful."[3] That protected consumers against sellers only indirectly, in the course of protecting sellers against sellers. The specific purpose was to control not sellers' dealings with consumers but rather their competition with each other by prohibiting monopolies and other restraints of trade.

The earliest commissioners, however, exercised their imagination and decided sellers would compete unfairly and restrain trade if they deceived consumers. False claims, after all, would attract business a seller would not get otherwise. To cheat consumers thus would cheat competitors, so from its earliest years many of the commission's cases involved advertising and sales practices,[4] making it seem almost as though deception of the public was the principal focus. In prosecuting such cases, however, the commissioners were required always to assert that they were moving against a seller's unfair acts toward other sellers, because that was the only action they officially had the right to call illegal.

Sellers quickly became incensed over this bold acquisition of power. A new federal agency was hard enough when it merely instituted more efficient handling of traditional cases, but inventing new kinds of unfairness on top of that was, well, just unfair! When Sears, Roebuck & Co. became one of the first to suffer the indignity, it went to court to object.[5] Caught advertising falsely that its competitors were cheating the public, Sears acknowledged the deed and correctly claimed it hadn't been illegal prior to the FTC Act. The phrase "unfair acts of competition" was nowhere defined, Sears said, nor had any list of unfair methods been compiled. Accordingly, the company demanded that the "vague" phrase be held "void for indefiniteness" unless taken to mean no more than what was unfair under common law before 1914.

The court admitted the vagueness of "unfair acts of competition," but declined to accept Sears' argument that what was legal before must still be legal now. Congress, it said, specifically intended that the FTC define what was unlawful. The critical phrase was left vague deliberately to leave such judgments entirely to the commissioners. The failure to provide a list left the FTC "free to condemn new and ingenious ways [of unfair competition] that were unknown when the statutes were enacted." Because the FTC had defined Sears's operations to constitute such new ways, the court upheld the decision and declared the commissioners were obligated to "stop all those trade practices that have a capacity or tendency to injure competitors directly or through deception of purchasers, quite irrespective of whether the specific practices in question have yet been denounced in common law cases."

The justification for so liberal a privilege was questioned the first time a commission decision was appealed to the Supreme Court. In *FTC v. Gratz* of 1920,[6] the high tribunal declared that the courts, not the commission, must define "unfair methods of competition." It did so over the strong dissent of Justice Louis Brandeis, who reiterated that Congress had designated such determinations to be the commission's right. Brandeis' point later prevailed, and in any event Gratz was not concerned with claims made to consumers and so did not specifically rule the FTC out of that field.

Another problem was the commission's assumption that injury to consumers was sufficient evidence of injury to competitors. The

Sears decision had implied that it need not collect any evidence or even state its expert opinion that injury to competitors was actually a factor in its cases. Very possibly the FTC in the ensuing years took occasional advantage of that situation by aiding consumers without even caring whether injury to competitors was truly a factor. In 1931 the Supreme Court clamped down,[7] saying charges against advertising were not sufficient unless injury to competitors was demonstrated. That pulled the commission away from direct consumer protection momentarily, but in 1938 the Wheeler-Lea Amendments expanded the FTC Act to read "Unfair methods of competition in commerce, and unfair or deceptive acts or practices in commerce, are hereby declared unlawful."[8] Since that time the commission has expressly been in the business of regulating sellers' misrepresentations.

As such, the FTC has been a formidable supporter of the consumer interest. Prior to its existence, legal help for consumers was restricted largely to court suits instituted by individual citizens. Criminal charges against sellers could be brought by public authorities, but the requirements of proof of criminal action were so great, and the penalties likewise so great, that such suits were rare. Suits could be brought by competitors against each other, but such opportunities offered no consistent aid to the consumer cause. Our protection was left pretty much up to ourselves, and while the chance of success was much improved by the early twentieth century, there were still many reasons, cost most of all, keeping individuals out of court.

The FTC changed that situation by attacking misrepresentations itself, without individual consumers having to take an active role and often before any damages occurred. Consumers not only got help without initiating it, and often before realizing they needed it, but each FTC action represented thousands, often millions, of affected consumers at one time. Suits under common law must be carried out on behalf of specific individuals, usually a single person, and when successful they benefit no one else. But the FTC can relieve a problem for the entire public in one action. Unfortunately, with some exceptions it does not recover damages for consumers, and thus does not remedy the wrongs a practice has caused. Typically it only prevents the practice from continuing, yet there is no doubt that such prohibitions represent a mammoth contribution to consumer protection.

The agency's right to regulate what sellers say was only one of its consumerist surprises. Its means of regulating falsity was from the beginning as unique as its decision that such a thing was within its jurisdiction. Just as the commission superseded the common law by redefining unfair methods of competition, it also superseded those precedents by redefining what it means to misrepresent unlawfully. The common law of misrepresentation provided many pitfalls for buyers trying to establish a misrepresentation as illegal.[9] They might fail to show they had (1) been an actual recipient of the misrepresentation; (2) understood it to convey (literally or by implication) a fact; (3) relied upon its supposed truth (not just have heard it stated); (4) been justified in relying on it; and (5) been damaged by that reliance. And of course buyers might fail to show that the seller had consciously falsified—this being mandatory in most misrepresentation cases when the FTC was created, 1914, because liability for negligent or innocent misrepresentation was only weakly established then, and warranty law was not well established.

All those requirements were necessary to assure that a misrepresentation be remedied only if shown to have caused the damages for which redress was demanded. There was fairness in that, by providing that sellers be punished only if their personal responsibility was established. But it's also fair to say that consumers can use more protection than that. Where a consumer was damaged but could not implicate the seller on all the necessary points, the consumer could go remediless in situations where responsibility might fairly lie all or partly with the seller. An advanced form of consumer protection would try to do something about that, and would even try to aid consumers where sellers were entirely faultless in what consumers suffered. The ultimate in regulatory policy would be to keep damages from happening in the first place, regardless of fault or lack of fault.

That was the breach into which the FTC stepped. It began to call misrepresentations unlawful that were not proved to have been actually received by, understood as fact by, relied upon as true by, or damaging to, any consumers—or to have been consciously intended to deceive. None of those things were retained as necessary by the commission; rather, its prosecutions needed to assert only that a sales misrepresentation possessed a *potential to deceive*.

Now that was truly different! The message may have deceived no one; it merely needed to be able to do so. The idea was outlandish, it destroyed precedents, it did things never done before. But it was confirmed, the *Sears* decision saying, "The legislative intent is apparent. The commissioners are not required to aver and prove that any competitor has been damaged or that any purchaser has been deceived."[10] Of the legal requirements thus discarded, probably the biggest was that of finding fraud, of proving that the seller consciously intended to deceive. The absence of that requirement (and of negligence, too) meant that entirely innocent representations could be held unlawful, and innocent sellers thereby penalized. That was the biggest break from previous law, and the biggest target at which industry directed its objections.

In writing the FTC Act, however, Congress had cleverly subverted objections in advance by reducing the penalty against the seller at the same time it reduced the requirements for violations. Commission procedure made it easier than ever before to act against misrepresentations, but also made the penalty for unlawful misrepresentation the lightest ever by aiming the attack away from the seller and toward the message. Common law prosecuted the sellers; the FTC prosecuted their messages. The penalty was that they must stop those messages; that's all. Sellers technically were not adjudged guilty of anything, but were simply told to cease and desist what they were doing.[11] If they didn't stop they could later be guilty of violating a direct order, but otherwise the FTC did not convict them or punish them in any of the ways, such as fines or jail, traditionally associated with legal offenses.[12]

Of course sellers might feel that to stop an ad was to act against themselves as well as against their ad. It curtailed their behavior; it made them stop doing something they wanted to do. There was the chance, too, that the order to cease their sales messages might be interpreted by the public as a finding of guilt, with consequent loss of credibility, good will, and ultimately sales. Nonetheless, at least technically, the FTC typically does not find sellers guilty or punish them.

Consumerists have said such procedures are not strict enough with wrongdoers.[13] Deliberate crooks get off with no punishment, true enough, yet there are two sides to the story. Consumers have gained because a commission that does not punish severely has not been hesitant to act. Messages that might be harmful have been taken out of circulation, whereas many would never be prohibited if it were necessary to prove actual harm. The difference in strategy is that of prevention rather than punishment. The goal is to aid consumers maximally at the sacrifice of less than maximum punishment to offenders, rather than the opposite. Increasing the punishment would only result in fewer convictions and more deceptive messages continuing to run.

Readers may wonder how that can be stated with such certainty. How do we know the FTC strategy is the best, particularly in view of the complaints against it? Might not greater penalties create greater deterrents? Why not get the most consumer protection simultaneously with the most punishment by easing the requirements for guilt without easing the punishment?

It happens that was tried, and didn't work. In 1911 a law called the Printers' Ink Model Statute was proposed by the trade magazine of that name to the various states, and eventually adopted by all but three. It prohibited as a misdemeanor any "untrue, deceptive, or misleading" advertising.[14] The requirements for unlawfulness were similar to those later used by the FTC; in particular, conscious intent to deceive did not have to be proved. But the penalty was more severe because a misdemeanor is a criminal act—not a serious one, but criminal nonetheless. That was more severe than the FTC sanction, and more than the common law interpretation of misrepresentation as a civil act. A civil wrong is not a crime, and is subject only to restoration of damages—no fines, no jail.

The Printers' Ink statute resulted in few convictions and the removal of little advertising, owing undoubtedly to its imposing the criminal penalty without requiring proof of fraudulent intent.[15] Common law developments in 1911 were not yet close to relieving a plaintiff of having to prove such intent, particularly in criminal cases. Many legal observers felt such proof was so traditional it could not be omitted. In fact, eight of the states adopted the statute only after amending it to require proof of a knowing falsehood or a conscious intent to deceive. Eight others amended it to require proof that the advertiser ought to have known of the falsity, which was negligent rather than fraudulent behavior, but still not innocent behavior.[16]

Printers' Ink objected to such alterations, since they ruined the intent to make illegality easier to demonstrate.[17] A majority of the states agreed with the magazine that dropping the fraud requirement was constitutional, and they obtained confirmation of this in at least one instance. In Ohio the point was challenged, and the court declared that "The act was intended for the protection of the public; it was not enacted because of any assumption of turpitude on the part of the seller."[18] The primary purpose, in other words, was not to punish the seller but to get the undesirable advertising out of circulation.

Unfortunately, while the rule would presumably have failed that purpose by including the fraud requirement, it could also fail by dispensing with it. A criminal conviction tended to charge sellers with turpitude in the public eye whether prosecutors intended that or not. Charging sellers with a crime was in a sense more serious in the absence of a fraud charge than with it, so prosecutors just didn't do it. The Printers' Ink statute was a noteworthy experiment, but not a success. It was on target in attacking advertisement more than advertiser, but misfired in calling the offending advertiser a misdemeanant. That is why we can be relatively certain that the FTC is correct to attack ads simply by stopping them while otherwise leaving the advertiser alone. Crooks go free, of course, but misrepresentations are far more likely than ever before to be found unlawful. By that test the FTC Act has been successful indeed.

However, the commission did not gain such privileges without challenge. Advertisers may have appreciated the reduced level of penalty, but not the reduced requirements for liability. They fought all the steps the FTC took to eliminate what was customary at common law. They fought them, and usually they lost. Most significant was the matter of no longer having to prove intent to deceive. The privilege was implied in the *Sears* decision,[19] but not made clear until 1934. In *FTC v. Algoma*,[20] the Supreme Court told several companies wishing to continue using a name found misleading that they were "not relieved by innocence of motive from a duty to conform. Competition may be unfair within the meaning of this statute and within the scope of the discretionary powers conferred on the Commission, though the practice condemned does not amount to fraud as understood in courts of law. Indeed there is a kind of fraud, as courts of equity have long perceived, in clinging to a benefit which is the product of misrepresentation, however innocently made."

Thus ended fraud, although an occasional advertiser thereafter had to be reminded of the fact. Not only was fraud unnecessary to prove, but proof of its absence no longer automatically excused an advertiser as it had in *Derry v. Peek*.[21] In *Moretrench v. FTC* of 1942,[22] the appeals court agreed that the FTC's finding of unlawful misrepresentation in an ad was appropriate even though the statements were conceded to have been made in good faith.

In addition to removing fraud, FTC procedure also removed the need to show that any specific consumers had read, heard, or seen the misrepresentation, relied on it, been deceived by it, damaged by it, or even exposed to it. All that was necessary was for the five commissioners to conclude by majority vote that a representation had the capacity to deceive a substantial segment of the population.[23] The original version of the FTC Act had not designated such a severely reduced level of proof specifically, though the legislative intent was apparent.[24] In 1938 the wording was made explicit when the Wheeler-Lea Amendments[25] prescribed in section 12 that dissemination of "any false advertisement" for food, drugs, medical devices, or cosmetics should be included among the unfair or deceptive practices prohibited under section 5. The phrase "false advertisement" rather than "deceptive advertisement" may appear to blur the distinction described earlier between falsity and deception, but the amendments added in section 15 a definition of "false advertisement" as "misleading in a material respect" ("misleading" being insignificantly different from "deceptive," and "material" meaning "affecting a purchasing decision"). The claims the amendments prohibited, then, were the same as those the commission had been acting against already—those able to deceive in a way affecting the consumer's purchasing decision. They were deceptive whether or not they were literally false.

The broad separation thus produced between deception and falsity gave the law a substantial and hotly disputed turn toward consumerism. At common law a representation typically escaped liability if shown to have some relationship to truth. But the FTC now began finding deceptiveness even with factual statements that were technically true. *DDD Corp. v. FTC* of 1942[26] involved D.D.D. Prescription, the "Original Formula of Doctor Dennis," touted in ads as just the thing "for quick relief from the itching of eczema, blotches, pimples, athlete's foot, scales, rashes, and other externally caused skin eruptions." The FTC charged that by implication this represented D.D.D. as a remedy, notwithstanding use only of the word "relief." The deceptiveness was presumed to lie in the common confusion between a relief, which merely alleviates symptoms, and a remedy, which alleviates their cause.

D.D.D. rejoined that the statement nowhere said "remedy," and referred to relief only from the *itching* of eczema, etc., not to actual relief from the eczema, etc. The appeals court agreed that "there is merit in petitioner's contention that this and similar statements, when carefully scrutinized, may thus be construed." But the court then criticized the "weakness of this position," which "lies in the fact that such representations are made to the public, who, we assume, are not, as a whole, experts in grammatical construction. Their education in parsing a sentence has either been neglected or forgotten. We agree with the commission that this statement is deceptive."

The case legitimized the notion that deceptiveness might occur apart from clear and evident falsity, when the challenged claim was literally and technically true. It also confirmed FTC's lack of requirement to show actual deception; the commission brought forth no evidence of the latter, yet its evidence was sufficient.

The notion that literal truth may be deceptive enabled prosecution of many claims that were not otherwise liable. When the FTC leaps upon one of these "untouchables," the advertising industry screams bloody murder because the type of claim has been acceptable for years. In the 1970s a major fuss arose over the idea that an ad, when it truthfully claimed a brand to have ingredient "X," might be falsely implying to the public that ingredient "X" was present in that brand alone. The fight against such allegedly deceptive "uniqueness claims" began with a group from George Washington University's law school who called themselves Students Against Misleading Enterprises (SAME).[27] They filed a petition asking the FTC to rule that the various brands of aspirin, bleach, and other product categories in which all brands were chemically similar be required to disclose that fact. Deception is inherent in advertising such brands, they said, particularly in view of the price differentials gained by those with heavy advertising. Bayer, they said, sold more than 50 percent of all aspirin, despite its high price, and the same was true of Clorox in the bleach market.

Ralph Nader soon entered the fray with a letter to the FTC[28] arguing that ads for Wonder Bread tried to make consumers think it was more nutritious than other enriched breads with essentially the same ingredients. Wonder, he said, should be made to admit the sameness to avoid deceiving the public. The FTC agreed, calling Wonder a "standard enriched bread" with nutrients at about the same levels as other enriched brands. Therefore, its complaint said, Wonder Bread should make no "uniqueness claims" unless its specific differences were listed and accompanied by a statement that competing breads were in all other respects the same.[29] The maker, ITT-Continental Baking Co., sent its president to protest that "No one is saying that our advertising isn't true, but that there's an alleged implication in it of nutritional uniqueness. We say it's not there. We haven't said other brands don't have similar qualities."[30] Nonetheless, the FTC entered an order restricting opportunities to differentiate Wonder Bread from its competitors.[31]

Another situation in which the FTC began finding deception without literal falsity emerged in the case of Un-Burn ointment. Claims for

Un-Burn's effectiveness, a commission complaint stated,[32] implied falsely to the public that laboratory tests proved that effectiveness. The complaint did not call the claims false, but said rather that the maker, Pfizer Chemical Co., did not know with sufficient certainty whether they were true. Pfizer protested that there was every reason to believe the claims were true even though specific tests had not been made, and that the public, in any event, did not take the ads to imply anything about what testing had been done.

Pfizer won when the commission finally conceded the ingredients in Un-Burn were old ones previously proven effective. The particular formulation was new, and never tested as such, but the components had been tested sufficiently in earlier formulations to satisfy technical experts that they would be effective in Un-Burn. The FTC, nonetheless, established its general principle, which meant from then on that any claim of effectiveness would imply that the advertiser had substantiation in hand to prove the claim was true.

The Wonder Bread and Un-Burn cases made clear that the FTC would go to broad lengths to distinguish deception from falsity and find the former in the absence of the latter. The eventual extensive identification of implied claims by the commission will not be described further here, because this author has covered it elsewhere prior to this second edition.[33]

Another way the FTC expanded the concept of deceptiveness came in calling entire ads deceptive for what they omit even though no individual statements therein are deceptive. Permission to do so was incorporated into the FTC Act by the Wheeler-Lea Amendments, section 15,[34] and was confirmed in *Aronberg v. FTC* of 1942,[35] another case involving the term relief. The commission felt ads for a product promising relief of delayed menstruation were deceptive in failing to reveal the presence of dangerous drugs in quantities sufficient to endanger health. The appeals court agreed that "The ultimate impression upon the mind of the reader arises from the sum total of not only what is said but also of all that is reasonably implied." The impression users might get, "because of ignorance, alarm, or desire for quick relief," was that the medicine was perfectly safe not only in recommended doses but also in larger or more frequent doses. Nothing explicitly told consumers to think that, but they might think it nonetheless, the FTC said.

The rule behind *Aronberg* was restricted to ads for food, drugs, medical devices, and cosmetics, but the FTC has long since applied it to other products simply by construing the principle into its interpretation of section 5. This produced probably its most outstanding instance of determining deception on the basis of a message's net impression, the 1950 case of *Lorillard v. FTC*.[36] Lorillard quoted statements out of context so as to convey precisely the opposite of what a *Reader's Digest* article said about Old Gold cigarettes. According to the story, the smoker "need no longer worry as to which cigarette can most effectively nail down his coffin. For one nail is just as good as another. Says the laboratory report: 'The differences between brands are, practically speaking, small, and no single brand is so superior to its competitors as to justify its selection on the ground that it is less harmful.' How small the variations are may be seen from the data tabulated on page 7." Based on that, the ads then baldly claimed: "Old Golds found lowest in nicotine, Old Golds found lowest in throat-irritating tars and resins."

The decision pointed out that "the table referred to in the article was inserted for the express purpose of showing the insignificance of the difference in the nicotine and tar content of the smoke from the various brands of cigarettes." Yet Lorillard "proceeded to advertise this difference as though it had received a citation for public service instead of a castigation from the *Reader's Digest*." Here is some more of what Chief Judge Parker of the Fourth Circuit Court of Appeals concluded:

> The company relies upon the truth of the advertisements complained of, saying that they merely state what had been truthfully stated in an article in the *Reader's Digest*. An examination of the advertisements, however, shows a perversion of the meaning of the *Reader's Digest* article which does little credit to the company's advertising department—a perversion which results in the use of the truth in such a way as to cause the reader to believe the exact opposite of what was intended by the writer. . . .
>
> To tell less than the whole truth is a well known method of deception; and he who deceives by resorting to such method cannot excuse the deception by relying upon the truthfulness per se of the partial truth by which it has been accomplished.
>
> In determining whether or not advertising is false or misleading within the meaning of the statute, regard must be had, not to fine spun distinctions and argument that may be made in excuse, but to the effect which it might reasonably be expected to have upon the general public.

I have quoted from *Lorillard* at length to emphasize that this kind of legal response simply was not established previously. The confirmation by the appellate court promoted a conception of justice that may seem obvious today, but that took the FTC a lot of straining to achieve.

Another area opened up for prosecution was that of situations having no message at all. The commission was upheld in 1942 by the appeals court in *Haskelite v. FTC*[37] in ruling that a failure to reveal a fact relevant to the consumer's purchasing decision could be called a deceptive nondisclosure. Haskelite made buffet or lap trays composed of a hardwood core and surfaced with processed paper simulating walnut and Mexican capomo wood. The FTC ordered the company to print statements on the trays or their cartons disclosing that the surfaces were of paper. Haskelite objected that failure to provide such explanation could not be deceptive because no representation was made to begin with. How could "nothing" be deceptive? It could, the court said, when accompanying certain other practices: "The process used by the petitioner to simulate woods does great credit to the ingenuity of the petitioner, and is so skillfully carried out that the physical exhibits shown us in court were distinguishable from the real wooden trays only after the most careful scrutiny. The trays themselves were the best evidence of the possibility of confusion. Without some warning, the trays of themselves are almost certain to deceive the buying public. The Commission has a right to consider this fact."

The FTC, in other words, may *require* certain statements as well as prohibit certain statements. Such "affirmative disclosure" has been ordered in many cases; Geritol advertising, for example, was told to state that most cases of tiredness were not due to "iron-poor" blood.[38] The most publicized instance was the settlement with cigarette makers requiring that print advertising display conspicuously the health warning that was already on cigarette packages.[39] In addition to specific cases, the FTC also has written a variety of guides and trade regulation rules that require disclosure by sellers in certain situations. One, for example, required light bulbs and their wrappers to have figures for brightness and estimated life stated thereon.[40] Another required posting of octane ratings on gasoline pumps.[41]

Another widening of its privileges was accomplished when the commission established that deceptiveness need not affect the entire public to be unlawful. This extended its reach beyond those cases, *Lorillard* for instance, in which virtually everyone would be misled. In *Siegel*[42] the FTC found deceptive potential in advertisements for coats made of "Alpacuna," a name inspired by the terms *alpaca* and *vicuna*. Vicuna was the more expensive fiber, and was not contained in "Alpacuna." The FTC ruled "that while in some cases the name might not be understood by prospective purchasers as indicating the presence of vicuna fiber, in a substantial number of other instances it would indicate the presence of such fiber. . . . The commission therefore finds that the name 'Alpacuna' is misleading and deceptive to a substantial portion of the purchasing public."

In this way the privilege to find deceptiveness was extended to ads that would harm only a "substantial portion" of the public. Advertisers could no longer escape merely by showing that some or even many persons remained undeceived. The commission's findings in *Seigel* showed that many understood the truth accurately, but that was no longer a defense if another portion was misled. (In chapter 9 we will see further explanation of how many deceived consumers are enough to justify prosecution.)

In all of the ways described, the FTC has successfully found new ways to define unlawful misrepresentations. Of course mistakes may occur when the process is subjective, and the commission has not been immune. Perhaps its most famous "goof" was prohibiting Clairol from saying it will "color hair permanently."[43] In other cases, the commission challenged certain alleged deceptions but withdrew when further review suggested they didn't exist.[44] Such errors illustrate that the real criterion for unlawful misrepresentation, no matter how much accompanying explanation, is often fundamentally the staff's and commissioners' subjective conviction (or plain gut feeling!) that an ad can deceive. Research findings, *Advertising Age* said, "may be casting doubt on the long-standing legal doctrine that members of the FTC are qualified to determine on the basis of their own impressions the probable impact of an ad on a consumer."[45] People in official capacities need to know, not guess, and their own best judgment, although sincere and carefully considered, is often just a guess. Suggestions have been made about habits of data gathering that the FTC might develop, but generally the old ways of making decisions have continued.[46]

I ran into this situation personally when an FTC attorney asked me to participate as an "expert witness" in a case alleging misrepresentation in ads for Sunoco gasoline.[47] He showed me the ads, and I said, well, I thought they could deceive people. But that, I added, was just my own opinion; why did he think I would be an *expert* on the matter? He said it was because I had a Ph.D. and held a reputable university position in advertising and mass communications. I said, "Is that enough? It says something about my knowledge of ads generally, but not about the Sunoco ads in particular." The attorney answered that that's what they mean by an expert witness in FTC procedures. If the commission can put more "experts" on the witness stand than the other side does, it will give them a big advantage.

I eventually learned that the procedures involved a careful weighing of evidence, with a pretty good eye on what witnesses say as well as who they are. But the problem is that witnesses often can say nothing with assurance about what the consuming public actually perceived an advertisement to be saying. When they haven't asked the public what it thought the ad meant, they can only fall back on what they *think* it would think. That's where credentials come in, because when people testify that the public thinks such-and-such when they really don't know, you can bet their degrees, position, reputation, and related qualifications will have a lot to do with whether the commissioners believe them. It's an adversary proceeding, which means other people will testify for the other side about what *they* think the public will think. Witnesses for both sides, naturally, will say the public thinks things favorable to their side's position. The commissioners must straighten out that tangle of weeds in the best way possible, and when the time comes they may discover that examining their experts' professional qualifications is in fact the best way possible.

Where experts disagree, the FTC may decide which opinion to accept, with "opinion" here meaning an expert's objective opinion-as-to-fact, not subjective claims. Some early court appeals denied the commission the right to choose among conflicting opinions-as-to-fact. In *L. B. Silver v. FTC* of 1923,[48] a breeder was ordered to stop claiming his hogs were separate and distinct from another breed. The FTC had introduced expert testimony that the breeds were not distinct, but on appeal the court observed that other experts felt differently: "There is practically no substantial conflict in the evidence tending to establish the facts from which these breeders and experts reach different conclusions. . . . Each of the individual members of these groups . . . though differing in opinion based on the same state of facts, appears to be entirely honest, sincere, and equally firm in the belief that his conclusion is the right one."[49] Since the breeder's opinion was as valid as anybody's, the court reversed the FTC's prohibition of it. The case seemed to imply that conflicts in testimony would negate all testimony, so that to protect itself against deception charges a company need only get someone to testify the claim was not deceptive.

A similar rebuff occurred when the commission charged that Marmola, a remedy for obesity, was neither safe nor scientific as claimed. The appeals court[50] said determinations of both these points were matters of expert opinion rather than fact, "determined by the particular expert's conceptions of science and of safety." Since the evidence showed the experts could not agree, the FTC was not permitted to call the claims false.[51]

The commission then worked up an alternate strategy that produced a successful order against Marmola.[52] The misrepresentations it alleged were more "direct and specific" than the ones it had named earlier, and it worked hard to introduce and establish its witnesses as being the most expert available. Although conflicts of opinion still remained, the decision summarized that "the medical testimony offered in support of the complaint far outweighs that offered in behalf of the respondent. . . . Without intending to detract from respondents' expert witnesses . . . the expert witnesses who testified in behalf of the complaint, taken as a group, are more outstanding professionally and their opinions entitled to more credit. . . ."

See what I mean about citing credentials! The procedure worked marvelously, with the Supreme Court noting on the next round of appeals that "This time the commission found with meticulous particularity that Raladam [the manufacturer] had made many misleading and deceptive statements. . . ."[53]

Eventually the FTC gained even greater leverage in the use of expert witnesses, and appeals courts showed a willingness, contrary to the attitude in the *Silver* and *Raladam* appeals, to accept without independent assessment the commission's own decisions where a conflict of experts occurred.[54] The commission was required to have substantial evidence for the decisions it made, but where such substantial evidence existed on both sides the courts now more or less automatically accepted the commission's choice.[55]

With those precedents, there was no doubt that the FTC could bolster its position in the Sunoco case by bringing someone such as myself to Washington to give my "expert" opinion. Every Ph.D. added to the line-up would make the evidence more substantial! Even if the Sunoco attorneys did the same thing, the commission's attorneys could argue that its experts were just a little more expert. The whole setup was fine and dandy from the commission's point of view, but I didn't like it very much. It would be much more satisfactory, I thought, if someone went out to the public and asked people what they thought about the Sunoco ads. Each individual consumer was a separate expert on that, and I was only one among many. Why not get the responses of many! They couldn't all come to testify, of course, but they could "appear," in effect, if someone totaled their responses and presented the total as evidence.

So I said to the attorney, "Look, why don't you let me do a survey? Perhaps it isn't customary, but it won't cost much if I use the students who reside in great numbers at my university. I know they would not constitute a representative sample of the entire United States population, but their responses should give some insight into how the public sees the Sunoco ads. If I get some data about those actual perceptions, I can give you much more than just my own opinion on what the Sunoco ads mean to people." The attorney agreed, and I did the survey and presented it as evidence in the FTC's case against Sunoco.[56] I'm going to describe that survey here to show what kind of information one can obtain about what a message implies to people over and above what it literally states.

In three University of Wisconsin classrooms I showed a total of 303 students a sixty-second television commercial. It showed an automobile fueled with Sunoco gasoline and then driven, pulling an empty U-Haul trailer, up a ramp specially constructed over the seats in the Los Angeles Coliseum.[57] The Sunoco gasoline pump, capable of dispensing eight blends of gasoline having different octane levels, was shown and discussed. Finally, the run up the ramp was shown a second time. During all this a voice is announcing:

> We're at the famous Los Angeles Coliseum. We're going to drive a car pulling this trailer from the field to the top of the stands to demonstrate an unusual gasoline. A gasoline that will help this car's engine put out every bit of power it has. Okay, Bill, up you go. What makes this gasoline unusual? It's blended with the action of Sunoco 260—the highest octane gasoline at any station anywhere. With 260 action the car and trailer go up the ramp just like that. You can get the same 260 action at Sunoco. The custom blending pump blends just the right amount of 260 into every gallon of premium, middle premiums, even regular. Watch again as Sunoco regular delivers in this car. Let Sunoco with 260 action deliver in your car. Get Sunoco 260 action. Action to be used, not abused.

The students sat in their customary classroom seats and saw the commercial run two times. They then turned to a questionnaire sheet that read as follows:

> This is a test to determine how well an advertiser's message comes through to you. The statements below refer to the Sunoco commercial

you have seen. Each statement represents something that may or may not have been stated or implied in the ad. None of the statements are exact quotes from the ad, but some of them are accurate re-statements of the ad's content and some are not.

If you think the statement is an accurate re-statement or paraphrase of what the advertisement stated or implied, either in words or in the described action, put the letter "A" for "accurate" beside it.

If you think the statement is *not* an accurate re-statement or paraphrase of the content of the advertisement, put the letter "I" for "inaccurate" beside it.

Don't concern yourself with whether or not you believe or accept what you think the ad says or implies. We are interested *not* in what you think is true or what you would like to be true, but only what the advertiser appears to be telling you.

1. __ Sunoco 260 is the highest octane gasoline at any station anywhere.

2. __ We're demonstrating an ordinary gasoline here.

3. __ Sunoco 260 action is action to be used, not abused.

4. __ We're going to drive a car pulling a loaded trailer to the top of the Los Angeles Coliseum.

5. __ You can get the power supplied by Sunoco 260 action only by buying Sunoco gasolines.

6. __ When your gasoline is blended with the action of Sunoco 260 you will get all the benefits of using the highest octane gasoline at any station anywhere.

7. __ You're seeing a stunt which a car can perform only if it is powered by Sunoco 260 action.

8. __ Gasolines blended with the action of Sunoco 260 are unusual because they provide more power than you would get with other gasolines.

9. __ This demonstration shows that gasolines with 260 action are unusual.

10. __ Having 260 action means that you have the highest octane gasoline available at any station anywhere.

11. __ You're seeing here the performance of a car using Sunoco 260. Be sure to place "A" or "I" beside all statements.

What do you think the Sunoco commercial meant to those people? Try the questions yourself before reading on, to determine your own perceptions. See what statements you think were accurate indications of claims the commercial stated or implied. If you want to decide independently of the university students' responses, do so before reading the following paragraphs.

Now to explain the results. A key characteristic of many sales messages alleged to deceive is that important facts are not mentioned (which, in fairness, is not always unlawfully deceptive). The typical service station has multiple types of gasoline, each distributed through a distinctive pump that draws from its own separate underground storage tank. At the time of the "Coliseum" commercial, Sunoco stations were different; they had only one kind of pump, and it supplied all eight of their gasolines. There were two underground storage tanks, both linked to the special blending pump. One tank contained 190, the lowest octane Sunoco offered, while the other contained 260, the highest octane it offered. (The numbers were not true octane figures but were trade names that accurately indicated the relative octane levels.)

When a dial was set to dispense 190, the pump drew gasoline solely from the 190 storage tank; the same was true for 260. But when any of the intermediate gasolines were requested, the correct blend was obtained by pumping from both the 190 and 260 storage tanks (200 was regular; 210, 220, 230, were middle premiums; 240, premium; and 250, super premium). The proportion was varied; for 200 the gasoline was drawn mostly from the 190 tank, while for 250 it came mostly from the 260 tank.

A consequence of this technology was that seven of the eight available gasolines, all but 190, utilized to some degree the gasoline drawn from the 260 tank. Even regular (200), as the ad pointed out, contained some 260. Sunoco gave a name to this feature of utilizing gasoline from the 260 tank, calling it "260 action." Your choice of Sunoco gasoline had 260 action if it contained, at least in part, Sunoco 260.

At the time the commercial ran, 260 was the highest octane gasoline a motorist could buy. But what did it mean to say a blend that was only partly 260 had "260 action"? I shared the FTC's suspicion that people might take it to mean more than it actually should, and more than was literally stated in the ad. I felt people might confuse 260 action with 260 so as to think that 260 action would provide them with the benefits obtainable from 260. 260 was truly unique, but the blends that promised 260 action contained reduced levels of octane obtainable from many competitors. If "260 action" could describe these blends, then "190 action" could describe them just as well. They all contained some 190 as well as some 260. Sunoco would never want to use the term "190 action," of course, but an accurate description of its blends could be made only if both terms were used. Using only one of the terms without the other was inaccurate and, I thought, deceptive.

I chose the eleven statements in the questionnaire to help test that supposition, and also to test the charges the FTC had made.

In the chart below, the eleven are described in various ways. The first column tells whether they were actually true or false, based on Sunoco's own information. The second tells whether they were literally stated in the ad, literally denied, or neither. The third column states how people should respond to the questionnaire *if* they respond exclusively to the ad's literal content. If the ad literally stated the statement, they should respond "A" for "accurate"; if the ad did not literally state it, they should respond "I" for "inaccurate." The fourth column states the percentage of the 303 university students who actually responded "A" for "accurate."

The critical figures in the chart are those showing how many people responded "A" where they would have indicated "I" had they responded to literal content alone. The instructions asked them to respond with "A" if they thought the ad literally stated the given content or if they thought the ad *implied* that content. Therefore when they responded "A" where the ad didn't literally state the given content, they must have thought the ad implied it. The results indicate the latter happened for statements 4 through 11, which were all false and not literally claimed in the ad, but many students saw the ad as implying such beliefs.

Statement	T-F	Literal treatment	Response predicted on basis of literal treatment	Percentage of "A" response
1	True	Literally stated	A	80
2	True	Literally denied	I	10
3	True	Literally stated	A	95
4	False	Literally denied	I	41
5	False	Neither literally stated nor literally denied	I	78
6	False	Neither literally stated nor literally denied	I	61
7	False	Neither literally stated nor literally denied	I	48
8	False	Neither literally stated nor literally denied	I	79
9	False	Neither literally stated nor literally denied	I	71
10	False	Neither literally stated nor literally denied	I	68
11	False	Literally denied	I	92

Now let's look at the misrepresentations the FTC alleged were contained in Sunoco's advertising.[58] I have listed them below, with an indication in parentheses of the survey statements relevant to each:

1. Gasolines that have 260 action give the user the octane benefits of 260 (statements 1, 6, 10 most specifically—also 5, 8, 9).
2. 260 action provides the maximum available engine power and performance, and therefore more than competing gasolines (statements 5, 7, 8).
3. The demonstration of engine power shown (i.e., the steep climb to the top of the Coliseum) constituted actual proof that 260 action outdoes competing gasolines in giving engine power and performance (statements 7, 9).

The students' responses to the questionnaire suggested they saw the ad as making the alleged misrepresentations. The first was probably produced by the confusion the FTC thought would occur between "260" and "260 action." To see how that happened, note first that most students acquired the correct belief about 260 from statement 1—80 percent of them responded with "A" for "accurate." But then they apparently attributed that belief incorrectly to the gasolines blended with 260—that's from 68 percent of them thinking that statement 10, which the reader should compare with statement 1, was also "accurate." The same result is shown by statement 6 (61 percent said "accurate"), and by several others. There seems little doubt that my participants saw the ad as telling them that "260 action" gasolines give the user the octane benefits of 260.

In addition, the results for statement 11 strongly suggest confusion in understanding the ad. That statement was specifically denied by the wording that the car was using Sunoco regular, yet 92 percent took the ad to say the car was using 260. Perhaps they noticed the wording about using regular, but thought the ad was saying it amounted to using 260. Confusion between 260 and 260 action could have been so well established earlier in the ad that it affected people's understanding of the statement toward the end of the ad about using regular.

It's my own conviction that the Sunoco advertising people deliberately intended to produce confusion between 260 and 260 action. My survey questions gave no direct evidence on the point, nor do FTC procedures, as we saw earlier, need to determine whether the advertiser intended to deceive. But I believe the phrase "260 action" is inherently likely to be misleading because it so obviously refers to 260 and yet was used to describe gasolines not having the qualities of 260. That would make it what advertising people call a "weasel," a false suggestion intended to convey more than it can truthfully mean.[59] Even if the phrase were originally conceived in pure innocence, it seems unlikely to me that anyone analyzing it carefully, and knowing the background facts that the advertiser knew but my students did not, would not recognize the confusion it could produce.

I feel supported in that opinion by a falsity explicitly stated in the ads. It was the claim that the ad would "demonstrate an unusual gasoline," which certainly must have been false since the car was using regular, which was not unusual in its octane level. Ninety percent of the students in my survey recognized the claim of unusualness (i.e., only 10 percent specified "A" for statement 2), and the only way the demonstrated gasoline could have been perceived as unusual would be if they had perceived it to be unusual in its octane level because it was blended with 260. In other words, the explicitly false statement could be accepted by viewers *only* if the implied falsity about 260 action was accepted first. That's why I feel the writers of the commercial probably intended that implied falsity to be accepted.

I hope my survey helps show the difference it can make to get actual evidence of how people perceive and misperceive. It enabled me to represent 304 experts rather than just one. It gave me something more to take to Washington than just my own gut feeling about how the Sunoco ad worked.[60] Opinions stated by so-called "experts" aren't nearly as good because different experts have different gut feelings. The only real experts on what the ad is saying to any individuals are the individuals themselves. You can't ask the advertiser or its critics, because they will typically answer according to the result they want to have reported.

I saw that happen exquisitely at State of Wisconsin hearings on proposed rules to prohibit deceptive price comparisons. Under attack was the type of ad or sales tag saying ""Now $10, was $15," when it never was $15. The state was contemplating a rule to disallow such price comparisons unless true, and unless the higher price had been in effect for at least two weeks out of the previous ninety days. The purpose of the latter requirement was to assure that the object had been at the earlier figure for some honest period of time. Otherwise anybody could circumvent the rule's intent by listing the higher price for a day, or an hour, and then making an essentially phony claim about the new low, low figure.

In the hearing a lawyer for a retailers' association asked what the rule would do to a grocer who put strawberries on sale for 69¢ per pound in the morning and then marked them down to 59¢ in the afternoon so as to move them off the shelf while they were still fresh. That couldn't possibly be deceptive, could it, he asked me after I testified in favor of the rule. I said I thought you can't rule out the possibility, and you should have seen the industry representatives jump. It was like Oliver Twist asking for more porridge; they couldn't believe it.

When you tell industry people a sales message might be deceptive they always interpret you to be charging the seller with intent to deceive. They don't know or in the heat of the moment they forget that the ancient concept of fraud is not part of the legal definition of deception as the FTC and other regulatory agencies use the term today. When I said the strawberry ad might deceive I wasn't saying anything about the grocer at all; I was saying only that buyers might misunderstand and make their purchases on the basis of the misunderstanding. If so, it might be reasonable to help them even though the actions of a perfectly innocent seller would be impeded. That's straight from the philosophy of conducting regulatory activities with a preventive rather than remedial purpose.

Obviously the strawberry situation couldn't create much deception, which is precisely why that crafty lawyer used it as an example. (I of course agreed with him that the "two weeks" rule couldn't reasonably be applied to such perishable items, but I also thought it was ridiculous to bring up because no regulators would ever try to apply it to such products in the first place.) The lawyer also used the example because he thought no one could question it. The reason I questioned it was not that I thought there'd be deception, but that I thought we couldn't be sure. But why should we have sat there in a hearing room far from any strawberries and tried to figure out the answer by logic? The thing to do would be to have someone put a sign over the berries saying 69¢ with a line drawn through it and saying 59¢ below that, then ask people who come along to say what it meant to them.

I suspect different people would think the sign meant different things. If so, it's likely some would be meanings different from what the storekeeper meant the sign to mean. If we saw that happening we'd suspect there was a problem, and if we didn't we'd conclude there wasn't. Maybe every customer who came along would understand perfectly that the berries were marked down because they couldn't be kept fresh much longer. Whatever the result, if we got the information we would know what the message meant to the consumer rather than just guessing about it.[61]

There's always the critic of the FTC who'll say that if the concept of deception produces so many problems we ought to go back to falsity as a criterion. But there's no going back when the regulatory purpose is to protect the consumer. The giant strides made by the commission may have resulted at times in seeing deceptiveness where it did not occur, but undoubtedly also have resulted in properly identifying a much greater proportion of what does occur. There has been a net gain, in other words, of correct over incorrect identifications. In this way the FTC has added considerably to the movement away from sellerism and toward consumerism.

The next two chapters add two more dimensions to the FTC's approach to identifying deceptive messages. Chapter 9 involves what members of the buying public, or what proportion of them, must be deceived in order to justify legal action. Chapter 10 is about the commission's dealings with opinion statements and puffery.

9

Reasonable Consumers or Other Consumers? How the FTC Decides

Does the Federal Trade Commission choose to protect only reasonable, sensible, intelligent consumers who conduct themselves wisely in the marketplace? Or does it also protect those who act less wisely?

Since its origin in 1914 the FTC has varied its answer to these questions. It has always prohibited sellers' claims that would deceive reasonable people, but has taken different positions on whether to ban claims that would not deceive reasonable persons yet would deceive others. The difference is highly significant to the trend toward greater consumer protection, because when the commission chooses to protect the latter persons as well, it finds a greater number of claims to be deceptive.

The "reasonable person standard"[1] has a long tradition in law. To apply it is to say that the only people who deserve legal protection from being harmed, or legal recourse afterward, are those who did all they should reasonably have been capable of doing to avoid the harm in the first place. It has been a quite demanding criterion, meaning in the marketplace that consumers should make their decisions on the basis of all examinations they could reasonably make and all information they could reasonably obtain.

The alternative criterion could be called the "ignorant person standard,"[2] referring to people who are lacking in knowledge. Some ignorant people may be stupid or uneducated or both, while others are bright and educated, but the key to defining them is that in the given context or topic area they are poorly informed or utterly uninformed. They have not obtained all of the information that can affect the decisions they will make. Given the changing nature of the marketplace as discussed earlier, vast numbers of us, including myself, fit that category with respect to numerous products.

Deceptive claims vary in the way they affect reasonable and ignorant consumers. Some deceive only the most seriously uninformed, while others deceive that group plus those who are typically ignorant as just described. Still other claims affect those two groups and also many of those consumers who meet the standard of reasonable behavior. Most seriously deceptive are the claims that affect virtually all consumers, including those who obtain and assess information at the highest level of human capability.

So, when the regulators find a claim capable of deceiving a large number of people, they will probably conclude that the group includes many who meet the standard of reasonable behavior, whereas if they find that the claim can deceive only a smaller number, they may decide it includes no or very few such people. Thus while under the reasonable person standard they will prohibit the claim only if it can deceive many, under the ignorant person standard they will prohibit the claim in either case. Obviously many more claims will be found in violation when the ignorant standard is applied.

The FTC does not go so far as to prohibit the deceptiveness that involves only a few consumers. It works under the constraint that it may proceed legally only when its action involves a sufficient degree of public interest.[3] Over the years the commissioners have been sensitive to the argument that no public interest exists in prohibiting messages that could deceive only a small number of the most uninformed, careless, or naive people. Let's look at a deception that seems to have been that kind.

In my hometown of Pittsburgh, Pennsylvania, there appeared for many Christmastimes a brand of beer called Olde Frothingslosh. The quaint item was nothing but Pittsburgh Brewing Company's regular Iron City Beer in a holiday costume, decked out with a specially designed label to provide some laughs. The label identified the product as "the pale stale ale for the pale stale male," and there was similar wit appended, all strictly nonsense. One of the best was a line saying that Olde Frothingslosh was "the only beer with the foam on the bottom."

An old friend at Pittsburgh Brewing, John deCoux, the ad manager there, told me about a woman who bought some Olde Frothingslosh to amuse friends at a party, and was embarrassed to find the claim was nothing but a big *lie*: the foam was right up on top where it was on every other brand she'd ever seen! She wanted her money back from the beer distributor (another quaint Pennsylvania custom), but he said "no way," so she went to her lawyer to bring suit. The story (and it's true) ended right there; the lawyer told her to forget it. She would have less chance than poor Herbert Williams,[4] because air conditioners have been known to exist on automobiles but nobody in history ever saw a beer with the foam on the bottom.

Individuals must bring suit under common law, because the FTC does not prosecute on behalf of specific consumers. The reasonable person standard would be applied, her reliance on the belief about the foam would be judged unreasonable, and that would be the end of that. Suppose however that the FTC pursued the same case on behalf of all consumers, and applied the ignorant person standard. Perhaps that person and others who might potentially be harmed by the claim might still have lost, but they would have come closer. If a significantly large body of persons was found to believe the foam was on the bottom, the commission might favor their position. But if it were only a few, or just one—as seems likely—they would gain nothing from the switch to the newer standard. There will be no protection for those who see a message that hardly anyone else sees.

Another reason for not taking the ignorant person standard to the extreme is that the FTC does not have the resources to prosecute all cases;[5] therefore the ones they choose might better be those that endanger more people. Another factor is that concern for the ignorant taken to an extreme could lead to repression of much communication content useful to consumers, and could lead as well to possible violation of the First Amendment's freedom of speech guarantee.[6] Finally, probably the most important objection to the ignorant person standard is that the reasonable person standard was traditional in the common law that preceded creation of the FTC in 1914. The common law held that to avoid being negligent a person must act as a reasonable person would act under like circumstances.[7] Mention of the reasonable or prudent person first appeared in an English case of 1837[8] and has been in widespread use since.

I have described the concept of negligence in discussing misrepresentation law,[9] but am using it here in a different sense. The earlier use involved whether sellers (as defendants) were negligent: did they state misrepresentations they didn't know but ought to have known were false? Here, the question is whether "contributory negligence" may be charged against those who claim to have been deceived, the plaintiffs. When they sue for misrepresentation, the rules require them to assert and show that they relied upon the claim, and that the damages they suffered resulted specifically from such reliance. In addition, they must show their reliance was justified—that is, it must pass the test of the conduct of a reasonable person. If they claim to have relied on a statement that sensible and prudent people would recognize as preposterous, they can be held guilty of contributory negligence and have their suit dismissed.[10]

That rule usually does not apply when deceivers consciously know the claim was false and intentionally seek to deceive with it—fraudulent misrepresentation. In that case persons deceived may rely without having to justify the reliance as reasonable.[11] But an exception to the exception comes with puffery and the other false but legally nondeceptive claims that are the topic of this book. The law states that people know and understand they are not to rely on such misrepresentations, even when stated fraudulently.[12] With such statements the reasonable person standard, when it is the prevailing standard, applies.

When the FTC was created, the only specific law on these matters was the common law just described. The FTC Act said nothing explicitly about what persons the commission should protect; it said only that proceedings must "be in the interest of the public."[13] The most obvious way to pursue that mandate would have been to follow the common law precedents and embrace the reasonable person standard. Instead, the FTC did the unexpected and scorned the reasonable standard in many early cases. Neither that concept nor a replacement standard was discussed explicitly but numerous cases show that the commission was applying what I call an ignorant person standard, or a close approximation. In 1919 it ordered a manufacturer to stop claiming its automobile batteries would "last forever."[14] One might assume that no reasonable person even then would have relied upon such a claim literally, especially when the same ads offered a service by which "the purchaser pays 50 cents per month and is entitled to a new battery as soon as the old one is worn out." The FTC saw the latter phrase, however, as confirming the falsity and deceptiveness rather than the sheer frivolousness of "last forever." The case indicates the commission was developing a deliberate policy of stopping deceptions that would deceive only a minority.[15]

Switching to the ignorant standard appeared questionable legally; precedent did not support it. But much was working against the prevailing reasonable person standard, in common sense if not in law. The legal conception of buyers who failed to be reasonable in the marketplace was that of persons who made a stupid purchase through their own fault—they should have known better.[16] That's a conception with which common sense could disagree. Some so-called stupid choices in today's market may be made not through carelessness but through the impossibility of obtaining and assessing information even if applying great caution and intelligence. The world of goods and services was once simple, but is now terribly technical. Many poor choices came to be made by persons who couldn't know better.

These problems might have been addressed by adjusting the reasonable person standard to the realities of the market. Consider a store scene in which a product is available at six cans for a dollar while one can is sixteen cents. In considering whether reasonable persons would be deceived, the law might take into account that many people are slow at arithmetic, and that the bustle of a market and the need to make many other choices in the same few minutes render it unlikely they would fully use the mathematical capacity they possess. The competence assumed of a "reasonable person" might have been reduced accordingly, and the traditional standard, altered in this way, might still have been applied.

What actually occurred in legal actions bordered on the opposite. Reasonable persons came to be regarded as *better* than average persons, who were never negligent and whose conduct was always up to standard. As such, the concept became entirely fictitious beyond the courtroom.[17] Such a person was "an ideal creature. . . . The factor controlling the judgment of [his/her] conduct is not what *is*, but *what ought to be*."[18] The law in effect had created an unreasonable conception of the reasonable person.

That's the problem the FTC sought to correct. We do not know, because the point was never discussed as such, whether the commission regarded its new conception as a move to a separate standard or as a redefinition of the reasonable man standard by the method described above. But the practical effect was the same either way—the commission moved toward protecting the public from deceptions that regulators previously had ignored because they would not harm the fictitiously reasonable person.

Considerations of the reasonable and ignorant standards eventually became explicit in appeals court decisions. In *John C. Winston* of 1924,[19] the commission outlawed a sales method that offered an encyclopedia "free" provided a purchaser paid $49 for two supplementary updating services. The seller appealed, and the court reversed on the grounds that no deception was involved: "It is conceivable that a very stupid person might be misled by this method of selling books, yet measured by ordinary standards of trade and by ordinary standards of the intelligence of traders, we cannot discover that it amounts to an unfair method of competition. . . ."[20]

The FTC retained a posture of resistance to the reasonable person standard.[21] But when it stubbornly invoked a similar restraint against a different encyclopedia company, Standard Education Society, in 1931,[22] it was again reversed on appeal.[23] Circuit Judge Learned Hand was most adamant in declaring that "a community which sells for profit must not be ridden on so short a rein that it can only move at a walk. We cannot take seriously the suggestion that a man who is buying a set of books and a ten year's 'extension service,' will be fatuous enough to be misled by the mere statement that the first are given away, and that he is paying only for the second. Nor can we conceive how he could be damaged were he to suppose that that was true. Such trivial niceties are too impalpable for practical affairs, they are will-o'-the-wisps which divert attention from substantial evils."

This time, however, the case went on to the Supreme Court, where a new justice in his first opinion told Learned Hand that the misrepresentation *was* a substantial evil. Hugo Black in *FTC v. Standard Education*[24] restored the commission's use of the ignorant person standard: "The fact that a false statement may be obviously false to those who are trained and experienced does not change its character, nor take away its power to deceive others less experienced. There is no duty resting upon a citizen to suspect the honesty of those with whom he transacts business. Laws are made to protect the trusting as well as the suspicious. The best element of business has long since decided that honesty should govern competitive enterprises, and that the rule of caveat emptor should not be relied upon to reward fraud and deception."

Though Black mentioned neither standard by name, his words suggest he was rejecting the reasonable person standard rather than merely adjusting it. It was his decision, above all, that led to the concept of an "ignorant person standard" for the FTC in place of what went before.

Just how Standard Education was supported by precedent is a curious question, because Black's opinion cited none. It affirmed that the sales method not merely had deceptive capacity but clearly deceived many persons, and it also said the deception was committed knowingly and deliberately.[25] This suggests the Supreme Court was invoking the common law notion that the reasonable person standard should not apply to deliberate deception. Something left unclarified, however, is what significance such a ruling should have for an agency such as the FTC that routinely did not make findings of deliberate deception. The whole advantage of FTC procedure, compared with what went before, was that it could prohibit sellers' messages *without* the traditional requirement of proving intent. What was the advantage, then, of obtaining the right to use the ignorant person standard only in conjunction with proving intent to deceive?

The result, however, was that the FTC thereafter applied the ignorant standard liberally without regard for determining intent, and in some cases without regard for the fact that intent to deceive was almost surely absent. The appeals courts not only approved, but cited *Standard Education* in doing so. The change was accepted thoroughly, particularly by the Second Circuit Court of Appeals, the one reversed in *Standard Education*. In *General Motors v. FTC* of 1940,[26] a case involving a "6% time payment plan" that actually charged 11.5 percent interest, the Second Circuit's Judge Augustus Hand concluded: "It may be that there was no intention to mislead and that only the careless or the incompetent could have been misled. But if the Commission, having discretion to deal with these matters, thinks it best to insist upon a form of advertising clear enough so that, in the words of the prophet Isaiah, 'wayfaring men, though fools, shall not err therein,' it is not for the courts to revise their judgment."

The influence of the *Standard Education* reversal was unmistakable on the one Hand—and on the other Hand as well. When Judge Learned Hand considered an appeal to the Second Circuit of the commission's finding of deception in an admittedly untrue claim that "one Moretrench wellpoint is as good as any five others,"[27] he said, "It is extremely hard to believe that any buyers of such machinery could be misled by anything which was patently no more than the exuberant enthusiasm of a satisfied customer, but in such matters we understand that we are to insist upon the most literal truthfulness. Federal Trade Commission v. Standard Education Society. . . ." As to another literally untrue Moretrench claim, saying its product had an advantage to which "contractors all over the world testify," Hand stated: "It is again hard to imagine how anyone reading it could have understood it as more than puffing; yet for the reasons we have just given, if the commission saw fit to take notice of it, we may not interfere."

It was clear that the Second Circuit's Hands were tied. Substitution of the ignorant standard for the reasonable standard proceeded in additional Second Circuit cases,[28] and in others as well.[29] Under such liberal interpretation the FTC appeared during most of the 1940s to be knocking down right and left every advertising claim it thought had the slightest chance to deceive even the most ignorant person. There was unchecked exuberance in the spree, including the action against Charles of the Ritz's use of "Rejuvenescence" as a name for its face cream.[30] The FTC outlawed the term on the grounds that it referred literally to the restoration of youth and the appearance of youth. The company protested that it was merely a "boastful and fanciful word" used nondeceptively, but the Second Circuit agreed with the commission. I find it amusing that Charles of the Ritz has been using the trade name "Revenescence" ever since, avoiding the literal meaning while apparently retaining some of the persuasive value it once received from "Rejuvenescence."

The Second Circuit's thoughtfulness toward the ignorant person reached an extreme when it agreed with the FTC in forbidding Clairol to say its dye would "color hair permanently."[31] The commission thought the public would take that as a claim that all the hair users grow for the rest of their lives will emerge in the Clairol color. That expectation was based on the testimony of a single witness who said she thought somebody might think that—although she would not.

On Clairol's appeal one judge of the Second Circuit, Clark, agreed fully with the FTC: "Petitioner's [Clairol's] actual defense is that no one should be fooled—a defense repudiated every time it has been offered on appellate review, so far as I know, since it is well settled that the commission does not act for the sophisticated alone." But the majority of judges, Swan and Augustus Hand, disagreed, saying they couldn't imagine *anybody* believing the Clairol claim: "There is no dispute that it imparts a permanent coloration to the hair to which it is applied, but the commission found that it has 'no effect upon new hair,' and hence concluded that the representation as to permanence was misleading. It seems scarcely possible that any user of the preparation could be so credulous as to suppose that hair not yet grown out would be colored by an application of the preparation to the head. But the commission has construed the advertisement as so representing it. . . ."

Despite such feelings, the majority said they had no choice but to support the FTC position: "Since the Act is for the protection of the trusting as well as the suspicious, as stated in Federal Trade Commission v. Standard Education Society . . . we think the order must be sustained on this point." While basing the decision on *Standard Education*, the Second Circuit offered no judgment that the Clairol claim was used with intent to deceive, and made no acknowledgment that *Standard Education* might have been intended by the Supreme Court to apply only where such intent was evident. The inclination to apply the ignorant person standard apparently overrode any other consideration. It almost seems that if the Olde Frothingslosh matter had been appealed to the Second Circuit in the same year as the Clairol case, 1944, the purchaser might have recovered damages because the beer's foam wasn't on the bottom!

Eventually, however, emphasis on the ignorant person standard came to be diluted, following additional curious events. An arbitrary fact of life in American law is that the various circuit courts of appeal sometimes rule differently. The Second Circuit was the one reversed by *Standard Education*, and we have seen that in subsequent cases it applied the ignorant person standard assiduously. That included the prohibition of puffery in *Moretrench*, even though puffery had traditionally been called nondeceptive. With its long-standing immunity, puffery might have been expected to resist the courts even if nothing else did, but under the ignorant standard the Second Circuit moved to eliminate that kind of falsity along with everything else.

In 1946, however, a puffery case was appealed to the Seventh Circuit. *Carlay*[32] involved a claim that Ayds candy mints made weight-reducing easy, which the FTC said was false. On appeal the Seventh Circuit,[33] which had tended earlier to object to the ignorant person standard,[34] decided that "What was said was clearly justifiable . . . under those cases recognizing that such words as 'easy,' 'perfect,' 'amazing,' 'prime,' 'wonderful,' 'excellent,' are regarded in law as mere puffing or dealer's talk upon which no charge of misrepresentation can be based." The court cited some of the previous non-FTC cases that allowed puffery,[35] and completely ignored those stemming from Justice Black and the Second Circuit that would have supported the FTC's outlawing of "easy."

The commission now had a contradiction to deal with. While the Second Circuit had told it to protect ignorant persons, the Seventh now told it to permit puffery that could deceive such people. The problem might have been resolved by the Supreme Court, but was never considered there. Instead, the FTC let the contradiction stand by allowing puffery everywhere thereafter, even though diluting the ignorant person standard in the process.

There were cases following in which the FTC retained a strong protective stance on behalf of ignorant consumers.[36] But in 1963 the commission finally commented that such protection could be carried too far. *Heinz W. Kirchner*[37] involved an inflatable device to help a person stay afloat and learn to swim. Called Swim-Ezy, it was worn under the swimming suit and advertised as invisible. It was not invisible, but the FTC found it to be "inconspicuous," and thought that was all the claim of invisibility would mean to the public: "The possibility that some person might believe Swim-Ezy is, not merely inconspicuous, but wholly invisible or bodiless, seems to us too far-fetched to warrant intervention." The decision added:

> True . . . the commission's responsibility is to prevent deception of the gullible and credulous, as well as the cautious and knowledgeable. . . . This principle loses its validity, however, if it is applied uncritically or pushed to an absurd extreme. An advertiser cannot be charged with liability in respect of every conceivable misconception, however outlandish, to which his representations might be subject among the foolish or feeble-minded. . . . A representation does not become "false and deceptive" merely because it will be unreasonably misunderstood by an insignificant and unrepresentative segment of the class of persons to whom the representation is addressed.

That is the position the FTC has followed since. It clearly rejects a strict ignorant person standard that would protect everyone from everything that may deceive them.[38] It would reject consideration, for example, of the Olde Frothingslosh claim that apparently fooled only one stray individual. Instead it protects only those cases of foolishness that are committed by significant numbers of people. Some observers might rather call the new stance a modified reasonable person standard in which what is reasonable has been equated more closely than before with what is average or typical.[39] Whatever the name, however, the FTC's present position appears to remain closer to the spirit and practice of the ignorant standard than to the reasonable standard of ancient tradition.[40]

While a new definition in the 1980s of "deceptive acts or practices" might be construed as a change of mind by the FTC on its standard, I interpret the change to be insignificant. The earlier understanding was that such acts had the "tendency or capacity to deceive a substantial number of consumers." The new definition said the commission would find deceptiveness in claims that were "likely to mislead consumers acting reasonably under the circumstances."[41] At first glance the latter might seem to refer to consumers who are reasonable in the old traditional sense, and thus to indicate a reversal that returned advertising regulation to its origins.

It did not indicate such a change; the ensuing cases show no evidence of decisions different than before.[42] There seems little doubt that "acting reasonably under the circumstances" is interpreted more in the manner of the ignorant person standard described above than of the traditional reasonable person standard. There is also little doubt that the FTC has continued the understanding brought upon it long ago by the appellate courts that it must forsake the ignorant standard and return to the reasonable standard in the case of puffery. That factor is very pertinent to the events described in the next chapter's examination of how the FTC has regulated puffing claims.

10 _____

The FTC and Puffery: Some Wins and Some Losses in the Fight for Consumerism

The Federal Trade Commission's encounter with puffery is a story of an original firm resistance against sellerist tradition, that softened into a court-enforced return to the past, then semitoughened into a stance of renewed although modified resistance that prevails today.[1]

Early Resistance

As seen in chapter 9, early FTC cases rejected the old notion of immunity for puffing. It was not an explicit rejection, but rather the omission of acceptance in situations where prevailing common law precedents would have called for acceptance. In the 1919 case, for example, the ruling against the automobile batteries said to "last forever"[2] simply ignored the possible defense that the phrase might be merely opinion. Traditionally its maker might have succeeded in suggesting it was only puffing to claim that the batteries would last a long time. But the claim was factual in a way, too, and the tradition-scorning FTC would have none of it.

There were several such early cases where the puffery defense was conspicuous by its absence.[3] One involved a maker of electric belts and insoles who advertised "so as to mislead the general public into the belief that [the] articles possess wonderful curative values."[4] The apparatus made no general medical contribution, so the ad was outlawed. But might there have been a psychological placebo effect? The possibility had been implicit for years in decisions permitting puffery, but the FTC in 1920 had no patience with such arguments. There was no room for the subjective viewpoint, no speculation about the "eye of the beholder."

That policy was maintained despite common law cases that continued to encourage puffery. Using the flamboyant phrases quoted in chapter 7, Judge Learned Hand in 1918 excused a seller of a patented vacuum cleaner for claims that "even though consciously false, were not of a kind to be taken literally by the buyer."[5] The claims were that the product was excellent, had the most economical operation and greatest efficiency of any vacuum cleaner, was easily operated, would give perfect satisfaction, would last a lifetime (maybe using the batteries that "last forever"), and so on. The evidence showed that the company that invested on the basis of those claims found the cleaner to have no value and no marketability whatsoever.

Thus while the advertising for the electric belt, which might have comforted users who believed it would, was outlawed by the FTC, the "consciously false" commendations for a vacuum cleaner having no chance of working, even for believers, was legally sanctioned by a tradition-serving court. Clearly a new direction was under way in the new agency.

However, the FTC eventually collided with the common law precedents when certain depuffed sellers asked the courts for review and relief. The first jolt came when the commission charged Ostermoor & Company in 1926[6] with unlawfully illustrating the insides of a mattress expanding to a height of thirty-five inches when its outside bindings were cut away. Although such expansion presumably indicated the powerful support features of the product, impressive if true, on actual test the mattresses expanded only three to six inches. The FTC thought the exaggeration in the illustrations implied a "resiliency or elasticity far beyond the fact."

The majority's order was dissented from by Commissioner William E. Humphreys, who said the prohibition "allows no room whatever for exaggeration. It eliminates the thrilling and time sacred art of 'puffing.' " Obviously hearing a different drummer than previous commissioners, Humphreys added that the enforcement of such a "rule of exactness" would destroy half the magazine advertising in America. The appellate court supported Humphreys' position and threw out the order, saying that "the slightest pictorial exaggeration of the qualities of an article cannot be deemed . . . a misrepresentation. . . . The time-honored custom of at least merely slight puffing . . . has not come under a legal ban."[7]

The commission, though reversed, proved unrepenting—perhaps because a technicality made the Ostermoor ruling ambiguous. The FTC's charge of deceptiveness assumed that the ad illustration showed the mattress interior freed of its bindings after first having been compressed as it would be in the finished product. But the appellate court ruled that the illustration showed the mattress material during construction, prior to being compressed for fitting inside the finished mattress. Its thickness prior to compression would naturally be greater than it would be after compression and release, which meant the illustration depicted a much less severe exaggeration than the FTC thought it had. This aspect of the decision may have encouraged the commissioners to think of the appellate reversal as due primarily to inadequate identification of the alleged misrepresentation rather than to adherence to the traditional immunity granted to puffery. Through such a rationalization the commission could recognize the court's reversal without perceiving the court to be forcing it to recognize and permit puffery.

The FTC went ahead with its attacks. In 1934 it took Fairyfoot Products[8] to task for its bunion plaster advertising and successfully weathered a challenge that the claims were only puffs.[9] Fairyfoot said its product would stop pain instantly, dissolve and remove bunions, return a deformed foot to its original shape, and perform other convenient miracles. The company defended those claims as "largely" justified by the facts and said that "where exaggeration appeared it was only such 'puffing' of the article as is not violative of the law." The FTC saw it another way, as did the appeals court, the latter stating, "Just where lies the line between 'puffing,' which is not unlawful and unwarranted, and misleading misrepresentations in advertising, is often very difficult of ascertainment. But in our judgment this case does not present such embarrassment, since the advertising here condemned is well beyond any 'puffing' indulgence."

In 1939 the commission was not equally successful in charging that Kidder advertised its motor oil in a misleading way.[10] As in *Ostermoor*, the order was overturned on appeal.[11] The appellate court agreed with the FTC that Kidder exaggerated in calling its product a "perfect" lubrication that would enable a car to operate an "amazing distance." But, the court said, "Such terms are largely a matter of personal opinion. What might be an amazing distance to one person might cause no surprise to another. So far as we know, there is nothing 'perfect' in this world, but still it is a common term, which undoubtedly means nothing more than that the product is good or of high quality. . . . We are of the opinion that [these claims] are nothing more than a form of 'puffing' not calculated to deceive."

The court's rejection was certainly in keeping with the intent of one author of the 1938 Wheeler-Lea Amendments to the FTC Act.[12] Although the amendments generally strengthened the commission in opposing deceptive advertising, Senator Burton K. Wheeler had wanted puffery to be excluded. He explained his position in debate on the Senate floor:

> Mr. Copeland (New York): I remember that years ago, when I was a medical student doing graduate work in Germany, I used to see the sign, 'Das beste in der Welt,' 'the best in the world.' Suppose a manufacturer of rayon in Cleveland, Ohio, should advertise, 'My rayon is the best in the world. It is superior to any other rayon.' What could the Federal Trade Commission do about that?
>
> Mr. Wheeler (Montana): It could do nothing about it.
>
> Mr. Copeland: Why not?
>
> Mr. Wheeler: If he said in his advertisement that it was the best in the world, and he was honestly of the opinion that it was the best in the world, the Federal Trade Commission could ordinarily not do anything about it, because it would be difficult for the commission to convince the Supreme Court that "seller's puff" was an unfair practice. The object of the proposed legislation is not to stop the issuing of exaggerated opinions with reference to one's own articles.
>
> Mr. Copeland: The Senator means "trade puffing"?
>
> Mr. Wheeler: Yes; trade puffing. What the Commission has tried to do is to stop the issuing of a definite statement with reference to a fact which was not true. There is a vast difference between a statement of a concrete fact with reference to some article and the mere puffing of one's own goods.
>
> Mr. Copeland: There may be, but I fail to see it.
>
> Mr. Wheeler: The law recognizes a vast difference. . . .[13]

Wheeler's comments made no apparent impression on the FTC. In 1939 it brought a complaint against puffery claims by Moretrench,[14] and survived the company's appeal through the fortuitous intervention of the ignorant person standard.[15] The judge who wrote the *Moretrench* decision, Learned Hand of the Second Circuit, had been reversed earlier in *Standard Education* by the Supreme Court's decision calling for application of the ignorant standard.[16] That standard clearly implied a prohibition of puffery, because puffery possesses the capacity to deceive those who would take it literally, which uninformed and careless members of the population probably would do. Thus Hand saw little choice in *Moretrench* but to support a complete shackling of puffery: "We understand that we are to insist upon the most literal truthfulness."

As other cases followed (see chapter 9), it seemed that the substitution of the ignorant person standard for the reasonable person standard would wipe out puffery for good. In *Gulf Oil v. FTC* of 1945,[17] the court interwove two of the well-known quotations about protecting ignorant men and fools into its finding that Gulf's puffery defense could not be accepted. The die appeared cast and puffery appeared doomed.[18]

A Court-Imposed Return to Tradition

Surprises were in store for the commission, however, in cases against Bristol-Myers in 1942, attacking such phrasing as "Ipana for the Smile of Beauty," and against Carlay Company in 1944. The latter was the advertiser described in chapter 9 that called its weight-reducing plan "easy." FTC prohibition of that claim was reversed on appeal in 1946,[19] so that the commission was forced to permit Carlay's puffery even though otherwise required to invoke the ignorant person standard.[20] That unseemly contradiction posed a problem for the FTC in deciding the Ipana case. Maintaining the ignorant standard would leave no room for puffery, while maintaining puffery would substantially deteriorate that standard. The pending complaint against Ipana loomed as the "playoff" to determine which of the two would win.

The Ipana decision (*Bristol-Myers*) was not handed down until 1949, seven years after issuance of the complaint.[21] The latter is the FTC's official imposition of a charge that could result in finding a violation. Complaints are made with the confident presumption that the facts will bear out such expectations, although the result is never certain until a hearing is conducted and the facts and legal conclusions are established. In *Bristol-Myers* the time required to complete that process was unusually long, perhaps owing to the demands of World War II. The delay allowed for the intervention of events that changed the commission's feelings about the charge. The 1942 complaint called the phrase "Smile of Beauty" false and misleading, seeing it to imply that Ipana's "use will result in the user possessing a beautiful smile and increased popularity." The complaint argued, in passionate protection of the ignorant man, though perhaps somewhat witlessly, that

> In truth and in fact, the smile is a change in facial expression, the most notable components of which are a brightening of the eyes and an upward curving of the corners of the mouth. It does not necessarily involve a display of teeth or gums. A smile not otherwise pleasing will not be rendered so by the possession of good teeth. Beautiful teeth will not insure a beautiful smile or social popularity. The beauty of human teeth depends primarily upon their conformation, color, arrangement in the mouth and other natural physical features, and teeth which do not possess these natural qualities will not be rendered beautiful by the use of Ipana tooth paste.

In other words, the commission had seen "Smile of Beauty" as a claim that Ipana will straighten out your crooked teeth. That's much like a commercial I recall in which Secret deodorant was touted to a woman who wore glasses. Once she began using Secret it apparently improved her vision so much that by the end of the commercial she didn't need to wear glasses anymore. I doubt that many consumers would believe that, or would believe the implication about the crooked teeth. But the protection of ignorant persons, prompted by the decisions in *Standard Education* and *Moretrench* among other cases, had become a primary criterion in 1942 for FTC decisions.

By 1949, however, *Carlay* had intervened to force the commission to acknowledge puffery. Accordingly, it concluded that Ipana's "Smile of Beauty" could not be attacked: "The reference to beautification of the smile was mere puffery, unlikely, because of its generality and widely variant meanings, to deceive anyone factually. As used in the advertising, the expression 'brighten and whiten the teeth,' according to the opinion evidence, means simply cleaning the teeth, and the record shows that while the use of Ipana will not alter the shape . . . of the teeth, it will assist in the cleaning of them."

Perhaps the flat-footedness of the complaint's remarks about the anatomy of the human smile prompted some realization of the absurdity of aiding just *every* ignorant person. In any event *Carlay* prevailed,[22] and the ignorant person standard was eroded to the extent of its application to puffery. FTC policy now provided that ignorant consumers would be protected from many false claims, but not from puffery. That involved a conclusion, in effect, that while such consumers would act less than reasonably toward many claims, they would always display the characteristics of the traditional reasonable person in their responses to this particular type.

From *Bristol-Myers* onward the FTC adapted itself to the realities of puffery and gave the concept full consideration. In several cases it dropped charges on the grounds that only puffery was involved. Mushroom growing, for example, was permitted to be called an "easy" occupation.[23] The commission said it realized the task was difficult work, yet accepted the claim because many people might find it easy compared with other occupations. An insurance plan was allowed to imply that it provided "adequate insurance" because what was adequate differs from person to person.[24] A brand of sewing machine was allowed to be described as "almost human and gives the housewife a tailor's skill." It might be overgenerous to designate the reference to "tailor's skill" as puffery, the commission observed, but it extended the generosity nonetheless.[25] A shoe company was allowed to represent that its special innersole would assure comfort and perfect fit, even though it would not be so for all individuals. The grounds were that the innersole would give an advantage that would not be present in its absence.[26] The case, *Tanners Shoe*, invoked the Supreme Court's explanation from *New South Farm* of 1916,[27] that the distinction between puffing and falsity was the difference between exaggerating qualities a thing possessed as compared with asserting qualities it did not possess at all.[28]

A Renewed but Modified Resistance

Still, the FTC did not acquiesce entirely. Steelco Stainless Steel claimed its statements were only puffery even though clearly factual. The company had made disparaging claims that food handled in its competitors' aluminum utensils would cause cancer, stomach trouble, anemia, blood poisoning, and other ailments. The FTC said it was not impressed with the "suggestion that representations relied upon can be excused on the basis that they are only 'puffing'. . . . Statements made for the purpose of deceiving prospective purchasers and particularly those designed to consummate the sale of products by fright cannot properly be characterized as mere 'puffing.'"[29]

More significantly, the commission several times rejected or ignored the puffery defense even when the literal form was that of opinion, describing claims instead as misrepresenting facts by implication. A medicine called N.H.A. Complex was said to "make one well and keep one well," a phrase perhaps innocent in itself but prohibited because the nostrum was claimed to prevent and cure a remarkable variety of diseases for which it had no effect.[30] In *Tanners Shoe*, although one instance of puffery was permitted as seen earlier,[31] the manufacturer was denied the right to claim that its shoe "provides support where it is needed most." The latter phrase, said the commission, carried an orthopedic or health connotation, which made a difference. Nor was puffery seen in claims by another shoe manufacturer that its insert would give "increased foot health and comfort," provide "more normal foot action," make "foot pains disappear as if by magic," and so on.[32]

Reweaving was not allowed to be called "easy to learn" when it seemed likely no one would find it easy.[33] The commission still regarded "easy" as a flexible term, harking back to when the appeals court let Ayds candy mints be called an easy way to diet.[34] But the flexibility with Ayds was that some people truly might find the task easy even though others would not. In contrast, the commission thought *no one* would find reweaving easy; therefore the term was no mere exaggeration of a true quality but a false fact misrepresenting the quality's absence.

In these and other cases a new strategy of resistance to puffery was created to replace the earlier one that failed. After originally prohibiting such claims, the FTC after *Carlay* no longer fought the appellate decisions saying the common law precedents gave such claims immunity. Instead, its strategy was to accept the category as a legal oasis for the seller, but to argue more strongly that sales claims should be denied admission because they were fact rather than opinion. That can be described as a modified resistance to puffery because the commission was no longer acting to remove the category; yet it was guarding the gate so that claimants to entrance would not necessarily be granted their wish. Of course, whether or not that actually amounted to much resistance would depend on the criteria chosen.

The criterion was strong in a 1958 case in which the FTC banned a representation that traditionally had been called puffery. *Liggett & Myers*[35] involved attempting to hide behind the puffery rule in describing Chesterfield cigarettes as "milder." The hearing examiner's initial decision sympathized with the advertiser: "For more than 20 years the term 'mild' . . . has been in wide use by cigarette manufacturers in advertising. . . . The present case appears to be the first in which the use of the word has been challenged. This would indicate that through the years the commission has regarded the term as harmless or innocuous, as merely a laudatory or 'puffing' term noting high quality or pleasant sensory reaction, not as a term relating to the amount or degree of irritation produced in the nose, throat or accessory organs." However, although initial decisions may be allowed to stand as FTC rulings, this one was not. Previous commissioners may have responded as the examiner[36] said they did, but the present ones now decided "milder" was factually false. In the twinkling of an eye a long-term item of puffery disappeared.

The resistance was extended with more cases. In *Lifetime*[37] claims of "first class craftsmanship and materials" were prohibited although defended as "a customary claim of American suppliers and artisans and . . . no more than puffing." The commission ruled that grade and quality distinctions were commonly made and depended upon in the given business and were of prime importance to prospective purchasers. In *Dannon*[38] a claim that yogurt was "nature's perfect food" was called misrepresentation of a material fact rather than puffing. The same era also produced the case of *Colgate*, the famous sandpaper caper.

Colgate[39] is best known for the use of a television mock-up, a category of falsity we will see in chapter 14. To describe the case briefly here, the advertiser said sandpaper could really be shaved after soaking with Rapid Shave shaving cream, but claimed it could depict the event accurately on the screen only by faking the scene with a piece of plexiglas on which large grains of sand had been sprinkled, loose. This "mock-up" was necessary, the argument went, to demonstrate something the product actually could perform. The FTC thought the mock-up was not necessary and therefore illegal.

A separate line of defense offered by Colgate was that no reasonable viewers would have regarded the demonstration as serious; they would have seen it only as puffing. That argument was fairly ridiculous; the lawyers who devised it must have realized that were it true it would have been unnecessary for Colgate to use the mock-up in the first place. There would be no need to convince viewers they were actually seeing something if they wouldn't have taken it seriously anyway. But lawyers will be lawyers! Probably they were not surprised to find the mock-up defense to be a stronger argument (though not strong enough), while the counterfeit angle about puffery was disposed of swiftly: "The argument that respondents [Colgate] only indulged in a little harmless puffing is obviously out of place. They represented, unqualifiedly, that 'Rapid Shave' will dramatically facilitate the shaving of sandpaper and that they were demonstrating this fact before a television audience to prove it. Both of these were factual representations; neither is true."

Though Colgate was only puffing with its puffery defense, the argument gave the FTC the chance to comment on its new strategy of resistance. From an earlier era Colgate had cited *Ostermoor, Kidder,* and *Carlay* as precedents,[40] to which the commission answered that in the present era the precedents that ruled *against* puffery were more significant than those that favored it. The earlier cases, it said, were now "inconsistent with the prevalent judicial and administrative policy of restricting, rather than expanding, so-called puffing." At this point the commission's resistance level remained high.

Further cases illustrated the policy of restricting puffery by refusing to admit various claims into the category.[41] One involved the nutritional values of Carnation Instant Breakfast, the ads having called the product equivalent to a pictured breakfast of bacon, toast, eggs, and juice. The FTC insisted on a revised illustration containing fewer eggs. "That may seem like a very small change," a spokesman said, "but it accomplishes what the commission considers proper: it prevents the advertiser from using a visual which exaggerates the true quantity of major nutrients in the product."[42]

In addition to cases against individual advertisers, the commission also wrote rules applying to entire industries. In one, rather than condemning puffery per se, the solution was to require affirmative disclosure of the facts the puff implied. Lightbulb makers were found to use fact-related puffs such as "long life," "extended life," "better light," and "stays brighter longer." It was true that one brand of hundred-watt bulb could burn brighter than another, but only at the expense of living a shorter life. Its maker naturally advertised the gain in brightness without mentioning the shortened life, and its competitor of course advertised longer life without mentioning the lesser brightness. Rather than outlawing the comparisons, however, the commission required them to be accompanied by disclosures of light output in lumens and expected hours of life along with the customary statement of wattage. The manufacturers could still communicate their vague phrases, but consumers now could check the precise facts behind them.[43] In that way puffery, though remaining, was deprived of its former potential for implying false facts.

Despite such instances of resistance, however, the FTC remained firm on protecting puffery as a category into which many claims fit. In 1971 it shunned a contrary argument that no ad claims could really be called puffs. Commissioner Mary Gardiner Jones argued, "In face of the huge dollar outlays expended by industry for its advertising campaigns, it is difficult to take seriously their arguments that any segment of their messages should be regarded as so unimportant and with so little effect on their audience as to justify being called mere puffing. . . ."[44] Despite her logic, the commission shortly thereafter reiterated that "There is a category of advertising themes, in the nature of puffing or other hyperbole, which do not amount to the type of affirmative product claims for which either the commission or the consumer would expect confirmation."[45] Jones' term ended in 1973, and no commissioner since has opposed the general idea of puffery's existence.

In the 1980s the FTC strongly asserted its acceptance of puffery in both a case and an influential rule. In *Sterling Drug* it said that " 'Bayer is 100% aspirin—the world's best aspirin,' and 'Bayer works wonders,' are merely puffing because the ad does not discuss any comparison of Bayer's 'quality' with other brands of aspirin."[46] That not only reflected acceptance of the category but also showed how wide it could be by drawing the remarkable conclusion that "best" is not a comparison. True, the commission declined to excuse another Bayer ad having a similar puff, but only because it also had false factual claims for Bayer's superiority. Thus, containing a puff would not excuse a total ad as puffery when it also had objectionable nonpuffing elements. But still, ads making claims that were nothing more than puffery were acceptable.

The influential rule was the 1983 Policy Statement on Deception,[47] in which the FTC broadly restated its definition of deceptiveness. About opinion claims in general it said:

> [T]he Commission generally will not bring advertising cases based . . . on correctly stated opinion claims if consumers understand the source and limitations of the opinion [Footnote: An opinion is a representation that expresses only the belief of the maker, without certainty, as to the existence of a fact, or his judgment as to quality, value, authenticity, or other matters of judgement. *Restatement of Torts, Second* § 538A.]. Claims phrased as opinions are actionable, however, if they are not honestly held, if they misrepresent the qualifications of the holder or the basis of his opinion or if the recipient reasonably interprets them as implied statements of fact [Footnote: *Id*, §539. At common law, a consumer can generally rely on an expert opinion. *Id*. §542(a). For this reason, representations of expert opinion will generally be regarded as representations of fact.].

About puffery specifically, the statement then said:

The Commission generally will not pursue cases involving obviously exaggerated or puffing representations, i.e., those that the ordinary consumers do not take seriously [Footnote: [see statement at this chapter's note 45]. The term 'puffing' refers generally to an expression of opinion not made as a representation of fact. A seller has some latitude in puffing his goods, but he is not authorized to misrepresent them or to assign to them benefits they do not possess. . . . Statements made for the purpose of deceiving prospective purchasers cannot properly be characterized as mere puffing. *Wilmington Chemical*, 69 FTC 828, 865 (1966).]. Some exaggerated claims, however, may be taken seriously by consumers and are actionable.

These portions of the Policy Statement on Deception reiterate both that the puffery category exists and that some claims do not belong in it. The latter include those that ordinary consumers take seriously, or that are made as representations of fact and thus could deceive consumers. They also more generally include opinion statements that (1) have limitations consumers do not understand, (2) are not honestly held, (3) misrepresent the basis for stating them, (4) can reasonably be interpreted as implied statements of fact, or (5) are expert opinions.

All of that seems to indicate that many claims in the form of puffery will be excluded from the category and prosecuted instead as deceptive. Nonetheless I have little faith in that possibility, for two reasons found in earlier content of this book. The first reason is the large number of puffs cited in chapter 3 and the other is the similarity of the FTC's position to that earlier described for the common law. In the first section of chapter 7 we saw how an immunity from deceptiveness was created for opinion claims, but in the second section we saw ways of tightly controlling such claims. Although the latter ideas seemed to suggest the immunity was very narrow, in the third section we saw that the tight control did not apply to opinion claims that also constituted sellers' puffery. The immunity for the latter was thus not narrow at all; it was very broad and strong.

I believe that the large number of puffery items that the FTC allows to run free indicates, just as in chapter 7, that the expressions stated above that seem to curtail the freedom of opinion statements are actually not applied by the commission to puffery claims. That is, the FTC assumes that examples such as those of chapter 3 are not taken seriously by consumers, are not understood by consumers as implying facts, do not represent the expert opinion of sellers, etc., etc.

Nestlé's, for example, claims to make "the very best chocolate." In disagreement with the FTC position, I believe that means to many consumers that there exists a standard for the best chocolate, and that Nestlé's ranks highest on that standard. I do not believe consumers understand what the standard is, but only that many of them believe there is such a thing, and that they believe Nestlé's is ranked highest on it by those experts, including Nestlé's competitors, who do understand what the standard is. Thus consumers *do* take the claim seriously, and *do* understand it to be implying facts, and *are* deceived if those facts are false, as such facts probably often are.

Buttressing my interpretation of the FTC position are the Bayer decision described above, and other recent commission actions involving puffery. In 1989 Firestone Tire asked it to change an order prohibiting representations that the company's "tires will be safe under all conditions of use," and requiring substantiation for representations that the company's "tires have any safety or performance characteristic."[48] Firestone asked that the order be interpreted by the commission to exclude what it called "generalized safety claims," such as "Quality you can trust," "Because so much is riding on your tires," and "Performance, safety, and price all rolled into one." The company contrasted such claims to "specific safety claims" that "refer to any particular safety or performance characteristic."

Thus Firestone wanted its "generalized safety claims," which of course are puffery claims, to be free from having to be substantiated. Notice the irony in what it was asking: the company wanted to be able to ask consumers to trust the company and its tires, yet also to have the law rule, in effect, that consumers must know not to trust that claim. Of course if consumers realized that legally they were obligated to distrust Firestone's claim that they could trust it, they would consider the company to be making no sense and to be terribly untrustworthy. If consumers did not know that, however—which most probably do not—then many would trust the claim and the company, as Firestone surely hoped they would, while at the same time Firestone would be utterly free of any obligation to support that trust.

Perhaps such reasons were why one commissioner, Andrew Strenio, dissented that "[T]he rationale for treating 'generalized safety claims' more leniently than 'specific safety claims' is strained at best. It seems illogical to allow a possibly lower level of substantiation for the broad claim of overall safety than for narrower claims of quality regarding a subset of safety attributes, such as puncture resistance. . . . In my view, generalized safety claims such as 'Our tires are safe' are objective and verifiable claims covered by the commission's ad substantiation doctrine."

Bravo Strenio! Yet the other commissioners agreed with Firestone and allowed the request. The moral of the story for consumers: do not trust Firestone's claim that you can trust it unless you realize that you are supposed not to. You need to know that the FTC encourages a company to ask for your trust while at the same time being fully and consciously aware that it need have no basis for its own belief that it can be trusted.

In 1995 the FTC agreed to a request from C & H Sugar[49] to reopen an earlier order prohibiting C & H from puffery claims while its competitors were not so prohibited. The commission ruled: "This modification is justified on the narrow facts of this matter. In particular, the homogeneous nature of the product means that there are few truthful, nondeceptive comparisons that can be made among competing products. In order to promote their brands, sugar refiners must rely on the sort of subjective endorsement claims described above, or objective product source and origin claims. . . . We are persuaded, therefore, that modification to permit puffery is warranted."

Of course I have no objection to having the rules be the same for all competitors. But the result is now that if companies cannot find a factual way to differentiate their brands from the competition, then let's by all means supply them with a puffing means for doing so. Despite whether any real basis exists for claiming to be different, the right to claim to be so must be protected at all costs!

To summarize this section and chapter, the FTC first resisted the very existence of puffery, then was rebuffed by the courts for doing so, and finally developed a new means of resistance by ruling certain claims out of the category. However, such renewed resistance is greatly modified and is very modest; the resistance level now seems not very high. As anyone can see in a few moments with television or a magazine, puffery has the commission's blessing and strongly lives on.

A Brief Note on Lanham Act Cases

Since the first edition of this book, advertising cases involving the Lanham Trademark Act have become frequent. While the act relates mostly to trademark law, it also lets advertisers sue each other in federal courts, and they have adopted the habit freely. However, as I have described at length in law review articles, the treatments in such cases of deceptiveness in general[50] and puffery in particular[51] are essentially the same as for the FTC. Consequently, I have decided not to discuss Lanham cases specifically.

11

Additional Kinds of Puffery, Beginning with Obvious Falsity

The story of puffery cannot be complete without examining some other false but legally nondeceptive sellers' claims having similar sellerist effects. To avoid confusing the reader who may encounter these topics elsewhere, I have used "puffery" thus far in its narrow legal meaning only. But in any practical sense it is appropriate to think of the term more broadly, as comprising the wider field of all related claims.

The other types of claims do exactly what puffery does; they describe the object for sale in ways that may be deceptive, although the law says they are not so even if false. They have the same characteristics as puffery in that they "blow up" the object. They have attained their legal status for roughly the same reasons and their notoriety for roughly the same problems as we have seen for puffery. Although the law says that sellers' claims will not necessarily be admitted to these categories, in practice the law lets many of them in. The first type is discussed in this chapter, and the others in the following three chapters.

Obvious falsity has already been mentioned in the story about the "air conditioning" on Herbert Williams' car.[1] By using it, the salesman puffed up the automobile to be worth more in Williams' estimation than it would otherwise have been. The presence of the air conditioner was not exaggerated, as with puffery, but rather was falsified as a matter of objective fact. That would ordinarily be a worse problem, but the law calls such falsity permissible where it presumes the truth is obvious.

Whether the air conditioner's absence was truly obvious might reasonably be argued, yet no one would question the general possibility that obviously false claims might be made. A car, for example, might be described as in good condition when it had no tires, or no steering wheel. As with puffery, the law is inclined toward calling such falsity nondeceptive because any buyers who examine the car will see the truth and so will neither believe nor rely on the claim. Buyers are not permitted to rely on representations that contradict what they presumably know.

The obvious falsity rule began in Anglo-American law with this statement by Justice Brian in 1471: "If a man sells me a horse and warrants that he has two eyes, if he has not, I shall not have an action of deceit, as I could know this at the beginning."[2] Spelled out more precisely later, it meant caveat emptor would apply when truth or falsity was obvious even though the claim would otherwise be a false warranty or fraudulent misrepresentation (deceit, in Brian's usage). Those two exceptions were held to be voided because buyers were not justified in relying on falsities they presumably knew were false.

Of course the rule was meant to apply only to what was really obvious. If you notice something about a product right away, virtually automatically, just by being around it briefly, then it's obvious. If you can't do that, then it's not. Regulators who have any doubt about which is which can ask consumers for their opinions, and decide accordingly. Mistakes are not impossible, but presumably the proper conclusion will usually emerge.

If that were all to be said about the obvious falsity rule, its story would be easy to tell. But much more happened; sellerist developments made the rule much more likely to have adverse effects on consumers. Regulators and courts, as typified in the case of Herbert Williams and the air conditioner, developed a tendency to treat obvious falsity as they treated puffery, assuming in the absence of any observation of actual consumer perceptions that certain falsities must be obvious to consumers (just as they assumed puffery was automatically distrusted by consumers). The rule thus acquired a systematic sellerist bias.

Why? The answer, as with puffery, lies in the rule's ancient history. Let's return again to the days when the law favored the seller overwhelmingly, and so decided that many things were "obvious" legally whether or not they were so factually. It happened as early as the year 1615 in that strange case of *Baily v. Merrell*.[3] Merrell, you'll recall from chapter 7, lied to Baily about the weight of the wood piled on the wagon. But when the overload killed the horses Baily couldn't make his damage suit stick because the court felt the actual weight was so apparent that he must have known it. The court said its decision was based on Brian's rule.[4]

Was the load's weight obvious in the same way the existence of a horse's eyes would be? Surely not. One of the judges said, in fact, that if Baily doubted the weight he could have weighed the load and found out. If you have to weigh things to determine their weight, the precise amount must not be obvious. Any observation for which we need an aid to measurement should certainly not be called "obvious" if that word is to retain its meaning of being something people notice instantly on sight. Another judge in the case may have recognized that problem and sought to reconcile his opinion with it. He also voted against Baily, but on the grounds that it should have been easy, presumably without weighing, to see the difference between 800 pounds and 2,000 pounds. The *difference* should have been obvious to Baily even if the precise weight was not. Under that view, "obvious" would still mean really obvious, and the rule would have been held to a fairly narrow scope.

Whatever may have been the better argument, later courts interpreted *Baily v. Merrell* as sanctioning expansion of the rule to cover much more than what was instantly noticeable. The rule came to be treated as virtually equivalent to the requirement of inspection under the rule of caveat emptor. That is, it came to apply to anything buyers might observe either instantly or by *inspection of the object*. A seller's false statement about anything capable of being inspected became an "obvious falsity" and therefore could not legally be relied upon by its recipient.

American law adopted the idea with great vigor, finding it attractively compatible with the rising tide of caveat emptor that marked the nation's early decades. In *Sherwood v. Salmon* of 1805,[5] Sherwood had described some land to Salmon and another man as "excellent bottom land," "side-hill fine for pasture land," and "good timber land." It was worth one dollar per acre, he said, except for one tract that was worth two. But he was willing to sell it for twenty-five cents per acre! The buyers were in Connecticut while Sherwood's land was in Virginia, 500 miles away, probably equivalent today to about 5,000 miles. When the buyers eventually saw their land, after buying without examination, they found the descriptions false and the value per acre far less than the twenty-five cents they had paid. They won a suit for misrepresentation, but had to defend themselves in an appeal in which Sherwood's counsel blithely conceded the misrepresentations had been false.

"It is agreed," the record stated, "that [Sherwood] falsely and fraudulently misrepresented the quality of the land; that his assertions were untrue, and known by him to be so." That's not a good way, ordinarily, for a lawyer to begin when trying to get a defendant off the hook. But in this case the concession laid the groundwork for Sherwood's winning argument: "The defects complained of must, from the nature of the subject, be visible. . . . The rule of caveat emptor relative to visible defects was without exception, if the purchaser has eyes to see, and the subject misrepresented did not require peculiar skill to discern its real condition [citing *Baily v. Merrell*, among other cases]."

Counsel for the aggrieved buyers protested futilely that the caveat emptor rule should be relaxed because it was overly difficult to inspect the land personally before purchase: "Where the quality of the article can be ascertained with *ordinary diligence*, the buyer shall stand by the loss; but to say, that in all events, he is to inform himself, is to place an honest man, in many instances in the power of a swindler. It is often said, in our books that courts should, as far as possible, enforce the duties of morality. The principle advanced [by the seller] seems to be rather a protection to fraud." Sellers, counsel for the buyers added, shouldn't "throw dust in a man's eyes, and then say that he might have seen." The buyers could not know the seller had lied; therefore the seller should be liable.

If that wasn't a winning argument, what could be? Unfortunately, it wasn't. The court declared the buyers could have won only by going to Virginia before the purchase. Failing to do so was fatal because "the maxim caveat emptor applies forcibly in this case. The law redresses those only who use due diligence to protect themselves. . . . The purchaser can see, if he will but look. . . . Whatever morality may require, it is too much for commerce to require, that the vendor should see for the purchaser. It is enough for him, in point of law, that he does not conceal the knowledge of secret defects, nor give a warranty, express or implied."

There again was the difference between the law of the market and ordinary morality. The absence of the claimed bottom land and pasture land was *no* secret. If you stood there and *looked*, you could see! It might take some effort to reach where you had to stand, but that's what you had to do. "Whether lands be five, or five hundred miles from the purchaser's residence," said the judge, "does not vary the requisition of due diligence, though it may the expense of complying with it."

Was the meaning of "obvious" getting less obvious? In *Baily* the qualities of the object were called obvious even when not seen instantly, although at least the wood was in front of Baily and he was looking at it. But in *Sherwood v. Salmon* the qualities were called obvious even though the purchase was entirely out of sight and would require extraordinary diligence to go to where it could be seen.

A similar viewpoint was offered in *Gordon v. Parmelee* of 1861,[6] in which the sellers claimed their piece of land was fifty acres when the true figure was twenty-eight. This time the buyers looked before they bought, although they failed to see the truth. When they sued for misrepresentation the court ignored the falsity of the sellers and said—shades of *Baily v. Merrell*—that the buyers had to do more than just take a glance when they purchased land: "They omitted to measure it, or to cause it to be surveyed. By the use of ordinary diligence and attention, they might have ascertained that the statement . . . on which they placed reliance, was false. They cannot now seek a remedy for placing confidence in affirmations which, at the time they were made, they had the means and opportunity to verify or disprove."

To read between the lines, these cases were establishing more than just a rule about obvious falsity. They were aiming toward a caveat emptor entirely without exceptions. No matter how much a sellerist device it may have been, caveat emptor had traditionally acknowledged the protection of buyers against false warranties and fraudulent misrepresentations. But here were attempts to eliminate even that, and impose an absolute caveat emptor. It was the most extreme sellerist form ever achieved by the law of sales statements, offering the least protection (i.e., none) against the most clearly fraudulent lies that could be told. If the obvious falsity rule may be thought of as Dr. Jekyll, this absolute caveat emptor was the Mr. Hyde that it spawned.

The U.S. Supreme Court never supported such a rule, but in 1871 it lent its weight to a milder form of the obvious falsity rule in *Slaughter's Administrator v. Gerson*.[7] Slaughter had wanted a boat that drew no more than 3½ feet when fully laden, but the one he purchased from Gerson went aground in deeper water. Slaughter's estate charged Gerson had claimed the draught was only 3½ feet, although other evidence suggested Gerson said it merely as something asserted by another and not known to himself personally. The suit also claimed Slaughter was unable to measure the draught, because "Unless the sea was calm—which does not appear—it was impossible to make an accurate measurement of the draught of water."

Slaughter, however, had taken two ship carpenters to the boat prior to purchase, and one of them reported to him a draught of 4½ feet measured at midships. When this evidence was revealed, it turned the case around. The Supreme Court declared that *even if* Gerson fraudulently misrepresented, he would not be liable because the truth had been obvious to Slaughter, not because he might determine it but because he *had*. Therefore he was bound to rely on it: "The neglect of the purchaser to avail himself, in all such cases, of the means of information, whether attributable to his indolence or credulity, takes from him all just claim for relief."

The Supreme Court thus supported the obvious falsity rule under circumstances where buyers held the primary responsibility for their own fate. Unfortunately it said nothing about applying the rule where buyers were more clearly the innocent victim of sellers' false acts, but cases on that point eventually doomed this absolute version of caveat emptor.

In *Roberts v. French*,[8] an 1891 case very similar to *Gordon v. Parmelee*, a buyer of land again failed to check false information about its size. But this time the seller not merely stated the acreage falsely but assured the buyer that the land had been most carefully and accurately measured. The court felt that made a difference, and ruled for the buyer: "When a man 'conveys the notion of factual admeasurement,' . . . still more when he says that he has measured a line himself and found it so long, his statement has a stronger tendency to induce the buyer to refrain from further inquiry. . . ." The buyer was not physically restrained, but the court perceived what would today be called a psychological lack of opportunity to inspect. As a matter of social intercourse one simply finds difficulty in examining something for oneself when the action would affront another who claims to have done so sufficiently for both. In that context the correct acreage was not obvious, and the buyer was not held at fault.

The case did not really reduce the scope of the obvious falsity rule, although it kept it from expanding further. The implication remained that measuring land was "obvious" in the sense of being open to ordinary diligence. But as the century mark passed, the consumerist thinking that affected so many rules caught up with that one, too. In *Judd v. Walker* of 1908,[9] a court finally decided that determining exact acreage was beyond what should be expected of a buyer who looked at his land before purchase. Judge Lamm of Missouri eloquently gave one of the strongest consumer orientations ever offered up to that time. To set the stage, he described the rule of obvious falsity as he felt it was meant to be stated, with "obvious" really meaning obvious: "The vendee is held to know what his own eyes would disclose, and knowing, could not be deceived. . . . For instance, if B. wants oats, and A. shows B. an open sack of beans (both . . . knowing beans when the bag is open), and A. tells B. they are oats, B. ought not to complain when he buys the sack because he gets beans. . . . In such case the fraud is made innocuous by the fact that it was patent to the vendee."

After that background, Lamm rejected the idea that measuring land was as easy as looking at beans in a bag. "Such defect," he said, "is not a patent defect to be got at by the use of natural facilities and the exercise of ordinary diligence. . . ." Further, he focused not only on the buyer's capability but also on the seller's culpability, the latter until then a rare consideration in the history of the obvious falsity rule. Earlier comments on the rule had referred exclusively to the buyer's responsibility, ignoring any obligations the seller might have. Lamm reversed that attitude strongly:

> Due diligence does not require that the vendee should suspect the vendor of lying, nor that the vendee should survey and measure the land to prevent being deceived by the lies of the vendor. . . . If the rule be construed to mean that a vendee must survey the land and measure it . . . and cannot rely on the positive assurance of the vendor as to his knowledge of the number of acres in his own land, then we do not agree to it as good doctrine. . . . It has sometimes been loosely said that the negligence of the vendee will prevent recovery for the fraud of the vendor. . . . That such an act in the vendor should not be actionable because of the mere negligence or inadvertence of the vendee in preventing the fraud ought to be neither good ethics nor good law.

It was time, Lamm added, to question the ancient principle of distrust: "Until there be written into the law some precept or rule to the effect that the heart of man is as prone to wickedness as is the smoke to go upward, and that every one must deal with his fellow man as if he was a thief and a robber, it ought not to be held that trust cannot be put into a positive assurance of a material fact."

Court decisions concerning false representations have rarely been accompanied by so direct an examination of the underlying foundation of the marketplace. Lamm recognized that the change from sellerism to consumerism meant in its depths a change in marketplace attitudes from distrust to trust. The law, he felt, should be written to protect and support those who trusted, rather than maintaining the earlier attitude of protecting those who distrusted. His comments were predictive of the criticisms of the reasonable person standard, as seen in chapter 9, that eventually developed.[10] It is probably no great coincidence that Lamm was echoed in Justice Black's statement in *Standard Education*: "There is no duty resting upon a citizen to suspect the honesty of those with whom he transacts business."[11]

Judge Lamm's consumerist tendencies have been strongly developed in the present day, particularly in warranty law, where no trace remains of the absolute version of caveat emptor.[12] Protection is assured against false warranties whose falsity is not patently obvious, and the law has shown in addition a "growing tendency" to retain warranty protection even when the falsity is obvious: "There seems no reason if the seller contracts in regard to an obvious defect or if he makes representations upon which the buyer in fact relies, why the seller should escape liability. It can hardly lie in his mouth to say that though he was making false representations or promises to induce the buyer to make the bargain, and the buyer was thereby induced, he should not have been."[13]

In misrepresentation law the consumerist change has not been so great. The obvious falsity rule has been specifically retained, as the *Restatement of Torts* indicates:

> §541: REPRESENTATION KNOWN TO BE OR OBVIOUSLY FALSE. The recipient of a fraudulent misrepresentation is not justified in relying upon its truth if he knows that it is false or its falsity is obvious.[14]

The appended comment favors the consumer, however, by declaring falsity to be obvious only where it may be determined by a "cursory inspection" or at a "cursory glance." If it is not so instantly obvious, the rule today is:

> §540: DUTY TO INVESTIGATE. The recipient in a business transaction of a fraudulent misrepresentation of fact is justified in relying upon its truth, although he might have ascertained the falsity of the representation had he made an investigation.[15]

Section 540's difference from the sellerist adherence to caveat emptor was reflected in 1936 by one of the authors of the *Restatement*'s original edition, Francis Bohlen, who said: "Had this been stated fifty years ago it would have been regarded as great heresy. I think it represents, however, a view that while starting as an inconspicuous minority is now approaching a majority view."[16] Since 1936 the majority has increased, and the obvious falsity rule now strongly reflects contemporary consumerism. While under sellerism "obvious" had ballooned into meaning anything a person might determine by inspection, under a consumerism orientation the term is contracted to mean only what is instantly noticeable.[17]

In addition, there exists today the opportunity, with obvious falsity disappearing from warranty law, to make a case on breach of warranty rather than unlawful misrepresentation. Herbert Williams founded his air conditioner suit on misrepresentation, and the court's decision noted pointedly, "This is an action brought in fraud and not an action for a breach of warranty."[18] The court may have been suggesting that Williams could have won under warranty law. Still, why didn't he win under misrepresentation law? Such an extremely sellerist consequence of the obvious falsity rule happened as late as 1969 because outmoded precedents of the past were not yet obliterated from judicial thinking. The memory of Baily and his unweighed load of wood still looms.[19]

Because it does, the obvious falsity rule joins the puffery rule in postponing the disappearance of sellerism. Just as the law may decide without checking that the public automatically distrusts puffery, it may decide without checking that the falsity of a representation is obvious. Both types of decisions should be regarded as prime candidates for change as the replacement of sellerism by consumerism moves toward its ultimate completion.

We should not conclude the story of obvious falsity without mentioning the Federal Trade Commission. In FTC considerations the common law rule plays no formal role, but the question of whether the public is deceived is always at issue. In some cases it is evident that people will know a falsehood immediately, Olde Frothingslosh's claims being a good example. Prominent among today's obvious falsities are the spoofs shown regularly in television commercials. The famous basketball players Larry Bird and Michael Jordan bounce the ball off odd surfaces such as the side of a building or the Goodyear blimp or even the moon, then straight into the basket ("Nothing but net"). That's a lie, of course, if you want to be literal about it, but the FTC assumes nobody does. There is probably always *some* potential for deception in such things, but only for those stray ignorant persons whom the commission no longer worries about.

I've enjoyed many spoofs myself because I know what I'm seeing is false, and because I believe the advertiser is not attempting to make me think otherwise. Particularly amusing was the Dr. Scholl's foot deodorant ad in which someone seated in an airliner took off his shoes and socks and everyone else immediately fainted dead away from the odor. Readers will have their own favorites, such as those from the major beer brewers (for example, the frogs: Bud, Wise, and Er).

I personally see no problem with spoofs when it's really obvious that what's literally stated is being offered as such. A physical event occurs that nobody has ever seen happen and that no one would expect to happen on the basis of anything they *have* seen. Without question that is truly innocent falsity, though I hasten to add that the comment applies to adults only, not to children. With children much less may be obvious, and the FTC should be properly concerned with whether youngsters are taking presumably innocent falsities literally. The same might be said for other vulnerable or disadvantaged types of people, such as ethnic minorities, ghetto dwellers, and the elderly or sick or infirm.

Such special cases aside, the spoof probably should not be the target of those who want to remove falsity from the marketplace. An example occurred in 1993 when the Marriott and Hyatt hotel chains sued the Ramada Renaissance chain for showing Frank and Cindy Marriott, and Donald and Sally Hyatt, exhibiting their preferences for the latter. A small-print disclaimer said these individuals whom Ramada had discovered (probably in the phone book) were not related to their innkeeper namesakes and their claims did not constitute endorsements by the Marriott and Hyatt chains. The latter sued for deceptiveness anyway, but the judge decided, "It is obvious from even a cursory reading that [these ads] are clearly tongue-in-cheek. I cannot see that any reasonable person would be misled—even absent the disclaimer."[20]

I said at the outset of this book that the goal should be to eliminate all falsity, but of course that means only where harm is done. When the seller's misrepresentation is not only obviously false, but also obviously intended to be taken that way, there typically should be no harm. Another way to make the point is that I believe spoof claims invariably are immaterial. The law says misrepresentations must be material to be illegal—that is, they must refer to something that actually plays a role in purchasing decisions.[21] Falsehoods occurring in spoofs, such as the Ramada ad, or an automobile flying like an airplane, simply will never be placed in that category because consumers (apart from the stray ignorant ones) will not purchase the advertised item on the basis of such a claim.

However, if all that is so, then why do I have any concerns with obvious falsity? It's because the line between spoofs and other representations, between what is correctly and incorrectly identified as obvious, is hard to draw. There was a TV demonstration for Bounty towels, for instance, which I have never been certain whether to call a legitimate spoof. When that brand, claimed to be The Quicker Picker-Upper, was touched to some spilled milk, the milk raced up into the towel with a loud slurping sound. It was a clearly impossible physical event, which would point the ad initially toward the spoof category. On the other hand, the representation was made in a straightforward manner, which would move it away from the spoof category. The ad would more clearly qualify as a spoof if it showed, for example, a magician pulling a rabbit from a hat and then doing the same with the paper towel. But the actual ad had no such indication that the representation was false, and so might be taken to represent that the towel has extraordinarily fast action. Such implication would be deceptive even if the Bounty towel were extraordinarily fast, because the act seen on the screen falsely overstated the speed.

So was the ad a spoof or not? I don't know. It has never been examined by the FTC, although possibly the commission commented by analogy on such matters when it rejected a commercial for All detergent in which water was shown rising around an actor clad in dirty garments. The water reached the man's chin, then receded quickly to show his clothing free of stains. Noting that the cleaning action was accomplished so quickly, the FTC decided that "even humorous commercials have actionable capacity to deceive where, as here, they depict the product in use and exaggerate the results ostensibly achieved from such use."[22] In other words, even if accompanied by some spoofing elements, an ad might convey something that consumers would take as truthfully factual and material.

The theory apparently was that the ad, by exaggerating something that could actually happen rather than something impossible, was no spoof. Apparently it wasn't puffery, either, because the exaggeration was just too great. That's fine, except that if such explanation were applicable to All detergent, one would think by analogy it should also apply to Bounty and to many other ads that generally have not received FTC criticism. Such actions, as already seen with puffery, indicate an arbitrary case-by-case resolution rather than pursuit of a definite policy.

That the FTC had not made its position clear on spoofs v. non-spoofs was suggested by testimony from hearings it held in 1971. Eugene Case, an advertising executive, described as false an Alka Seltzer commercial depicting "professional pie eaters."[23] The ad showed some fat men taking Alka Seltzer to ease their stomachs after participating in a contest that one of them said took place on the "professional pie-eating circuit." The ad was false, Mr. Case said, because there was no such circuit and no such professionals. He assumed therefore that the ad, though he admired it very much, would be vulnerable to FTC attack.

Mary Gardiner Jones, the commissioner taking the strongest pro-consumer stance at the time, disagreed with Mr. Case. "I would take very strong umbrage with your implication that we would take that off the air," she said. The only fact she saw implied to the public by the commercial was that the product gives relief from overeating. She was concerned only with whether that fact was true, and not at all with the obvious unreality of the professional pie eaters. Jones did not formulate a rule for identifying spoofs. however, nor has the commission as a whole ever done so. As a result, the misunderstanding experienced by Mr. Case could repeat itself forever as advertisers continue their accustomed habits of operating in close proximity to legal borderlines.

In summary, although spoofs and other obvious falsities certainly can occur, I find it appropriate to emphasize that when misrepresentations can reasonably be called material, and cannot reasonably be called obviously false, they should be banned from the marketplace as deceptive.

12

Puffing with Social and Psychological Claims

Another type of falsity the law says is nondeceptive associates the advertised product or service with sociological or psychological values that it does not provide literally, objectively. Doritos "flavor the way you look at life." Frosted Mini Wheats are "for the adult in you, for the kid in you." Post Raisin Bran "makes everybody feel like somebody special." And of course, "You deserve a break today." All these things are true in a certain sense if you choose to think they are. But they are not *really* true.

With such claims, the advertiser puffs the product's value by talking about a characteristic it doesn't have at all. If you deserve a break, or if you don't, the feature is in you, not in the product. But just as with puffery and obvious falsity, the law assumes that social-psychological misrepresentations are always nondeceptive, and again, I feel it's wrong to assume that automatically. The answer in any individual case should be determined by observation, not decided as a matter of law without observation.

Undoubtedly some of these statements are accepted as objective values by some consumers—why else would the advertisers use them? And that means they deceive the public to some significant degree. Yet, in reflection of its ancient attitudes the law is reluctant to look and see, choosing often to decide dogmatically that no adverse effects could possibly be happening. In fact, the law has been reluctant even to discuss these claims, which have thus been declared legally nondeceptive by default rather than by, as with puffery and obvious falsity, deliberate rulings.

A social or psychological misrepresentation is a claim that a product possesses a feature that in truth exists only in consumers' social environments or within their own personalities or mental states of mind. "Reebok believes in the athlete in all of us." Such an expression of self-image is not truly part of the product, but is associated with the product only in the representation. The message implied to the consumer, however, can be that the feature will accompany the product with such certainty that it may be treated as if it were an actual part of the product.

"What sort of man reads Playboy?" Such features or values are attached to products in an entirely arbitrary manner, there because the message says they are, and *only* because the message says they are. They are different from inherent product features, which are present in an objective sense. An ad stating that Doritos contains certain ingredients or that a car has an automatic transmission would be describing an inherent feature—a thing that is physically there. By contrast the social representation describes a feature not of the product at all, but of the consumer's social environment ("Your friends will love you for serving such-and-such . . ."). And the psychological representation describes a feature of the consumer's own personal nature ("Be the person you've always wanted to be . . .").

Of course the advertising industry does not regard such claims as misrepresentations. It regards them as suggestions about results that can in fact occur for the lucky purchaser. Don't tell the advertiser that "You'll meet the nicest people on a Honda" is false. You might go out on your Honda and meet some fantastic folks! Some people will, and every buyer might. It's one of those projective things you can make seem true by wanting it to be true, by a process of wishful thinking.

Yet I believe the advertisers are lucky they have not been challenged on the possible deceptive content in these claims. Clearly it is false to promise features that buyers have little prospect of actually getting. You might make some friends with your Honda, but it is false to imply you will for sure. All you actually get are the tangible components of the cycle, the parts made of metal and rubber and leather. Dealers do not physically hand you any social values, nor would they respond favorably if you asked them to guarantee any such thing as part of the product warranty. Social-psychological values are literally not there, and any representation that states or implies they are is false. If advertisers are ever taken to court on these matters, they will no doubt admit such falsity, but will feel safe in defending it as not deceptive.

One such defense might be to claim that social and psychological misrepresentations are obviously false to any but the stray unreasonable person. The answer the industry deserves on this point is the same I have given it for puffery.[1] If the public knows that what it literally gets is only the Honda and not the social values, then why are advertisers so idiotic as to use such claims? Of course they think it's not obviously false to consumers at all. And there are reasons why it shouldn't be.

For one thing, the absence of a social or psychological feature is never obvious in the sense of being instantly noticeable. If such a claim is false consumers will find out only by using the product, not merely just by looking at it. And of course that means it will happen only after making the purchase, not before. You can look at a cycle and see whether there's a steering wheel, but you can't look at a cycle and see whether you will or won't meet the nicest people on it. The absence of the claimed benefit is not observable by the "cursory inspection" or "cursory glance" that we saw in discussing obvious falsity. That, of course, is precisely the value of such claims from an advertiser's standpoint. Consumers can think they will be present later even though they don't see them at the store. They don't expect to see them at the store; therefore their absence at that point does nothing to inform consumers that they'll be absent later. That's subtle falsity, not obvious falsity, and accordingly there seems little chance of invoking the obvious falsity rule in its defense.

Another defense of social and psychological misrepresentations might be to claim they are only puffery, in its narrow legal definition of having opinion form.[2] However, these claims are not opinions; they are facts. They are facts about consumers rather than about the product, but they are facts. There's really no good defense, I believe, for an assertion that false social-psychological representations are not deceptive. The only thing that has permitted them to exist as nondeceptive is that they have not been challenged. When the challenge comes, the lack of legal precedent could work against them, since while the law has never condemned such representations it also has never specifically condoned them; it has only ignored them. Puffery and obvious falsity at least have the weight of some shaky precedents behind them, but social-psychological misrepresentations have none. Thus their only hope is that the issue continues to be ignored.

To have no history of regulation is to have a situation quite different from those seen elsewhere in this book. The difference is that social and psychological misrepresentations are a product largely of the twentieth century.[3] They were developed because competitors began desiring to differentiate their own brands of goods from other brands that were virtually similar in inherent physical characteristics. Before the 1900s the makers or processors of soap, bread, grain, salt, milk, and numerous other commodities had not been much concerned with such a desire. They had been producing their goods with no thought of making them distinct from the production of their fellow makers. They didn't care, because demand traditionally was greater than supply and everyone was selling all they could make. Other companies that today we call competitors were not really competing in the sense of threatening to drain off sales a maker would otherwise get.

Conditions eventually changed. Manufacturing increased to the point where supply overtook demand and passed it. Individual producers became threatened with an absence of markets, and began seriously to compete for those that remained. As this competition heightened in the late nineteenth century, producers became painfully aware that the nondistinctiveness of their product was a liability. With overdemand it had not mattered, but with oversupply it became crucial.

Yet the ultimate customer did not care. The flour in the bin at the store might come from anywhere; flour was flour. The question producers began to ask was, "How can I get the public to want mine?" The solution was to differentiate one's flour as a brand and build a demand for the brand's distinct attributes. If the process worked and people demanded Smith's flour, they could get it only from Smith. Even if there were a slack demand for flour in general, the traditional overdemand might nonetheless be created for Smith's brand.

In the twentieth century many markets have changed in that way from selling products to selling brands. The marketing goal is to make the brand appear to the customer as though it is the product. "When you're out of Schlitz you're out of beer" was a perfect modern statement of that purpose. Not all consumers will accept so extreme a suggestion, of course (indeed, they did not do so with Schlitz). But when they write "Kleenex" on their shopping list instead of "paper handkerchiefs" they are reflecting the strength with which such changes can occur.

Successful brand distinctions were difficult to achieve at first. Producers could each put their distinctive name on the product easily enough, but efforts to differentiate beyond that point were hampered because the soap or flour or sugar was basically the same in its inherent features as that of all competitors. Those who tried to add, augment, or alter inherent characteristics typically found that the differences did not make enough of a difference, and the competition in any event could generally match the gains by making the same adjustments.

This is not the place to recount the story of all the steps taken to solve the problems of scarcely differentiable brands. In short, the producers eventually followed the advice of advertising specialists who saw that apparent product differences could be achieved in sales messages even if not in the product itself. With that insight, sales communication turned to stressing features that were not inherent parts of the brand but could be associated with the brand in the public's mind *as if they were inherent*. Today we have many features such as social status in our automobiles that we didn't have before. We have all those social and psychological features, but we have no law concerning them.

Well, we have a tiny bit of law, because of two complaints the FTC filed in 1971. In the first, advertisements for Wonder Bread were alleged not only to have made several false nutritional claims, but to have falsified the bread's contribution to people's mental and social states.[4] The advertiser, said the complaint, "tends to exploit children's aspirations for rapid and healthy growth" and also their parents' concern for their growth and development. "This part of the complaint," a contemporary law review article stated, "is concerned with the psychological effects on both parents and children. It is not concerned with the misrepresentation of the inherent product qualities and is, therefore, a departure from previous FTC policies."[5] Unfortunately for the departure, however, that portion of the complaint was eventually decided in Wonder Bread's favor, with no restraint of social-psychological claims.

In the other case,[6] ads for a pill called Vivarin told women their husbands would be more attracted to them if they used it, apparently implying some sort of sexually based arousal to renew the lagging instincts of tired old married folks. To quote the ad directly:

One day it dawned on me that I was boring my husband to death. It was hard for me to admit it—but it was true. . . . Often by the time he came home at night I was feeling dull, tired and drowsy, and so Jim would look at television and, for the most part, act like I wasn't even there. And I wasn't.

I decided that I had to do something. I had seen an advertisement for a tablet called Vivarin. It said that Vivarin was a non-habit forming stimulant tablet that would give me a quick lift. Last week . . . I took a Vivarin tablet . . . just about an hour before Jim came home, and I found time to pretty up a little, too. It worked.

All of a sudden Jim was coming home to a more exciting woman, me. . . . The other day—it wasn't even my birthday—Jim sent me flowers with a note. The note began: "To my new wife. . . ."

All very nice, except that the contribution of Vivarin was to provide merely the equivalent of two cups of coffee. No miracle aphrodisiac, just good old caffeine at a premium price! However, although the major allegation of the FTC's complaint involved a social-psychological misrepresentation, the Vivarin ads were also challenged for not disclosing caffeine as the critical ingredient. Thus, as with Wonder Bread, the commission again did not attack the social-psychological element alone but only in conjunction with misrepresentations about inherent features. That suggests that the former may merely have been thrown in to help prosecute the latter, just to fatten up the case, so to speak. The FTC obtained a prohibition, but such successful prosecution does not necessarily indicate it could effectively prosecute a social-psychological misrepresentation standing alone.

Nor can two cases in any event make much impact on a business that produces hundreds of social-psychological misrepresentations annually. The general conclusion can only be that such claims are essentially unregulated at this time. They are a case, again, of the law's assuming without checking that the falsity is nondeceptive. And they are a case, again, where reasons exist to think the law is wrong. Many of them may cause no problem for consumers, but not all of them.

Postscript to This Topic

My rewriting of this chapter for the second edition has been affected by my 1994 book, *The Tangled Web They Weave*, which also examines deceptive advertising. It examines puffery only briefly and says almost nothing about obvious falsity and various other topics from this book. However, it takes up the issue of social-psychological claims very extensively, calling them "non-brand facts." Although the latter term is slightly broader, including all fact claims about things other than the advertised brand, most such claims in practice are social-psychological ones. Consequently, while elsewhere in this edition I offer much analysis beyond that of the first edition, I have not done so in this chapter. No additional cases on the topic have occurred, however; it remains a dead area in the law.

13

Puffing with Literally Misdescriptive Names

This chapter introduces another kind of puffery: names that are literally false in describing the advertised object. Although they puff up the object's value in doing so, these claims typically are called nondeceptive by the law because the public understands their true meanings. I feel the law is often correct about that, although there can be a potential for deceptiveness.

Let's start with some of the most innocent examples. Danish pastry need not legally come from Denmark, nor china from China, nor Irish potatoes from Ireland, nor Boston baked beans from Boston. The law says people are not deceived because they know the name is merely a description and not a literal claim.[1] People understand that Swiss cheese may come from America, and Idaho potatoes may come from Maine. They know French toast isn't French, and permanent waves aren't permanent (how can you have a permanent wave when you've only got temporary hair?).

Probably most consumers will agree with the law in assuming that the public generally recognizes these literal misdescriptions as such, and interprets them by secondary meanings that have superseded the original literal meanings. Consumers understand that the "Swiss" in Swiss cheese refers to a style (a strongly established secondary meaning) rather than to a point of origin (the traditional primary meaning). Certainly the law is correct in the general proposition that such secondary meanings exist.

However, let's try some other names. What is the reader's understanding of a substance called Stone China, used to make dishware? What do you think is the nature of Plyhide, as in "Lounge chairs, upholstered in 'Plyhide'—with that tailored leather look"? What fact do you believe about a product called Six Month Floor Wax? What does "Made in USA" mean when it is stamped on a product? What business do you think the National Laboratories of St. Louis engages in?

Aren't those are a little tougher than Danish pastry! Stone China is the material known as earthenware or stoneware. Plyhide is vinyl, with nothing made of or associated with leather or other animal hides. Six Month Floor Wax will not last six months. "Made in USA" has been stamped on goods made in Japan in a town whose name was changed to Usa. National Laboratories of St. Louis operates and services vending machines and has no connection with any laboratory. If you didn't know these secondary meanings, then those puffing names could deceive you. As a matter of fact, there is reason to believe they *have* deceived people and should rightfully be taken out of the marketplace. The FTC has banned the terms Stone China, Plyhide, Six Month Floor Wax, Made in USA (where not true), and National Laboratories of St. Louis.[2] The effect on the public was considered, and judgments were rendered that the names were misdescriptive not only literally but also in fact. The companies claimed the secondary meanings were established in the public's eye, but the commission decided they were not.

In these cases the FTC has demonstrated a willingness to act that we have not seen elsewhere. It has refused to let develop a category of representations receiving automatic immunity. Puffery and social-psychological misrepresentations, and obvious falsity to some extent, are such categories; they are like umbrellas, under which the seller may run to be safe. But with misdescriptive names the law has allowed no such safety. It has taken each case on its own merits, allowing secondary meanings to be used only when established in the public's mind. The burden is on the user of the name to prove the change to the new meaning has occurred.

The commission's right to ban misdescriptive trade names came from the Supreme Court in *FTC v. Winsted* of 1922.[3] Winsted Hosiery had been selling underwear labeled as "Merino," "Natural Merino," "Gray Merino," "Natural Wool," "Gray Wool," "Australian Wool," and "Natural Worsted." All those labels were found by the FTC to mean to "a substantial part of the consuming public" that the underwear was made entirely of wool, whereas the real material was mostly cotton with a small portion of wool. Winsted claimed the terms were understood within the trade to indicate goods made partly of cotton. The manufacturers and dealers, it said, had created secondary meanings that in their minds fully superseded the original ones. There could be no unfair competition, therefore, if everyone involved knew how the words were being used by everyone else.

But "everyone," said the Supreme Court, meant not just members of the trade but the consuming public as well. For the latter, the Court found that "wool" or "worsted" had no trace of any secondary meaning, but only the primary meaning of "all wool." A secondary meaning was found only for terms containing the word "Merino," indicating a wool-cotton combination. But even that was said to be "not a meaning so thoroughly established that the description which the label carries has ceased to deceive the public." The public, in other words, was only somewhat aware of the secondary meaning of "Merino," relying generally on the primary meaning which was therefore deceptive in describing Winsted underwear. The Supreme Court affirmed the FTC's position and outlawed the use of all the disputed terms as descriptions of underwear that was not all wool.

While Winsted's customers were not getting what they thought, a more subtle problem may occur when consumers get what they expect but from a source different from the one they expect. There is probably less harm done by this kind of deception than the other, but the FTC banned it, too, and was upheld by another Supreme Court ruling in 1933, *FTC v. Royal Milling Co.*[4] The commission had attacked several companies that had "milling," "mills," or "millers" in their names, but did not mill wheat (i.e., grind it into flour) themselves; they only blended and packaged flour obtained from actual millers. The variations of "mill" were found to be commonly understood by dealers and the public to indicate companies that *did* grind wheat into flour. On appeal, the Court agreed a legal remedy was necessary: "If consumers or dealers prefer to purchase a given article because it was made by a particular manufacturer or class of manufacturers, they have a right to do so, and this right cannot be satisfied by imposing upon them an exactly similar article, or one equally as good, but having a different origin. . . . [S]uch purchasers are deceived into purchasing an article which they do not wish or intend to buy, and which they might or might not buy if correctly informed as to its origin."

The point was reinforced in *FTC v. Algoma*,[5] when the commission sought to prohibit confusion in the lumber industry between "white pine" and "yellow pine." Genuine white pine was adjudged superior to yellow pine, and deemed worthy of being correctly identified. But a practice had developed within a portion of the industry to refer to some yellow pine as "California white pine," resulting in some buyers' getting a product other than what they expected. The Supreme Court decided the confusion thus produced should be prohibited *even if* the yellow pine received were equivalent to the white pine ordered, because "The consumer is prejudiced if upon giving an order for one thing, he is supplied with something else."

The Court also explained, however, that confusion does not necessarily occur when a name is literally misdescriptive. If "California white pine" had been found to have "two meanings with equal titles to legitimacy" (a secondary meaning of "yellow pine" as well as the literal "white"), then no confusion would occur. That can happen, the Court said, when "by common acceptation the description, once misused, has acquired a secondary meaning as firmly anchored as the first one." That has become the FTC's test, and many terms pass it and remain in use. The secondary meaning of "Danish pastry," for example, is far better established in the United States than the primary meaning. The falsity of the original meaning could deceive consumers who have not learned the secondary meaning, but that probably will not happen with any appreciable portion of the public.[6]

The wide range of misdescriptive names prohibited as deceptive by the FTC will be indicated here by mentioning only a few of those it has pursued. The "Institute of Hydraulic Jack Repair" was called deceptive because it created the false impression of being a bona fide institution of higher learning.[7] "Madras," unless describing "fine cotton, handloomed and imported from the Madras section of India," may not be used except with a clear and nondeceptive statement of the way the fabric actually resembles India Madras fabric.[8] "Scout," "Eagle Scout," and "Cub Scout" sleeping bags may not be so designated when the manufacturer has obtained no affiliation with or approval from the Boy Scouts of America.[9] A cigar maker situated in New Jersey may not misrepresent itself as the "Havana Florida Company."[10] The word "liver" was removed from "Carter's Little Liver Pills" because the pills had no medical effect on that organ.[11] A furniture company was denied the use of "Grand Rapids" in its name because its furniture was not manufactured in Grand Rapids, Michigan.[12] "Virginia" may be used only to describe hams from hogs raised in Virginia and given the specific Virginia curing and processing that imparts a distinctive flavor; it may not be used on hams given Virginia processing but from hogs raised outside the state.[13] The United States Testing Co. was banned from implying it had connections with the United States government.[14] The National Commission on Egg Nutrition was neither public nor independent nor associated with government; its members were egg producers.[15]

While the above names were in use before being outlawed, others have been restricted from the start to their primary meanings so that no secondary meanings could develop. Typical of these are names for European liquor and wine. United States government regulations state that liquor distilled in America may be called "brandy," but none may be called "cognac" or "cognac brandy" unless distilled in the Cognac region of France.[16] A similar rule applies for Scotch whiskey.[17] Wines called "champagne" must be produced in the Champagne district of France; so-called American champagnes must be labeled "sparkling wine" first, followed by the place of origin (i.e., California) preceding the word "champagne."[18]

Another European name protected under American law is Roquefort cheese, which may be sold by that name only if made in a single place: the village of Roquefort in the Aveyron region of France, population 1,300.[19] Blue or bleu cheeses are made elsewhere, but none may be called "Roquefort" unless aged a minimum of three months in the caves of the mountain, the Rocher du Cambalou, on which the village stands. Production is limited, which explains the delicacy's high cost.

The result of all such activity is that the category of literally misdescriptive names, unlike the others we have seen, is carefully subdivided into categories of deception and nondeception. We might ask why the law has discriminated so effectively for these claims while simultaneously making its automatic and nondiscriminatory assumptions of nondeceptiveness about so many claims in the other categories we have examined. The answer could be, in part at least, the newness of misdescription law. Puffery and obvious falsity were founded in the ancient heritage of caveat emptor, and attempts to change them crash on the reefs of that still-powerful precedent. But elements of the law created only in the twentieth century have no such backing, a point the manufacturer in *Winsted* tried to exploit by saying such practices never before amounted to unfair competition against one's competitors. When the argument backfired,[20] there was no chance for the caveat emptor mentality to shape regulation in that area.

Social-psychological misrepresentations, on the other hand, are also a post–caveat emptor phenomenon, yet are regulated as they would have been under that rule. If they are so relatively new, why has the FTC not attacked them as it has attacked misdescriptive names? I believe the answer is related to the relative degree of threat sellers perceive in those two kinds of falsity. A seller's competitors probably feel more directly affronted by its literal misdescriptions than by its social-psychological misrepresentations. A company making real china, for example, might be more threatened by a stoneware company's use of the name "Stone China" than by its false claims about social satisfactions to be achieved. That's because the social misrepresentation does not so directly negate the quality differential that real china possesses. The "Stone China" claim contradicts the china-stoneware distinction, while the social satisfaction claim, though inconsistent with the distinction, does not contradict it so directly. In fact, any competitor can copy the social satisfaction claim and so cancel it out.

Whatever the reason, the decisions about literally misdescriptive names reflect the modern consumerism trend, and suggest directions the law might take toward controlling the other forms of allegedly nondeceptive falsity. They also show, however, how sticky problems develop when the law assesses the deceptive potential of such misrepresentations. Mistakes are always possible, as the case of the Milan hats demonstrated. *Korber Hats v. FTC*[21] was an appeal of an FTC decision that Korber's hemp hats could not be called "Milan" because the public understood that term by its primary meaning— made in Italy from wheat straw with a distinctive weave or braid. Therefore hats of hemp, the commission thought, should not be called Milan. But Korber argued back that a secondary meaning was well established as identifying the category solely by the weave or braid, which would mean Milan hats with such features could be made of hemp and could be made outside Italy.

The appellate court accepted Korber's claim of the presence of the secondary meaning, but decided it developed alongside rather than in place of the primary meaning, with the result that both understandings of "Milan" were held by considerable portions of the public. So the court decided to let Korber use the terms "hemp Milan" or "imitation Milan." That would retain use of "Milan," in recognition that the hats fit the new secondary meaning, yet allow it only qualifiedly, in recognition that the hats did not fit the original meaning. The name "Milan" unqualified would be allowed only for wheat straw hats made in Italy.

It may have been the best solution available, yet one can imagine the dissatisfaction produced. Korber Hats would dislike using a qualifying word in front of "Milan," and the makers of "genuine" Milan hats would dislike Korber's using the name at all. And since virtually no one, neither public nor trade, would use the term in both meanings, everyone would be upset to some degree by official recognition of the meaning they didn't use. Still, what else can be done when both meanings are popular!

Readers may have their own experiences of confusion produced by names' not meaning what they literally say. I once went to a lumberyard to get some boards to make a brick-and-board bookshelf. I already had the bricks, so I asked for some boards similarly twelve inches wide. When the clerk brought some out, I picked up a ruler and found they were only about 11¼ inches wide. When I said I wanted them twelve inches wide, the man said, "Those are twelve-inch boards." I said they weren't. He then related that twelve-inch boards weren't really twelve inches wide, but they called them that anyway. And I couldn't get boards that were really twelve inches wide, because boards come only in standard sizes—such as twelve-inch! I took that size home because I wanted the bookshelf and they were the closest I could get.

As I eventually learned, the workmen start with raw lumber that they saw to twelve inches, then plane it to smooth out the surface. The latter is what gets the width down around 11¼. So there is a reason for referring to the result as a twelve-inch board, and the practice probably wasn't originated with any intention of deceiving or even accidentally misinforming. It began back when most customers were familiar with sawmills and understood what they were going to get. It was only much later that folks like me began showing up who didn't understand.

Does that justify keeping such names? It's curious how it always works out to disadvantage consumers. The only exception I know is the baker's dozen, which happened in the guild days before caveat emptor[22] when the law controlling falsity was so strict that bakers packed a thirteenth item for safety. The baker who counted one short by occasional accident would still be supplying twelve and would avoid serious penalties. His "dozen" was thus a literally false name whose falsity favored buyers in order to protect sellers.

After caveat emptor arrived, however, the penalties were systematically weakened or eliminated. So it's no surprise to see today's literally false names always favoring the seller, as McDonald's "quarter-pound hamburger" illustrates. When the company first used that name, a Nassau County, N.Y., official said it wasn't so. His inspectors checked 150 McDonald's outlets in the county and found the hamburgers averaging 3⅞ ounces. A spokesman at company headquarters quickly came up with what we might call a "lumberyard explanation." He said McDonald's weighs the hamburgers before they're cooked, and they lose weight during the cooking.

Both the lumber and hamburger people, forced to work with items that begin at one size and end at another, feel justified in using their misdescriptive names. Isn't everyone, after all, supposed to know those things? Well, Nassau County thought otherwise and charged eight counts of false advertising.[23] Shortly thereafter McDonald's commercials began including the legend "Pre-cooked weight one-quarter pound" superimposed over the visual representation. Notice the contrast in such cases between what people *should* know and what they *do* know. People probably should know meat loses weight when cooked, but the charge against McDonald's assumed they should not be expected to understand that the advertised weight was the precooked amount. If they thought they would get four ounces of meat, postcooking, then the regulators thought they should get that.

Here's another example to test your opinion against. A woman complained of buying a nine-inch pie and finding the true diameter was only 7¾ inches. The explanation was that industry practice includes the rim of the pan in determining the stated size![24] Did you know that? *Should* you know that? I suspect such usages are not widely understood by consumers, who are thereby hurt because the smaller hamburger or pie is not equivalent. In the lumber business, on the other hand, literally misdescribed twelve-inch boards have been sold by the millions to buyers who typically fare well because in most cases the misdescribed board is functionally equivalent to the one the name literally indicates.

My personal situation was different because I was not in the trade, and because I wanted the boards for an untypical purpose. My bookshelf plan was to match sizes close enough that the bricks and boards would not be noticeably different. Another factor was that I had stated clearly to the man that "I would like some boards that are twelve inches wide." I didn't say just "twelve-inch boards," but rather used a description that he incorrectly interpreted as a label. That might create a valid complaint. Perhaps someone should take such a case to court, because buyers could benefit if sellers ceased using names that have a deceptiveness potential.

You'll be glad to know, however, that everything turned out just fine with my bookshelf project. When I got home with my boards I found my twelve-inch bricks weren't twelve inches, either!

14 _____

Puffing with Mock-Ups

The final type we will see of the expanded definition of puffery is the mock-up, associated most often with the visual media of photographs and television. You make a mock-up by artificially altering your product to get a good picture of it. TV cameras cannot photograph a dish of ice cream, because it melts almost instantly under the hot studio lights. So technicians substitute mashed potatoes, and in the finished commercial the product looks just like ice cream.

That practice is acceptable legally if you cannot get your picture otherwise. Shampoo or soap suds are used to form the head on beer because natural heads won't stay fluffy long enough. Wine is used for coffee because filming gives coffee a murky color, less attractive than what the naked eye sees. Similar problems of appearance occur with orange juice and iced tea. And while it's not a problem with today's color cameras, blue sheets and towels and shirts were substituted for white in the days of black-and-white TV, because anything white threw a hazy blur over the rest of the picture.

All such arrangements puff the product falsely and therefore deceive, but the law calls them nondeceptive.[1] There's no reason to disagree generally with such rulings, because the values that such mock-ups may add deceptively to the product are not especially likely to attract customers. Few people care to eat ice cream under hot studio lights anyway, so implying it can be done adds no particular enticement. Besides, the mock-up contributes in many ways to *removing* deception rather than producing it. It is the only way certain perfectly true and nondeceptive representations about a product's features can be made. It is *technically required falsity*, which cannot be said for the other types of falsity we have examined.

Still, the existence of mock-ups can produce problems. To alter before photographing invites abuse by encouraging advertisers to devise illustrations in which the consumer perceives the product as having qualities it truthfully lacks. The Aluminum Company of America[2] did that in a TV demonstration that contrasted "New Super-Strength Alcoa Wrap" with a brand of "ordinary" aluminum foil, both wrapped around hams. The foils were said to have been wrapped and unwrapped a number of times, resulting in the "ordinary" foil's being wrinkled and torn and its ham dried out. The Alcoa Wrap had held up perfectly, and the ham inside it was seen to be fresh.

Was anything wrong with this demonstration? Only the fact that the "ordinary" foil was deliberately torn before filming, and the ham it "protected" was already less fresh than the other at the time they were first wrapped. Had a freshness test genuinely been conducted and Alcoa Wrap found superior, the alterations might have been defended as simply reenacting in a studio something that truthfully happened elsewhere. If a test couldn't be conducted in a studio and pictures couldn't be taken in a laboratory, then an artificial reconstruction would be technically required. But this time there was no prior test, and the mock-up was a construction, not a reconstruction.

In Colgate-Palmolive's "invisible shield" commercial,[3] objects thrown toward the announcer were deflected before hitting him by a sheet of scarcely visible glass. The announcer implied that Colgate Dental Cream's protection was similar in fighting tooth decay. If the toothpaste's effectiveness was precisely similar, meaning no harmful substances could reach the teeth, the mock-up would be defensible as a demonstration device, illustrating by analogy a process that could not be illustrated literally. The truth, however, was that the implication was false; the use of Colgate could not guarantee that decay would never happen.

On behalf of Blue Bonnet margarine,[4] TV commercial makers devised "Flavor Gems," which were drops of moisture glistening on the surface of Blue Bonnet but not on butter or another margarine. The Flavor Gems were offered as the reason Blue Bonnet tasted more like butter than did other margarines. Although they might have illustrated by analogy some feature of Blue Bonnet that could not be shown on film otherwise, in truth these drops of liquid, applied artificially and magnified, stood for nothing but themselves. Even if Blue Bonnet did taste more like butter than other margarines, it could not have been because of the Flavor Gems or anything they stood for.

When Libby-Owens-Ford Glass Company[5] demonstrated the "superiority" of its automobile safety glass, it smeared a competing brand with streaks of vaseline to create distortion, then photographed it at oblique camera angles to enhance the effect. It "showed" the distortionless marvels of its own glass by taking photographs with the windows rolled down.

Carter Products[6] promoted Rise shaving cream with a mock-up equally unfair to poor old Brand X. A man was seen shaving with an "ordinary" lather that dried out quickly after application. He then switched to Rise and showed it fulfilling its slogan, "Stays Moist and Creamy." Unbeknownst to viewers, the substance used on the first try was not a competing brand or a shaving cream at all. It was a preparation specially designed to come out of the aerosol can in a big attractive fluff and then disappear almost immediately.

As with literally misdescriptive names, mock-ups that deceive have been carefully discriminated by the law from those that do not. There is no systematic permissiveness that recognizes this kind of falsity as automatically immune from liability. The FTC's actions, in fact, have come closer to blanket condemnation than to blanket immunity. All the commercials just mentioned have been stopped by the commission, severely warning the industry of the limits beyond which it may not go.

The case most responsible for that legal stance was that of the "great sandpaper shave." Colgate-Palmolive's Rapid Shave shaving cream was shown enabling a man's razor to slice the grains of sand from sandpaper just as easily as you please. It was "apply . . . soak . . . and off in a stroke," the commercial said, and it was entirely phony. What was shown being shaved were loose grains of sand sprinkled over plexiglas. The FTC became involved when numerous complaints arrived from people who said they couldn't shave sandpaper that way. The commission agreed and sued Colgate,[7] which then turned the matter into one of the most heavily contested advertising cases on record by maintaining the demonstration was a legitimate mock-up.

You *could* shave sandpaper, the company said, if it was very fine. But fine sandpaper couldn't be photographed for TV because it would look like smooth paper on the screen, and so ruin the demonstration's credibility. Coarse sandpaper would look like sandpaper, all right, but couldn't be shaved. The only thing to do therefore,

Colgate said, to illustrate the legitimate fact of shaving sandpaper, was to do the test with fine sandpaper but illustrate it with a mock-up using the coarse variety.

That may have made a satisfactory argument except for certain other facts. For one, fine sandpaper could be shaved by a blade only after much more prolonged soaking than implied by the phrase "apply . . . soak . . . and off in a stroke." At the FTC hearing Colgate's attorneys cited the dictionary meaning of "soak" to be "wet thoroughly, saturate," which they said implied a long time. But their argument was undercut by the accompanying phrase "off in a stroke" and the fact that the shaving in the commercial came almost instantly after the application of Rapid Shave.

An even more significant feature of the ad was the implication to the audience of seeing an actual demonstration. Ice cream ads utilizing a mashed potato mock-up typically do not emphasize to viewers that they are actually seeing ice cream. But the Rapid Shave commercial implied not only that the demonstration was true but that viewers were seeing it actually happening.

The FTC not only called Colgate's defense worthless but, shockingly to the industry, made a ruling much more far-reaching. All mock-ups were unlawful unless disclosed, it declared, because they all showed the viewer something that was not so. Undisclosed substitution of plexiglas for sandpaper would be unlawful even if the sandpaper could be shaved easily, because viewers thought they were seeing something they were not. Let there be, accordingly, no more shampoo heads on glasses of beer, no more colored water substituting for iced tea, no more mock-ups at all. The commission was demanding utter elimination of this entire category of misrepresentation.

In *Colgate v. FTC*,[8] the First Circuit Court of Appeals disagreed with that extreme view. What could be wrong, it asked, with undisclosed mock-ups that merely involved appearance, as in the mashed-potatoes-for-ice-cream switch? Moreover, what was wrong with those that depicted the product's performance, if that performance was accurately shown? Shouldn't the only mock-ups prohibited, the court asked, be those giving inaccurate depictions? The court agreed with the FTC that the Rapid Shave commercial was one of the latter, but it returned the commission's order for rewriting to correct its concerns over the general rule.

The FTC tried reformulating the rule,[9] and the First Circuit again rejected it.[10] This time the commission appealed to the Supreme

Court,[11] which made the determinative decision about mock-ups by considering three questions:

(1) Were undisclosed mock-ups of mere appearance acceptable? The FTC said no; the appellate court said yes.

(2) Were undisclosed mock-ups demonstrating true performance acceptable? The FTC said no; the court of appeals said yes.

(3) Was the Rapid Shave undisclosed mock-up acceptable? The FTC and court of appeals both said no.

The Supreme Court ruled in favor of the appeals court on the first question and in favor of the FTC on the second. On the third, it agreed the Rapid Shave mock-up was unlawful, but because the commercial implied the actual seeing of a demonstration by leaving the mock-up undisclosed, not just because the performance supposedly demonstrated was false. Even if the performance in the mocked-up demonstration was true, the mock-up would be still be deceptive when undisclosed because viewers understood they were actually seeing such performance in the commercial.

The operative rule, then, is that undisclosed mock-ups are acceptable only where no value is placed on the idea that viewers are actually seeing what appears to be shown. If the mocked-up appearance is presented without fanfare, with no accompanying claim that what appears to be so is actually being seen, the mock-up is acceptable without disclosure. The concept of technically required falsity is accepted. But if the appearance is presented with fanfare, with the implication that viewers are seeing something real when they're not, then the mock-up is illegal unless disclosed.

That distinction presumably is clear enough to the regulators, but I saw an indication that it had not trickled down to the public. Ed McMahon had just finished a Smucker's commercial on the *Tonight Show*, soon after the Supreme Court decision, when Johnny Carson asked him, "How long will it take to melt?"[12] The commercial was done live in the studio for Smucker's butterscotch topping, which was poured over a bowl of ice cream. "It depends on the temperature of the room," said McMahon, trying not to spill the beans. But Carson persisted with, "You made it and you were talking about how wonderful it was. It does look wonderful on television." McMahon finally admitted the "ice cream" was a vegetable spread used for cooking, which prompted Carson to harangue: "There ought to be a certain amount of honesty. . . . When they show that woman cleaning the floor and say, 'One swipe to it,' did you ever see that floor? It's the filthiest thing you have ever seen and they go right through. . . . They put graphite on the floor, powdered graphite. . . . I don't think that's fair."

Johnny was right in his comments about the graphite, but unfair to Smucker's when he mixed the two examples together. The floor cleaning portrayed an utterly phony demonstration, while the Smucker's ad merely showed the ice cream without comment. It wasn't even for ice cream but for the butterscotch topping, which removed the mock-up further than usual from illegality. The discrimination between legal and illegal mock-ups apparently still needed to be learned by many laymen.

That the discrimination eventually was well learned by the industry was illustrated by the memory of a friend of mine for a demonstration he rigged up prior to the Colgate case. As advertising manager for a chemical company, he wanted to show the effectiveness of a chemical designed to retain the natural color of meat placed on display in stores. Many meats when sliced and exposed to fluorescent lights will oxidize and take on a gray discoloration after a short period, which ends their sales life at a time when they actually still are fresh. The chemical, when included in the curing process, could slow down that oxidation and retain the meat's natural color. Although some might call that an undesirable mock-up in itself, I am inclined to accept it as long as the meat indeed remains fresh.

When my friend went to the photo studio to make comparison shots of meat with and without the chemical, he was dismayed to find the treated piece turning gray almost immediately, matching the untreated one, because of the hot lights. The chemical could keep meat red under store conditions, but not here. What could he do to get a picture? He could run to the nearest drug store, buy some Mercurochrome, and daub it on the chemically treated meat.

Without a second thought he did exactly that and got the picture he wanted. The resulting ad included a caption under the picture that said "Actual unretouched photograph." As my friend pointed out, it wasn't the picture that was retouched; it was the ham.

His mock-up was legal when he used it, but in retrospect he found it amazing to recall that the question of legality or illegality never crossed his mind in that pre–Rapid Shave age of innocence. Later, though, he learned not to act on such ideas without consulting the company's lawyer first. Caution became the primary rule where mock-ups were concerned. Ad agency creative experts who never talked to lawyers in their life were curbing their instincts until the legal beagle said OK.

One agency, doing a cleanser commercial in which a bathtub ring was shown being scrubbed away, grew frustrated over the fact that the ring had to be replaced for each of many retakes.[13] There was no question the cleanser could do the job, so the producer wondered why the prop department couldn't just whisk a new ring onto the tub each time with some water-soluble spray paint. No, said the lawyer, if we're going to demonstrate removal of a bathtub ring, the public has got to be shown exactly what we're telling them they're seeing. So some poor production assistant was recruited to take half a dozen baths that day while expensive cameras and filmmakers stood around waiting for yet another batch of dirty suds. An agency executive later asked an FTC official if all that tub time was necessary, or was the agency's lawyer just running scared. The FTC man said he would have given the same advice.

Another victim of mock-up worries was that venerable figurehead of General Mills, Betty Crocker. Mock-ups usually involved pictures of products, but she was an exception. Thousands of women yearly were writing her letters and getting answers with her signature, but there was never any real Betty. She was invented in 1936, and for most of her "life" the company apparently worried no more about her fictional existence than my friend did about his Mercurochrome caper. So the board of directors must have been jolted in 1973 when they saw a newspaper story headlined "Betty Crocker is a lie—so is Aunt Jemima."[14] The story implied no legal charges against those unreal ladies, but suggested consumers were wondering about practices that had never brought a murmur in times past. A spokesman for General Mills thought it was still unimportant, however; he claimed it wasn't the company's fault that women insist on believing in Betty Crocker.

Spurred by such sellerist attitudes, mock-up problems occasionally continued, with some advertisers unable to resist the temptation. Campbell Soup Co., for example, put so many marbles in its bowl of vegetable soup that it created a deceptive practice out of something that might have been perfectly legitimate. Campbell's problem was that picturing the solid ingredients seemed vital to making sales, but when the soup stood still the solids settled to the bottom of the bowl and the resulting photograph showed nothing but the broth. The company's solution was to place marbles in the bottom of the bowl before pouring in the soup. That would make the solid ingredients poke above the surface and be shown attractively.

So far so good—it seemed legitimate because it would show the product only as it really was. Things got out of hand, though, when the executive in charge of marbles put so many in the bowl that the photographed soup displayed a far greater proportion of solid ingredients than the soup actually had. The result was an FTC-imposed settlement in which the company consented to avoid such practices in the future.[15]

Meanwhile, a Borden's ad "showed" Kava instant coffee to have far less acidity than other brands.[16] A needle swung far to the left side of a scale to show Kava's low acidity and far to the right to show the others' high acidity. Though the difference was true, the FTC was concerned that the portion of the acidity scale shown on the screen was only a small part of the total scale. It was as if a household thermometer, typically about ten inches high and calibrated from 120 degrees to -50 degrees, was revised to show a range of only 70 to 75 degrees in the same ten inches. On such a thermometer a temperature drop of two or three degrees would look like a mammoth change, but would really be insignificant. Although most consumers would see what was unusual about such a household thermometer, they would not likely know that the top and bottom ends were missing from the unfamiliar acidity scale. Therefore, said the commission, the Kava ad was deceptive for overexaggerating a true difference. The case involved both mock-ups and puffery, showing that puffing exaggerations may be made not just with words but also with rigged demonstrations.

The FTC has not been free of mistakes on mock-ups, as when it charged Zerex with misrepresentation in a can-stabbing demonstration in which a container of the product was pierced with a sharp instrument. The antifreeze began to flow out but its sealing qualities quickly closed the hole, just as it would do, the commercial implied, in an automobile radiator. The commission complained that the pressure and other conditions in the punctured can did not reflect conditions inside a radiator and therefore misrepresented Zerex's ability to stop leaks. Of course the conditions were different in some senses, but the eventual finding was that they were similar by analogy. The FTC withdrew the charge and conceded the demonstration did not misrepresent Zerex's performance.[17]

Numerous other mock-ups were attacked appropriately by the commission,[18] and by the mid-1970s advertisers apparently were thoroughly informed about mock-ups, because such deceptiveness disappeared and was absent for a long time. Suddenly in 1990 the Volvo mock-up burst onto the scene in what appeared as a remarkable lapse of legal memory by a major advertiser and ad agency. Since in the meantime I have told the story elsewhere,[19] I will say here only that the demonstration of the monster truck driving over the Volvo station wagon without crushing it, as well as the simultaneous crushing of various other cars, was accomplished by utterly illegal mock-ups. The Volvo's roof was reinforced with extra metal beams; the other cars had their roof supports cut.

I do not believe the Volvo incident means we are returning to the use of such deceptive demonstrations. The precedents against them are as clear as anything can be in the law, so I am sure that more such incidents are unlikely to recur in any significant number. A few have happened since then,[20] but do not seem to indicate a new trend.

To summarize the discussion of mock-ups, they are controlled by a legal orientation very similar to that applied to literally misdescriptive names. The law accepts both types of claims as legitimate but also declines to grant them immunity indiscriminately. Such handling shows that the law is fully capable of testing false representations for possible deceptive potential. The fact that it does so vigorously in these areas serves only to highlight the contrasting way in which it glosses over the many cases of puffery, obvious falsity, and social-psychological claims that deceive. There is no really acceptable reason for taking such differing approaches to the various subcategories of what should be a unified regulation of deceptiveness. If the law can recognize the deception in some of these types, it should be able to do so for the others as well.

15

Puffery's Immunity Should Be Eliminated

This last chapter discusses what should be done. My recommendation is not for a blanket condemnation of puffery, but definitely for removal of the blanket immunity the law has given it. Although the regulators exert some control in disallowing certain claims from entering the puffery category, they grant an automatic across-the-board immunity to the immensely greater number they let in. Anyone who doubts that the category is bulging in size need only look back to the examples in chapter 3. There is no question that massive numbers of puffs exist in American advertising.[1]

The assessment here treats puffery in its narrow legal definition. Obvious falsity, literally misdescriptive names, and mock-ups are controlled by existing rules that generally reflect a contemporary consumerist orientation. True, they sometimes function in effect as sellerist loopholes, letting deceptiveness go free, but where that happens I feel the problem is in the interpretation rather than in the rules themselves. In contrast, social-psychological misrepresentations have the same immunity as puffery—not because the law has excused them, as with puffery, but because it has scarcely considered them at all. Accordingly, I recommend that the treatment proposed here for puffery be applied to social-psychological claims as well. For both types, the existing legal treatment continues to represent the traditional sellerist tradition derived from the caveat emptor rule that has generally otherwise been eliminated.

I would remove that automatic immunity and instead consider each puff potentially open to a search for the factually deceptive content it may imply. Any that imply no factual claims, or imply factual claims that are not deceptive, will go free. Of course I feel that much puffery does imply factually deceptive content, and thus merits being prohibited, and that the removal of the immunity will help achieve the desirable result of truly bringing caveat emptor to an end.

That would be an important improvement over the law's current procedure of committing claims to the puffery category simply by examining their form. The examples of chapter 3 typically have been excused by the law not through searches that reveal no deceptive implied facts, but rather by perfunctory conclusions involving little more than noting them to be of opinion form, subjective and evaluative on their faces, rather than objective and factual. That of course tells us nothing about what the claims do or don't imply to consumers; it tells us only that the regulators continue to reflect the old precedents that presumably explain all that needs to be known about such claims—i.e., that consumers know they should not, and do not, rely on them in making their buying decisions, and so are not affected by them.

Those precedents are wrong because form alone determines neither the perceptions of messages nor the buying responses based on them. Removing such rules seems doubly justifiable when we realize that they developed accidentally and incorrectly both as conclusions about consumers' behavior and as reflections of the decisions from which they purportedly derived. Let's return to our earlier analysis to review the twists and turns that brought the law improperly to this point.

We saw in chapter 7 how *Harvey v. Young* created the distinction between fact and value claims (the latter "bare," i.e., unsupported by facts). The case also created the rule that value claims should be excused from deceptiveness because buyers have the duty to regard them as unreliable bases for their own judgments. *Ekins v. Tresham* explained value further by saying it will vary legitimately among people, and can be checked and determined separately by each, and so one person's evaluation cannot deceive another even though it may not be appropriate for that other. An individual thus is negligent in relying on another for such claims because only that individual and no one else can determine his or her own evaluation. *Baily v. Merrell* added that recipients of fact claims can often check the truth for themselves, and when they can, their failure to do so renders them negligent and renders the claim immune from being legally deceptive, even when the speaker speaks fraudulently.

In *Pasley v. Freeman*, Justice Grose not only put those ideas together but expanded them significantly by declaring that opinion claims also were immune even when fraudulent. Justice Buller objected, and seems to have been more accurate about the existing law. But Grose's view prevailed, resulting in the eventual summation derivable from Lord Ellenborough that sellers' false claims of value ("quality") even when spoken fraudulently were immune from deceptiveness when buyers had equal means of knowing. That rule traveled to America, as seen in chapter 7, in the conclusions of Justice Kent and the opinion of *Medbury v. Watson*.

The idea that an opinion can be stated fraudulently was unusual not only because the precedent from which Grose created it involved only fact claims, but also for the question of how an opinion can be fraudulent in the first place. To be fraudulent it would have to be capable of being found true or false, which by definition is not supposed to be possible for opinions. Today's explanation for that apparent inconsistency is that opinion claims can indeed be capable of truth or falsity if and when they imply fact claims. The early cases used no such modern terminology, but we can apply it retrospectively. On doing so we see the cases just cited to have held that buyers could understand sellers to be implying that they knew of a factual basis for their opinions, and therefore to be implying that they knew those claims to be true, and thus to be speaking fraudulently in those instances where their actual belief was that those claims were false.

That early law went on, however, to say that such fraudulent speech did not matter because the buyers typically had equal opportunity with the sellers to examine the underlying facts, and so could rely entirely on themselves. They could arrive at their own opinions with the same efficacy that sellers enjoyed. Further, because opinions are personal things—yours is yours, and cannot be anybody else's—the buyers were obligated to rely entirely on themselves. It would be improper for you to rely on anyone else in formulating what was your own personal assessment. There would of course be some instances in which buyers could not examine the facts, and where that occurred they could not formulate their own opinion claims and so were entitled to rely on the sellers' opinions as being true.

Had the puffery rule stopped evolving at that point, I would have no complaint about it today. However, to continue with events from chapter 7, it did not. In the series of cases beginning with *Brown v. Castles*, the point was added that buyers not only knew not to rely on opinions, but did in fact always decline to rely on them. That was a huge change because it switched from being a normative rule, about what people ought to do, to a finding of fact, saying what they did do.

Further, what consumers were presumed to do was not merely always to check the underlying facts for themselves before formulating their opinion. The presumed behavior was stronger than that; it was that they typically were so certain that such claims were unsupported that they rejected them out of hand, immediately. They never actually checked the underlying facts for themselves because they understood instantly that those facts were unreliable and so must be dismissed automatically.

Based on that understanding of consumer behavior, the rule followed that false opinion claims should be considered immune from being called legally deceptive even when spoken fraudulently, and—this is what was new—even when they could not be checked. It was a complete turnaround, in which a rule that originally said opinion claims could be relied on if they could not be checked now provided that they could not be relied upon whether they could be checked or not.

The essence of the change was to give complete immunity for opinion claims even when the sellers knew they had no factual basis for them and knew they did not believe them. Although that did not mean the claims would always be false, it meant that sellers would be charged with no responsibility for them and thus could speak falsely without penalty. As Prosser put it with appropriate bluntness, "The 'puffing' rule amounts to a seller's privilege to lie his head off, so long as he says nothing specific, on the theory that no reasonable man would believe him, or that no reasonable man would be influenced by such talk."[2]

That of course reflects the traditional reasonable person standard, which is what will be applied today when individual buyers charge misrepresentation or breach of warranty. But today we also have the Federal Trade Commission, and have we not seen that the FTC made a big difference in the law? Well, it has made many big differences, and it originally tried to do so with puffery. As we saw in chapters 9 and 10, the Federal Trade Commission at first abandoned the reasonable person standard and attacked puffery. It seemed successful in doing so as late as 1942 when its action against Moretrench was upheld by the judge who in 1918 had made one of the key historical statements validating puffery as a category.[3] Judge Learned Hand's

Second Circuit, however, was now controlled by the 1937 case[4] that replaced the reasonable person standard with the ignorant person standard, and he was forced to concede the FTC's right to pursue its long-standing desire to prohibit puffery.

That privilege lasted only until 1946, however, when it was removed by the decision in *Carlay*[5] that made the commission allow puffery even though continuing to apply the ignorant person standard to other claims. The Seventh Circuit in *Carlay* ignored the precedents that controlled Judge Hand, and cited instead the precedents establishing puffery in the common law. That brought puffery at the FTC to the place where it remains to this day, under the thumb of the line of cases beginning with *Brown v. Castles* that found consumers to disbelieve and decline to rely on all instances of puffery.

The FTC might have tried, and in my opinion should still try, to resolve the contradiction. The Supreme Court said the commission need not apply the traditional reasonable person standard, and the Second Circuit, reflecting that decision, said the commission could prohibit puffery. The Seventh Circuit, however, said the FTC could not prohibit puffery, which meant in effect that for puffery the commission would have to apply the reasonable person standard.

The commission might have asked the Supreme Court to reverse the Seventh Circuit or otherwise reconcile the conflicting decisions, but didn't. Instead, it simply accepted the contradiction, through which it accepted in effect the finding of fact that consumers typically behave in reflection of the reasonable person standard when they encounter puffery even though they typically do not do so otherwise.

The idea that consumers act in that way goes utterly against the custom of advertisers to use puffery in great quantity. Their actions must indicate that they believe consumers' decisions will be affected by such claims, since otherwise they would not have used them so often or continued such use for so long. Because advertising people are highly skilled in the art of persuasion, I have no hesitation in accepting their actions as sufficient evidence per se for believing the law is wrong to say that puffery does not affect the buying behavior of consumers.

There is also research evidence for the point. For example, a market research firm, R. H. Bruskin Associates,[6] surveyed a sample of citizens on whether they felt various advertising claims were "completely true," "partly true," or "not true at all." The puffery claims among them were rated as follows:

1. "State Farm is all you need to know about life insurance" (22 percent said completely true, 36 percent said partly true);
2. "The world's most experienced airline" (Pan Am) (23 percent and 47 percent, respectively);
3. "Ford has a better idea" (26 percent and 42 percent);
4. "You can trust your car to the man who wears the star" (Texaco) (21 percent and 47 percent);
5. "It's the real thing" (Coca-Cola) (35 percent and 29 percent);
6. "Perfect rice everytime" (Minute Rice) (43 percent and 30 percent).

And the highest score in the survey went to Alcoa's claim, "Today, aluminum is something else," appraised as completely true by 47 percent and partly true by 36 percent.[7] While those statements were of puffery form, the questions in effect asked the surveyed consumers to consider them as facts (by asking about their truth), and the consumers seem to have had no trouble in doing so. Further, they seem to have regarded such facts to a great extent as true, which suggests they would have relied on them.

The significance of that survey is this: *Had the questions been answered as the law assumes consumers will always answer them, they would have been answered "not true at all" one hundred percent of the time.*

A study titled "Is Advertising Puffery Believed?" was done in 1980, in response to the first edition of this book, by researchers at the University of Illinois. Rotfeld & Rotzoll[8] exposed 100 subjects first to 5 ads containing 13 puffing claims, then to a questionnaire asking whether those and other claims were communicated by the ads. There was some incidence of failure, but 80.5 percent of the time the subjects saw the ads to be making the puffing claims. The questionnaire also had 17 additional claims of factual form that the researchers thought might be seen as implied by the puffery claims. As with the Bruskin research, the law's assumption would be that such perceptions would never occur to consumers. However, the ads conveyed those puff-implied fact claims into the subjects' minds 44.7 percent of the time.

The researchers also asked, as did the Bruskin research, whether the subjects believed the claims. Such belief, when there is no basis for it, would bring consumers even closer to being harmed than would merely seeing the claims conveyed. Subjects believed the explicit puffing claims in 39.6 percent of the instances where they had the opportunity to see them conveyed. That amounted to 49.2 percent of the 80.5 percent of instances where they actually saw them conveyed.

To believe such claims to such a strong extent indicates the subjects must have seen factual content in them.

The same people believed the puff-implied fact claims in 11.4 percent of the instances where they had the opportunity to see them conveyed. That was 25.5 percent of the 44.7 percent of instances where they saw them conveyed. Although that degree of belief was lower, it was artificially so because there were 17 such puff-implied fact claims that the subjects could link with the 13 puffery claims. The degree of belief would have been higher if determined as the percentage of times subjects saw at least one fact claim conveyed impliedly by each puffery claim, and the percentage of times they believed at least one. I contacted the researchers to ask for that information, but unfortunately they had not retained it.

The researchers observed, however, that their subjects, none of whom were currently in college, were well above average in education. That gave good reason to expect that the true incidence of seeing the puff-implied fact claims conveyed, and of believing them, would be higher for the lesser-educated general public. In any event, all reported percentages were far above zero, and thus far different from the traditional legal expectation that consumers will pay no attention. The study strongly supports those who believe the law is wrong in that.

Additional research on puffery followed this book's first edition. Shimp[9] asked subjects what they saw implied from puffing statements that were also "incomplete comparatives" because they seemed to imply completions. For example, the puff "Mennen E goes on warmer and drier" could imply fact statements such as "Mennen E goes on warmer and drier than any other deodorant on the market." When questioned, subjects saw the ads conveying such completions in high percentages, some over 50 percent. And when asked whether those claims were "directly stated" or "intended but not stated," subjects very often called them "directly stated," which they were not.

Holbrook[10] exposed subjects to alternate versions of a foreign car ad, one stating 11 factual claims (e.g., "27 miles per gallon on regular gas"), the other stating the same claims in puffery form (e.g., "truly excellent gas mileage"). The results from asking subjects about the importance of each ad's claims, and their belief of them, could not reliably distinguish the two types of ads statistically from each other. That is, puff and fact claims generally were of equal importance and were given equal belief, contradicting the law's assumption that we always know puffery and treat it differently.

While bitterness in coffee might be measured objectively by experts, consumers treat it as subjective opinion, differing from person to person. When Olson and Dover[11] showed half their subjects a claim of "no bitterness" for a certain brand, belief in the claim became much higher than for the half not seeing the ad. Both groups then tasted the coffee, not knowing it was deliberately brewed too strongly to make them likely to sense bitterness. The tasting experience predictably reduced the high belief of those who had seen the claim, yet their belief remained higher than that of those who had not. Thus a puffery claim actually changed what people tasted, and so would surely have potential in real life situations to affect purchasing decisions.

Vanden Bergh and Reid[12] did similar research involving a ballpoint pen. Elsewhere, they[13] found people recognizing ads and ad components containing puffery no less often than ads that did not, another way of illustrating that consumers respond to puffery no differently than they do to fact claims.

All of the studies just mentioned, and additional related research, are described in greater detail in an article I coauthored.[14] In later work, Shimp and Yocum[15] showed puffery to be no less effective than factual claims in favorably affecting attitudes both toward advertised items and toward purchasing them. Vanden Bergh and Fink[16] identified degrees of believability of puffery claims in experimentally created ads. Vanden Bergh and Bartlett's[17] analysis of automobile magazine ads showed readership no different for ads with or without puffery; Kurzbard and Soley[18] made a similar finding for industrial magazine ads.

Wyckham[19] studied claims such as "Results no other powder can beat" that he considered to be "implied superiority claims" rather than puffery because they do not claim superiority explicitly. However, chapter 3's descriptions of puffery, separating it into various types not previously noted, included such phrases because they claim their products to be the best possible (i.e., none are better but some may be equal) even though they do not claim them to be the best (i.e., none are equal). Of course I expect them often to claim their products to be the best impliedly, and that was supported by Wyckham's finding that consumers saw them as implying superiority 55 percent of the time.

A final research study on consumer response to claims was not about puffery but about irrelevant attributes. Carpenter and colleagues[20] studied attributes that appear to differentiate brands but really do not, for example, instant coffee having flaked crystals. Though relevant for ground coffee, crystals are irrelevant for instant because the flakes dissolve. Some of Carpenter's subjects saw ads touting a product's attributes including such an objectively irrelevant one, while others saw ads mentioning only relevant attributes. Preference ratings were predictably higher for those told the product had the attractive irrelevant attribute. That, however, was only part of the study. The researchers also in advance had divided each group in half, with one of the halves of each told more about the attributes, including whether they were relevant.

The key finding was that preference ratings were increased by the irrelevant attribute for those told it was so, just as they were increased for those not told. Although the claim of the irrelevant attribute was not puffery, there is a similarity in that the law expects consumers to recognize attributes claimed in puffery to be irrelevant, to ignore them, and to decline to rely on them. Yet here consumers relied on the irrelevant attribute even when explicitly told it was so. For us to be affected by an irrelevancy, even when cautioned not to be, certainly supports a conclusion that we will be affected by puffery claims that we may very well judge to be relevant because the advertisers have invited us to think that.

While a number of research items have been described, there is always the problem that each is limited to certain puffs in certain contexts. The generalizability to further situations, however, is usually thought to be high when studies done in various ways show what researchers call convergent validity—results in the same direction, with nothing to the contrary. That is one of the most significant features of the research on puffery. There are no findings that back up the law's position that such claims are automatically rejected by consumers and have no impact on them.

Is it possible that advertising people and their lawyers have researched the topic? Probably not, because evidence that puffery works would hurt them, and they don't need evidence that it doesn't work as long as the law assumes it doesn't on the basis of no evidence at all. In fact, evidence of puffery's not working could hurt ad people by prompting those paying the huge sums involved to wonder whether they should keep doing so if the ads have no impact on sales. As a result, findings in either direction would upset the need of advertising agencies and their lawyers to keep their clients convinced that puffery works and to keep the FTC convinced that it doesn't.

What about the regulators doing research? That's exactly what I want to see, but the problem is that they have no incentive to do it when they've already decided what the results will be. That's a shame, because the FTC knows a great deal about how to determine what consumers see ad claims to be saying. The method essentially involves surveying, simply asking people for their perceptions of the claims being communicated.[21] The commission uses that expertise on factual claims, but not on puffery. In a practical sense, then, the recommendation of this book is nothing more than that the FTC and other regulators apply the same procedure to puffery.

The fact-finding process could benefit from using the breakdown of types of puffery offered in chapter 3. Such discriminations, not made in any previous writing on puffery (including this book's first edition), can be helpful in determining what puffs are most likely to imply fact claims. The first category given in chapter 3 seems most likely to do so, in my judgment, and the last category seems least likely. The distinctions seem intuitively predictive, since "best" is a stronger claim than "better," which is stronger than "good." The entire set of lists from chapter 3 includes those and additional categories as follows:

Best. That means unique, alone in the top ranking; no competitor is as good. Examples from chapter 3: "The best tires in the world have Goodyear written all over them." "Nobody gets the dirt out like Hoover."

Best possible. That type of claim is slightly weaker; nobody else is better, nor can be, and probably some are worse; however, some may be equally good. Examples: "Perfect rice everytime" (Minute Rice). "Nothing cleans stains better than Clorox bleach."

Better. That means some are worse, although allowing that others may be as good or better. "For my tough headaches, Advil just works better." "For dazzling, whiter teeth" (Aquafresh).

Specially good. That means very high in comparison to others, which could often mean as good as many and better than some. However, the exactness of the comparison is less clear than in the earlier categories. The claims are becoming weaker and more vague as we go down the list. "If it's Weber, it's great outdoors" (barbecue grill). "Doing it right" (J. C. Penney).

Good. That means just plain good, a relatively modest claim. The advertised items compare well enough with others to be valuable. They could be as good as many, perhaps better than some, but this is even weaker and more vague than the previous category. "M'm M'm good" (Campbell's soup). "We bring good things to life" (General Electric).

Subjective qualities. This is the weakest category of puffery claims. The qualities of course may suggest that the advertised items rank well in comparison with the competition. But these are the only claims not using comparatives explicitly, and so are the most oriented to sheer subjectivity, sometimes to the extent of being fancifully unreal. "There's a smile in every Hershey Bar." "Taste the future" (Budweiser Ice Draft).

Notice that two types of claims are omitted from these lists. The first involves truly individual opinions spoken by nonexpert users of advertised items, making statements such as "I prefer Coke." The puffs I am concerned about in this book are those in the form of "Coke is the best" that imply facts extending beyond the speaker's state of mind. Individual opinions will probably do that with relatively few people. For most consumers they are opinions that imply themselves to be nothing else, including implying no factual basis, and so I see little problem with them.

The second type is that of jokes or spoofs, which were used to illustrate obvious falsity in chapter 11. I would never have thought of these claims as puffery had not some recent press reports thought so by using examples such as the one for potato chips that says, "Betcha can't eat just one."[22] Statements made in an explicitly joking manner or format typically are not puffery, which does not offer a humorous context. There may be some borderline cases where the context is ambiguous, but any such examples could be placed only in the weakest puffery category ("subjective qualities"). On the whole, expressions not offered as serious claims are not what we are examining here.

Turning back to the listed categories, let's see how their impact on consumers differs. Although individual instances may vary, claims in the first category seem most likely in general, and those in the last category least likely, to prompt consumers to see advertisers as implying that a supporting factual basis exists. The first category seems also most likely, and the last category least likely, to be false in doing so. It's a natural result of "best" and its equivalents being the strongest puffery claims, while the weakest are the subjective qualities such as the "smile" in a chocolate bar.

To claim a product or service is the "best" should certainly imply to many or most consumers that underlying factual support exists. It's a value claim, to be sure, and certainly an opinion. But it's also enough more than that to justify not excusing it as something that will vary for all consumers and which we can all evaluate for ourselves. The latter is where the law of opinion statements began, with *Harvey v. Young*, but not where it ended. The claim that Ford Escort is the best small car is not offered to consumers as something we should all recognize as no more than one speaker's personal opinion. I am sure surveying would show most of us seeing it as implied by Ford to be based on an established standard or criterion for evaluating its cars. Consumers typically won't know what the standard is, of course, but they will assume it exists, and that it applies equally for all. By such analysis, "best" expresses the application of a factual standard. Thus it is not an opinion at all in the original sense of meaning an evaluation that exists separately for each consumer and each maker.

It's utterly impossible for consumers to draw their own personal opinions about which cars are best, because that takes both expertise and testing equipment we do not have. We do not evaluate because we *cannot* evaluate, and thus we do not have our own personal opinions. We do not have the opportunity equal to that of Ford, nor in fact any opportunity at all, beyond the examination of certain superficialities, to make such assessments. We rely on sellers' claims because we need to rely on something, and nothing else is available.

Granted, I am saying I think these implied meanings are what consumer surveys will show. I certainly don't know it for each specific claim, because such surveys haven't been done. Granted, too, that a certain number of consumers will see such claims as implying nothing, as meaningless. We know for certain, based on communication research, that messages typically receive a variety of interpretations, not just one. We also know, however, as discussed way back in chapter 2, that the regulators frequently discover that ads convey claims to consumers by implication. And, from later chapters, we know the regulators don't search for implications once they define a claim as puffery. Thus I am predicting that the process of consumer response I have just described, which can be called the Puffery Implication,[23] will often be found if the law simply begins looking for it.

Again, however, I believe it will be found most often and most strongly for the strongest puffs. While all of the forms of puffery will imply that they are supported by facts, the probability of their doing so will weaken as we move down the list. The second category, for example, the "best possible" claim, does not involve claiming to be superior to all others. So, to convey as strong a claim as the first category, it would have to imply being best and then imply what that implies as discussed above. Although that result would take more steps, it nonetheless seems highly likely, because the research by Wyckham discussed earlier in this chapter showed that claims such as "Nothing cleans stains better than Clorox bleach" implied superiority 55 percent of the time. Further, those consumers not seeing "best possible" as implying "best" but meaning only what it technically states, that nothing is better, could still see the implication that the speaker has a factual basis for that lesser claim.

While "better" is even farther down the line, the same analysis applies. A claim such as "Advil just works better" may be seen as implying "best" by some consumers, although probably fewer than for the "best possible" claim. It could also imply "best possible," and of course even if taken merely in its technical meaning it can imply existence of factual support.

The entire group of claims should work the same. Each can imply any of the higher types of claims, although the higher the reach the less the probability. Just as "better" is less likely than "best possible" to imply "best," "specially good" is even less likely to do so than "better," and so on. Claims in the last category of "subjective qualities" are not only the weakest of all but also the least predictable. That is, they will be taken by consumers to have the most different meanings, and so by fewer consumers for any given meaning. For that reason they will be the least likely to imply a factual basis.

Now for the matter of how false the various categories are. To reiterate a point made earlier, I believe puffs generally are false in implying factual support because when such support exists the advertisers will report it explicitly. Where they do, the issue becomes no longer the truth of the puff, but rather the truth of that factual claim. But that doesn't happen very often; puffery is usually "bare" in the sense we saw for the "bare assertions" identified in the earliest cases in chapter 7. The puffery examples in chapter 3 are typically that way. Where factual support exists it will surely accompany the puffery, because that will make the puffs more credible. No advertisers rely on a weaker claim while keeping a stronger one hidden; they always use the strongest claim they have. Unfortunately, though, they often don't have one that's very strong. So when you see them using the puff alone, you can probably conclude it's because the factual support doesn't exist.

Again, however, the likelihood seems to be greatest at the top of the list and smallest at the end. In cases where the Puffery Implication, saying that factual support exists, is found to be made, then the stronger the claim, the more likely it is to be unsupported and thus false. "Best" is stronger than "better," which is stronger than "good." It would be much easier for Campbell's to obtain support for "M'm M'm good" than for AT&T to prove it's "the best in the business."

Although I never thought to question Campbell's on its claim, I wrote a letter to AT&T asking what support it had. The answer from a marketing person said the claim referred to the company's "ability to complete a higher percentage of calls than our competition, to block fewer 800 calls, and to have the highest sound quality."[24] I was unsatisfied, because the claim was completely unqualified, yet the letter claimed as superior only three aspects of making telephone calls and nothing about the company's other activities. I wrote back, pointing out that I thought the puffery claim "would imply to many consumers seeing it . . . that your company is superior to its competition in each and every aspect of that competition." That one was referred to a company lawyer, who told me the phrase was used "not as a claim but as a service mark [trademark] to identify and distinguish [AT&T's] brand. . . . As a service mark, we did not believe we had to substantiate the expression and were never asked to do so."[25] Of course I wasn't surprised that they were never asked about the matter, but I sure disagree with one thing—I could swear "The best in the business" is a claim.

In summary, then, the claims at the top of the list ("best") are most likely to be more than opinion through implying factual support, and are also the most likely to be false and so deceptive in having no such factual basis. At the bottom, those that claim only "good" or boast of subjective qualities are the least likely.

These distinctions seem important because of the impression I have gained over the years that discussions of puffery suffer from treating all examples as the same. The critics will pick the worst they can find, while the supporters will pick the most benign, each identifying their choices as typical. Obviously our criticism will be better as well as fairer if we recognize the differences. Compare, for example, the FTC excusing Bayer for claiming to have the "world's best aspirin"[26] and excusing a foreign company for claiming its sports car to be "the sexiest European."[27] I expect the aspirin claim to imply factually to many consumers that an industry standard exists and Bayer performed best on it, but I expect relatively few consumers to see the car claim as implying either such a standard or such a performance. The description "sexiest European" may be utterly unhelpful to consumers in making the decision to spend $30,000 or more, but I see it as being much closer to the original idea of an opinion than I see with many puffs.

That difference, in the end, is what matters. It's one thing when consumers see opinions in the way the law originally conceived them, and another when they see them impliedly yet surely to be fact claims. In the first instance the opinion is truly something that varies from consumer to consumer and that we all have an equal opportunity to determine for ourselves. In the second instance, however, the opinion is something that does not vary from one person to another, and that we have no opportunity to determine for ourselves. Accordingly, when the latter occurs the puffery should be subject to the treatment that fact claims get. The traditional immunity should not be allowed to prevent that.

At this point I might be ready to conclude this book were it not for some recent activity that may change the treatment of puffery in the direction I recommend. It involves one of the periodic rewritings of the warranty provisions of the Uniform Commercial Code (UCC), cited several times earlier, mostly in chapters 5 and 6. The UCC is not a law itself but a model that the various states may adopt as actual law, with the purpose of achieving uniformity throughout the United States. The states are sovereign with regard to such decisions, but the fact that so much commerce operates nationally makes them appreciate the advantages of being similar. Consequently, they have based their laws to an overwhelming degree on the UCC. Over time, however, new conditions develop and court decisions adapt to them, and the code would become outdated if not rewritten to reflect such changes. The work is sponsored by the American Law Institute and the National Conference of Commissioners on Uniform State Laws, and undertaken by numerous lawyers who give those organizations large amounts of their time while continuing in their regular jobs.

As the second edition of this book is being written in 1995, a drafting committee is working on the UCC's article 2, covering the sale of goods, and is proposing changes in section 2-313, discussed earlier[28] as defining warranty in this way: "Any affirmation of fact or promise made by the seller to the buyer which relates to the goods and becomes part of the basis of the bargain creates an express warranty that the goods shall conform to the affirmation or promise." The section then asserts the immunity of puffery by adding that "An affirmation merely of the value of the goods or a statement purporting to be merely the seller's opinion or commendation of the goods does not create a warranty." (Those who work with the UCC customarily refer to the concepts cited in that sentence as being, collectively, "puffery.")

A significant change in the new draft is an addition to the above that says, "Any description, sample, affirmation, promise, or statement which relates to the goods made by the seller presumptively becomes part of the agreement with the seller and creates an express warranty that the goods will conform to the affirmation, promise, or statement."[29] In other words, and this is a bit confusing, a puffery statement first remains excluded as an express warranty in a direct sense, based on retention of the wording at the end of my previous paragraph. But it then amounts to an express warranty in the sense of being something that the seller is held to warrant to the consumer. The complexity is apparently due to the drafters' desire to retain the traditional identification of puffery statements as separate from fact statements by definition, yet also now to hold the sellers accountable for those statements in the same way as for factual statements.

The changed portion then goes on to say, "However, no obligation is created if the seller establishes by a preponderance of the evidence that a reasonable person in the position of the buyer would conclude that either the seller merely affirmed the value of the goods or merely stated an opinion or commendation. . . ." In other words, the seller gets the opportunity to prove in court that the puffery claim should be treated as no more than puffery, and thus not as an express warranty would be treated, by establishing that the buyer understood it only as puffery and not as fact, presumably rejecting it and refusing to rely on it.

Despite the opportunity thus given sellers to retain the traditional understanding, these changes if carried out would make a significant difference in puffery's fate. Exactly as this book advocates, its immunity from prosecution would be removed and replaced by the idea that it may be accepted and relied on by consumers to their detriment. Further, if the seller asks a court to find that consumers reject such a claim, the burden would be on the seller (defendant, in court) to prove the rejection rather than on the buyer (plaintiff) to prove the acceptance. Thus the idea that puffery may be relied on would be regarded not merely as a possibility but as a fact presumed to be true at the start of a lawsuit and until such time as the seller proved otherwise.

The proposed changes were first offered by the drafting committee's reporter, Richard E. Speidel, Professor of Law at Northwestern University. He told me that the reason was simply that court decisions and legal commentaries over the years were changing in the direction of showing sympathy for increased protection for consumers. That is fully consistent with this book's recommendation to continue the general trend of the law away from the rule of caveat emptor, and thus away from sellerism and toward consumerism, by removing the remaining sellerist remnant of caveat emptor that puffery represents.

The proposals are also consistent with the idea expressed herein that decisions about puffery should be made not merely by noting its semantic status as opinion rather than fact, but by finding how consumers actually react to it. The provision that sellers may try to establish consumer rejection suggests they must do so by looking not merely at statements of value, opinion, or commendation as forms of expression, but rather at how consumers respond to them. In that way the fancifulness of ancient assumptions about consumer behavior would give way to the realities of actual facts.

While these proposed changes thus are very exciting, the present moment unfortunately is an awkward time to be writing about them, because there is no guarantee they will be put into place. If they are, they will strongly affect the treatment of puffery. The drafting committee, however, has yet to make its final recommendation, and the proposed changes must later pass through higher-level committees of the sponsoring organizations in a process that will probably not be completed until 1997.

A factor working against ultimate change is that the advertising industry has mounted a strong resistance to it. The action has taken the drafting committee by surprise, not only by its vehemence but also by the unexpectedness of advertisers' being greatly concerned about the UCC. As the drafters well know, UCC warranty cases are generally brought by individuals dissatisfied over contract provisions or sellers' direct statements to them. What is at issue is usually centered on the buying-selling transaction itself. Most cases against advertisers are brought by FTC or other government regulators or by other advertisers, and not under the UCC.

Nonetheless, the advertising industry is strongly against the change, apparently feeling vulnerable to any move that would take away its traditional privilege. The industry's lobbying groups such as the American Advertising Federation have asked that no change be made, doing so largely on the argument that the law's precedents support puffery, and those precedents should continue to be followed. As I've made clear already, that line of argument seems utterly bankrupt, but the problem for the industry is that it has little or nothing else to support its position. Puffery exists today not because the law's analysis of its effects is correct, but only because its analysis is law. When and if a reanalysis is conducted as I have proposed in this book, the precedents will turn to dust and nothing will be left to hold up the industry's position.

Puffery is advertising people's Catch-22. They defend it because it's legal, but it can be legal only if it doesn't work. If consumers reject puffery as the advertisers claim, there is no reason to use it. They would be defending it for a reason that tells them there's no point in defending it. A sensible reason for using false puffery could only be that it works, which would then make it illegal. If consumers rely on it as I believe they do, there is a reason to use it all right, but then it is deceptive and the law's support for it must disappear.

The industry simply should not be allowed to have it both ways, treating consumers as dumb while describing them as smart. That famous advertising executive, author, French chef, and chateau collector David Ogilvy once declared, in defiance of the motivation researchers' mounting evidence to the contrary, that "The consumer isn't a moron, she is your wife."[30] But, responded another prominent industry observer, "Sometimes it seems that the consumer is not only your wife, she's also a moron; and what's more so are you and the kids." If some advertising is moronic, he added, there's a strong suspicion that much of the public responds to it, or otherwise it would quickly disappear.[31]

Another excuse ad people use, along with saying consumers know lying when they see it, is that consumers accept lying; they don't mind it. They treat it in the way they treat "little white lies." If you are impressed with such an argument, I recommend the book *Lying*, by Sissela Bok,[32] which examines conditions under which society might reasonably find lying to be justified. It's important that the liar incorporate the perspective of the deceived, Bok says, which could make lying acceptable in situations such as those in which people indicate they approve of being told lies. Many of us, for example, might prefer that others compliment us on our hair styling or clothing rather than express any negative opinion they may actually have. Can that rule be applied to false puffery, however? I think not, because I cannot imagine that consumers should reasonably be interpreted as having given their consent to be lied to in that way. If they haven't, the lying is not justified, and another of the advertisers' excuses disappears.

There *is* one, and only one, thing on which advertising people and I agree, and that is that the change I advocate in the law will change the nature and look of advertising significantly. To them it would be a loss, while I believe that to consumers, and thus to society as a whole, it would be a gain. Puffery is useless to consumers; it is useful only to one party to the sales transaction. Something so limited in its value to society should not be encouraged to exist.

Notes
Table of Cases
Index

Notes

This book is annotated in legal style, since so many of its references are to legal sources. Readers not experienced in researching the law might consult a librarian for help in obtaining the cited materials. The following explanatory comments are offered to keep such consultation to a minimum.

"65 U.S. 493" or "65 *Harvard Law Review* 493" means the case or article is in Volume 65, beginning at p. 493. "65 U.S. 493, 506" means the reference is to p. 506 of the item. "*Advertising Age*, July 2, 1 (1973)" means the article begins on p. 1.

Abbreviations used include:

U.S.: United States Supreme Court Reports.

S.C.: Supreme Court Reporter (alternate source of the reports in "U.S.").

L.Ed.: Lawyers Edition (third source of the reports in "U.S.").

F.: Federal Reporter (cases of federal courts other than Supreme Court).

F.2d: Federal Reporter, 2d Series.

1st Cir.: U.S. Court of Appeals for the First Circuit.

Wis.: Reports of the Wisconsin courts (same treatment for other states).

A., N.E., N.W., P., etc.: Reports for the Atlantic, Northeast, Northwest, Pacific, etc., areas (generally alternate sources for cases in state reports).

Wis.2d, A.2d: Wisconsin Reports, 2d Series; Atlantic Reports, 2d Series.

TRR: Trade Regulation Reporter.

FTC: Federal Trade Commission Decisions.

CFR: Code of Federal Regulations.

Eng. Rep.: English Reports (reprints of early English cases).

Y.B.: Yearbooks (early English law).

Chapter 2. Falsity without Deception

1. I am speaking principally of the activities of the Federal Trade Commission, which has acted against deceptiveness since its formation in 1914. Its actions are detailed in chapter 8. In common law the term *misrepresentation* is used rather than *deceptive*, and it is established that misrepresentation rather than falsity per se is what is illegal (see chapter 6).

2. Hot wheels: *Mattel*, consent order, 79 FTC 667 (1971); Johnny Lightning: *Topper*, consent order, 79 FTC 681 (1971).

3. The difficulties of this process are further detailed in chapter 8, at note 43 ff.

4. Reasons for assuming the falsity of virtually all puffery are stated in chapter 3, text following note 6.

5. See full discussions in chapters 7 and 10.

6. The Kraft case is published: *Kraft*, 114 FTC 40 (1991), affirmed on appeal, *Kraft v. FTC*, 970 F.2d 311 (1992). The other cases are not yet published but are available by contacting the FTC: *Jenny Craig* (1995), *Häagen Dazs* (1994), *Stouffer Foods* (1994), Honda and Toyota: *Nissan* (1994), Unocal and Seventy-Six: *Unocal* (1994), *Revlon* (1993), *Hasbro* (1993), *Mr. Coffee* (1993), *General Electric* (1993), Hefty: *Mobil Oil* (1992), Glad: *First Brands* (1992), *Campbell Soup* (1992), *Orkin Exterminating* (1992), *Volvo* (1991), Mazola: *CPC International* (1990). The Kraft and Stouffer orders resulted from litigation; the others were settled by consent.

7. The Kraft and Volvo cases are described extensively in I. Preston, *The Tangled Web They Weave* (1994).

8. Traditional common law holds that injury must occur specifically because of a person's justifiable reliance upon a message, if action is to be taken against the message. *Restatement of the Law of Torts*, §525 (1977); William L. Prosser and W. Page Keeton, *Prosser and Keeton on Torts*, 5th ed., §108 (1984). The Federal Trade Commission assumes the same in determining that a message is likely to deceive (see chapters 6 and 8).

9. See discussion of the "ignorant person" in chapter 9.

10. *Williams v. Rank & Son Buick*, 44 Wis.2d 239, 170 N.W.2d 807 (1969).

Chapter 3. Puffery

1. My definition is drawn from authorities such as these:

"It is settled that the law does not exact good faith from a seller in those vague commendations of his wares which manifestly are open to differences of opinion . . . and as to which 'it has always been understood, the world over, that such statements are to be distrusted' (Brown v. Castles . . .). . . ." *Deming v. Darling*, 148 Mass. 504, 20 N.E. 107 (1889). This statement by Justice Oliver Wendell Holmes includes a quote from a case described in chapter 7 as the origin of the portion of the puffery rule saying that consumers will know to disbelieve and refuse to rely on the claim.

"Puffing . . . is considered to be offered and understood as an expression of the seller's opinion only. . . . An opinion may take the form of a statement of quality, of more or less indefinite content. . . . The 'puffing' rule amounts to a seller's privilege to lie his head off, so long as he says nothing specific, on the theory that no reasonable man would believe him, or that no reasonable man would be influenced by such talk." William L. Prosser and W. Page Keeton, *Prosser and Keeton on Torts*, 5th ed., 757 (1984).

"[A]ny seller will express a favorable opinion concerning what he has to sell; and when he praises it in general terms, without specific content or reference to facts, buyers are expected to and do understand that they are not entitled to rely literally upon the words." *Restatement of the Law of Torts (Second)*, §542 (1977).

"An affirmation merely of the value of the goods or a statement purporting to be merely the seller's opinion or commendation of the goods does not create a warranty." *Uniform Commercial Code*, 10th ed., §2–313 (1987). The statement qualifies the following from the same source: "Any affirmation of fact or promise made by the seller to the buyer which relates to the goods and becomes part of the basis of the bargain creates an express warranty that the goods shall conform to the affirmation or promise." Under this law a buyer may sue for breach of warranty, but not when the claim is puffery.

"[T]he Commission generally will not bring advertising cases based on subjective claims (taste, feel, appearance, smell) or on correctly stated opinion claims if consumers understand the source and limitations of the opinion. . . . The Commission generally will not pursue cases involving obviously exaggerated or puffing representations, i.e., those that the ordinary consumers do not take seriously. *Policy Statement on Deception*, FTC document reprinted as appendix to Cliffdale, 103 FTC 110, 174 (1984).

Additional statements describe the phenomenon by emphasizing what it is not:

"[When the seller] assigns to the article qualities which it does not possess, does not simply magnify in opinion the advantages it has but invents advantages and falsely asserts their existence, he transcends the limits of 'puffing' and engages in false representations and pretenses." U.S. v. New South Farm, 241 U.S. 64 (1916). This Supreme Court case has been used by the Federal Trade Commission against factual claims defended as puffery; see chapter 7 at note 28, and chapter 10, at notes 27–28.

"Puffing refers, generally, to an expression of opinion not made as a representation of fact. . . . While a seller has some latitude in 'puffing' his goods, he is not authorized to misrepresent them or to assign to them benefits or virtues they do not possess." *Gulf Oil v. FTC*, 150 F.2d 106, 109 (1945).

" 'Puffing' does not embrace misstatements of material fact." Colgate, 59 FTC 1452, 1469 (1961).

See also definitions in the many cases cited in chapters 7 and 10.

2. A comment from "Is it or isn't it?" *Wall Street Journal*, February 25, 13 (1971): "The *Chicago Tribune* bars advertisers from using such superlatives as 'lowest prices,' but it bills itself as 'the world's greatest newspaper.' Is it? 'In a journalistic sense we definitely are,' declares H. F. Grumhaus, president and publisher. 'Of course we aren't,' says editor Clayton Kirkpatrick. 'It's not a literal statement, any more than the *New York Times* actually prints all

the news that's fit to print, or the *Atlanta Journal* covers Dixie like the dew. It's a poetic phrase that attempts to set some objectives.' "

3. See research support for this, as discussed in chapter 15.

4. I do not mean that the Federal Trade Commission has explicitly called each of these claims puffery. But it has not questioned them, either, which is the way most puffery is treated.

5. Some of the classic presentations in the field called general semantics are *ETC.: A Review of General Semantics*, a quarterly periodical; S. I. Hayakawa, *Language in Thought and Action* (1949); Wendell Johnson, *People in Quandaries* (1946); Alfred Korzybski, *Science and Sanity: An Introduction to Non-Aristotelian System and General Semantics* (1933); Irving J. Lee, *Language Habits in Human Affairs* (1941).

6. Ray L. Birdwhistell, *Kinesics and Context*, 227 (1970). See similar comment by a Federal Trade commissioner, chapter 10, at note 44.

7. See definitions in note 1. It is conceded that stray persons may be deceived, but that fact is given no significance; see discussions in chapters 9 and 10.

8. Sid Bernstein, "Puffery wins a smallish victory," *Advertising Age*, October 23, 16 (1972). Through a generous editorial policy, I was permitted a rejoinder to Mr. Bernstein in his own publication: "Challenges stand that puffery may be low-priority problem," November 27, 47 (1972).

9. See chapter 2 at note 10.

10. "FTC hits puffery claims at ad hearings," *Advertising Age*, October 25, 1 (1971); "Overholzer tackles the nuts and bolts of advertising," ibid., November 1, 181 (1971). Unfortunately, the commission has had no more recent hearings on the general nature of advertising.

11. Pamphlet, American Association of Advertising Agencies (1970).

Chapter 4. The Roots of Sellerism

1. Anthony Fitzherbert, *Boke of Husbandrie*, §118 (1534).

2. Under Sweden's Marketing Act of 1971 an advertiser may say nothing he can't prove. "You can't say a product is 'best,' for instance," according to a Swedish advertising executive. "It takes away a lot of cliches and stupid things. You have to talk about important things, not artificial things." Kathryn Sederberg, "Consumer ombudsman is feature of Swedish law," *Advertising Age*, May 22, 98 (1972).

Canada's Competition Act of 1971 prevented even harmless puffery and obvious exaggeration. A Canadian official stated that the courts would, should an appeal be taken, interpret the sections of the act dealing with misleading advertising as applying to the "credulous man" (called in this book the "ignorant man"; see chapter 9), thus eliminating the advertisers' defense that a reasonable man would not have believed the exaggeration. "Canadian law will prevent puffery claims," ibid., October 4, 77 (1971).

In Germany puffery was curtailed considerably, though not so outrightly as in Sweden or Canada. Highly subjective assertions, such as a florist's claim to have "the most beautiful flowers in the world," are still permitted. But the claim that "Wiscoat is the world's best coat" has been found deceptive. Warren S. Grimes, "Control of advertising in the United States and Germany: Volkswagen has a better idea," 84 *Harvard Law Rev.* 1769, 1794 (1971).

3. Walton H. Hamilton, "The ancient maxim caveat emptor," 40 *Yale Law Journal* 1133 (1931).

4. Ibid., 1156. "No Roman author whose works survive seems to have scribbled the two words down."

5. "Grolier ads tell consumer he's 'entitled to protection,' " *Advertising Age*, June 28, 56 (1971)

6. Hamilton, "Caveat emptor," 1157, note 166.

7. Ibid., 1136–63. Henri Pirenne, *Economic and Social History of Medieval Europe*, 176–88 (1937).

8. Hamilton, "Caveat emptor," 1138.

9. Ibid., 1137.

10. Ibid., 1141.

11. Ibid., 1141ff.

12. Pirenne, *Medieval Europe*, 180; W. J. Ashley, *An Introduction to English Economic History and Theory*, 90 (1919).

13. Hamilton, "Caveat emptor," 1153.

14. Ibid., 1158–59.

15. Ibid., 1162.

16. Ibid., 1163.

17. Ibid.

18. Ibid., 1153.

19. Ibid., 1169ff.

20. Ibid., 1163–69.

21. This exception was not set down explicitly in earlier times when buyers' normal distrustfulness usually made them decline items not available to examine. Later, when trust developed, the requirement of opportunity to examine was made specific: *Barnard v. Kellogg*, 77 U.S. 383 (1870); *Way v. Ryther*, 165 Mass. 226, 42 N.E. 1128 (1896); *Kell v. Trenchard*, 142 F. 16 (4th Cir., 1905).

22. Hamilton, "Caveat emptor," 1166–69, 1173.

23. Samuel Williston, *The Law Governing Sales of Goods*, §194ff. (1948); William L. Prosser and W. Page Keeton, *Prosser and Keeton on Torts*, 5th ed., §95A (1984); *Uniform Commercial Code*, 10th ed., Article 2 (1987). For broader discussion of warranty, see chapter 5.

24. Often shortened to "fraud." Also called, especially in early law, "deceit." Prosser and Keeton, *Torts*, 5th ed., chap. 18. For broader discussion see chapter 6.

25. Hamilton, "Caveat emptor," 1138.

26. Y.B. 42 Ass. 259, pl. 8 (1367). This case was acknowledged as a precedent in the later *Dale's Case* and *Chandelor v. Lopus*, being identified in both cases as "42. Ass. 8" (see notes 27 and 33 below).

27. Cro. Eliz. 44, 78 Eng. Rep. 308 (1585).

28. Samuel Williston, "Liability for honest misrepresentation," 24 *Harvard Law Rev.* 415, 417 (1911). See the discussion of *Dale's Case* in chapter 5, at notes 3 and 28.

29. See detailed discussion in chapter 6.

30. Anthony Fitzherbert, *Fitzherbert's Abridgment*, Monstrauns de Faits [A showing of deeds], pl. 16 (1577).

31. Anthony Fitzherbert, *Natura Brevium*, 94c (1534).

32. Hamilton, "Caveat emptor," 1138.

33. Cro. Jac. 4, 79 Eng. Rep. 3 (1603); Hamilton, "Caveat emptor," 1166ff.

34. Sir James A. H. Murray, ed., *The Oxford English Dictionary* (1933–). The word was also spelled "bezor," "bezer," and "bezoar."

35. Credit for unearthing these facts is owed to Grant Gilmore, "Products liability: a commentary," 38 *U. of Chicago Law Rev.* 103, 107 (1970).

36. *The Random House Dictionary of the English Language*, 2d unabridged ed. (1987).

37. Gilmore, "Products liability," 108.

38. Prosser and Keeton, *Torts*, 5th ed.

39. Hamilton, "Caveat emptor," 1169ff.

40. No indication is available that this original case was published; the sole reference made to it occurs in the Exchequer case. See note 33 above.

41. *Southern v. Howard*, Cro. Jac. 468, 79 Eng. Rep. 400 (1618).

42. "Chandelor v. Lopus," 8 *Harvard Law Rev.* 282 (1894). A footnote mention of this missing third case was made in 73 Eng. Rep. 160, but the editor's notation identified it as a reference to the second case—further bad luck. See R. C. McMurtrie, "Chandelor v. Lopus," 1 *Harvard Law Rev.* 191 (1887); and Emlin McClain, "Implied warranties in sales,' 7 *Harvard Law Rev.* 213 (1893).

43. Hamilton, "Caveat emptor," 1169.

44. Ibid., 1169ff.

45. See note 47.

46. Hamilton, "Caveat emptor," 1186.

47. 2 Caines (N.Y.) 48 (1804).

48. Coke's statement is quoted by Kent from *Co. Litt.*, 102a (1633).

49. *Barnard v. Kellogg*; see note 21 above.

50. Karl N. Llewellyn, *Cases and Materials on the Law of Sales*, 210 (1930).

51. *Burns v. Lane*, 138 Mass. 350 (1885).

52. "The central purpose of the provisions of the Federal Trade Commission Act . . . is in effect to abolish the rule of caveat emptor which traditionally defined rights and responsibilities in the world of commerce.

That rule can no longer be relied upon as a means of rewarding fraud and deception." *FTC v. Sterling Drug*, 317 F.2d 669, 674 (2d Cir., 1963). The case cites similar statements made by the Supreme Court in *FTC v. Standard Education Society*, 302 U.S. 112, 58 S.C. 113 (1937) (see chapter 9, at note 24), and by the court of appeals in *Goodman v. FTC*, 244 F.2d 584 (9th Cir., 1957) (see chapter 10, at note 33). George J. Alexander wrote that "Caveat emptor is dead" in his *Honesty and Competition*, 226 (1967).

Chapter 5. Warranty

1. See chapter 4, at note 33ff.
2. *Crosse v. Gardner*, Carthew 90, 90 Eng. Rep. 656 (1689); Holt, K.B. 5, 90 Eng. Rep. 900 (1689); also *Cross v. Garnet* (same case), 3 Mod. 261, 87 Eng. Rep. 172 (1689)
3. See chapter 4, at note 27.
4. Although Holt did not use the word "warranty" in *Crosse v. Gardner*, he did in the related decision of 1700, *Medina v. Stoughton*, 1 Salk. 210, 91 Eng. Rep. 188 (1700); 1 Lord Raym. 593, 91 Eng. Rep. 1297 (1700); Holt, K.B. 208, 90 Eng. Rep. 1014 (1700). A seller sold lottery tickets as his own when they were not, and Holt judged that "where one having the possession of any personal chattel sells it, the bare affirming it to be his amounts to a warranty."
5. Samuel Williston, *The Law Governing Sales of Goods*, §196 (1948).
6. 3 T.R. 510, 3 D. & E. 51, 100 Eng. Rep. 450 (1789).
7. Williston, *Sales*, §198.
8. See chapter 4. note 47.
9. 13 Mass. 139 (1816).
10. *Budd v. Fairmaner*, 8 Bing. 48, 131 Eng. Rep. 318 (1831).
11. *Borrekins v. Bevan*, 3 Rawle (Pa.) 23 (1831).
12. 9 Watts (Pa.) 55 (1839).
13. Thomas A. Street, 1 *Foundations of Legal Liability*, 391 (1906).
14. Williston, Sales, §199.
15. James Kent, 2 *Commentaries on American Law*, 11th ed. (George Comstock, ed.), 633 (1867).
16. 51 N.Y. 198 (1872).
17. See also *White v. Miller*, 71 N.Y. 118 (1877). For a discussion of the New York and Pennsylvania warranty cases, see K. N. Llewellyn, "On warranty of quality, and society," 36 *Columbia Law Rev.* 699 (1936), and 37 *Columbia Law Rev.* 341 (1937).
18. 1 *Uniform Laws Annotated* (Sales) (1950, 1967), hereafter cited as USA.
19. 56 and 57 Victoria, c. 71 (1894).
20. *Heilbut v. Buckleton*, A. C. 30 (1913).
21. *Walker v. Kirk*, 72 Pa. Super. Ct. 534 (1919); *Michelin Tire v. Schulz*, 295 Pa. 140, 145 A. 67 (1929); *Pritchard v. Liggett & Myers*, 350 F.2d 479 (3d Cir., 1965).

22. *Pritchard v. Liggett & Myers.*

23. *Uniform Commercial Code*, 10th ed. (1987), hereafter cited as UCC. Section 2-313 states: "(1) Express warranties by the seller are created as follows: (a) Any affirmation of fact or promise made by the seller to the buyer which relates to the goods and becomes part of the basis of the bargain creates an express warranty that the goods shall conform to the affirmation or promise. (b) Any description of the goods which is made part of the basis of the bargain creates an express warranty that the goods shall conform to the description. (c) Any sample or model which is made part of the basis of the bargain creates an express warranty that the whole of the goods shall conform to the sample or model."

The Uniform Sales Act had contained what it described as "implied" warranties on descriptions and samples in its sections 14 and 16. Williston has explained, "It is customary to call the warranty in a sale by description an implied warranty, and for that reason this nomenclature has been preserved . . . in the Sales Act. The warranty might more properly, however, be called express, since it is based on the language of the parties" (Williston, *Sales*, §233, and the same point is stated for samples in §249). In the Uniform Commercial Code, therefore, these warranties are called express. See distinction between express and implied warranties in the text following this note.

24. The idea was established prior to sellerist times as well, although not using the terminology of "implied warranty." See text following this note; also chapter 4, at note 7ff.

25. When Coke (as quoted in Seixas, chapter 4, at note 48) declared that "the common law bindeth him not, unless there be a warranty in deed, or law," this was the warranty in law to which he referred (an implied warranty, in modern terms, though he called it "express"). See Street, 1 *Foundations of Legal Liability*, 379.

26. See Lord Holt's cases, at notes 2 and 4 above.

27. See chapter 4, note 26.

28. See chapter 4, note 27.

29. 2 *Blackstone's Commentaries* 451 (1771). That was not the last word in England. As late as 1849 a court ruled there was no implied warranty of title: *Morley v. Attenborough*, 3 Exch. 500. But by 1864 it was established for good: *Eichholz v. Bannister*, 17 C.B.N.S. 708, 112 E.C.L. 708. In America the argument was settled earlier: "If the seller has possession of the article, and he sells it as his own, and not as agent for another, and for a fair price, he is understood to warrant the title": James Kent, 2 *Commentaries on American Law*, 1st ed., 478 (1827). Also see Arthur Biddle, *Law of Warranty in the Sale of Chattels*, 212ff. (1884).

30. USA, §13.

31. UCC, §2-312. The warranty of title in the UCC is not called "implied," though not called "express" either. This appears to be a technicality,

to exempt section 2-312 from certain qualifications imposed on implied warranties by section 2-316. Still, the warranty of title is based on the sale itself and not on words of the seller.

32. Williston, *Sales*, §228.

33. 2 East 314, 102 Eng. Rep. 389 (1802).

34. The matter had been aired in *Stuart v. Wilkins*, 1 Doug. 18, 99 Eng. Rep. 15 (1778). but the warranty idea was actually quashed in that case, the justice said, although the record might give the opposite impression.

35. 4 Camp. 144, 171 Eng. Rep. 46 (1815).

36. *Gardiner* may seem to have involved an express rather than implied warranty, since it was based on the words "waste silk" in the sale note. But Ellenborough felt the buyer deserved to receive a commodity that would be not merely describable as waste silk, but also salable (merchantable) as such, the latter not being expressly stated.

37. William Prosser wrote an authoritative article on the subject, but cited no leading case: see "The implied warranty of merchantable quality," 27 *Minnesota Law Rev.* 117 (1943). Some relevant New York cases are discussed in Llewellyn, "On warranty of quality."

38. USA, §15(2).

39. UCC, §2-314: "(1) Unless excluded or modified (Section 2-316), a warranty that the goods shall be merchantable is implied in a contract for their sale if the seller is a merchant with respect to the goods of that kind."

40. Prosser, "Implied warranty," says the earliest case was *Jones v. Bright*, 5 Bing. 531, 130 Eng. Rep. 1167 (1829). But *Hoe v. Sanborn*, 21 N.Y. 552 (1860), which contains a long discussion of the history and rationale behind implied warranties, says it was *Bluett v. Osborne*, 1 Stark. 384, 171 Eng. Rep. 504 (1816).

41. 110 U.S. 108, 3 S.C. 537 (1884). Also see *Gray v. Cox*, 107 Eng. Rep. 999 (1825).

42. USA, §15(1).

43. UCC, §2-315: "Where the seller at the time of contracting has reason to know any particular purpose for which the goods are required and that the buyer is relying on the seller's skill or judgment to select or furnish suitable goods, there is unless excluded or modified under the next section an implied warranty that the goods shall be fit for such purpose."

44. Ibid., §§2-314, 2-315, 2-316.

45. Williston, *Sales*, §234.

46. UCC, §2-316.

47. Ibid.

48. William L. Prosser, "The fall of the citadel," 50 *Minnesota Law Rev.* 791 (1966).

49. 168 Wash. 456, 12 P.2d 409 (1932).

50. William L. Prosser and W. Page Keeton, *Prosser and Keeton on Torts*, 5th ed., §107 (1984).

51. 32 N.J. 358, 161 A.2d 69 (1960).

52. A prominent earlier case that attacked the "privity of contract" requirement was *MacPherson v. Buick*, 217 N.Y. 382, 111 N.E. 1050 (1916). It did not involve a sales representation express or implied, however; it was concerned with strict liability for negligence in manufacturing, a topic beyond the scope of this book: see Prosser and Keeton, *Torts*, 5th ed., chap. 17; and Richard A. Epstein, Charles O. Gregory, and Harry Kalven, Jr., *Cases and Materials on Torts*, 4th ed., chap. 8 (1984).

53. 3 TRR, ¶10,377, Report on Automobile Warranties (1970). Stanley Cohen, "Pollution threat may do more for consumers than laws, regulations," *Advertising Age*, March 2, 72 (1970).

54. Michael G. West, "Disclaimer of warranties—its curse and possible cure," 5 *Journal of Consumer Affairs* 154 (1971).

55. UCC, §2-313.

56. Ibid. §2-316.

57. Prosser and Keeton, *Torts*, 5th ed., 692; and see articles and cases cited therein.

58. "Guides for the advertising of warranties and guarantees," 16 CFR chap. 1, part 239 (1995)

Chapter 6. Misrepresentation

1. See chapter 4, at note 33ff.

2. 1 Lev. 102, 83 Eng. Rep. 318 (1663).

3. See chapter 5, at notes 2 and 4.

4. *Bree v. Holbech*, 2 Doug. 654, 99 Eng. Rep. 415 (1781), had the more usual result when an aggrieved party asked a court to find fraud without proving knowledge of falsity. Bree received a document called genuine but actually forged. The supplier Holbech was an apparently innocent party who believed the paper was good security and stated without qualification that it was. The receiver acknowledged the supplier "might not know of the falsehood," but argued for fraud because of the firm nature of the representation. The notion was far ahead of its time; it would be another century before intent to deceive would be defined to include "knowledge of lack of knowledge" as well as "knowledge of falsity." See remainder of this chapter.

5. See chapter 5, note 6.

6. See chapter 4, note 47.

7. 2 East 92, 102 Eng. Rep. 303 (1801).

8. What would this have accomplished in *Seixas* (see chapter 4, at note 47), where the agent was presumed innocent because he did not know the wood was not brazilletto? He did not know it was, either, yet he said it was firmly.

9. 11 M. & W. 401, 152 Eng. Rep. 860 (1843). "It is not necessary to show that the defendants knew the facts to be untrue; if they stated a fact which

was true for a fraudulent purpose, they at the same time not believing that fact to be true, in that case it would be both a legal and moral fraud."

10. *Restatement of the Law of Torts (Second)*, §526 (1977).

11. William L. Prosser and W. Page Keeton, *Prosser and Keeton on Torts*, 5th ed., §107 (1984).

12. L. R. 1 H. L., Sc. 145 (1867).

13. 14 A.C. 337, 58 L. J. chap. 864 (1889).

14. Some writers say this finding of fact was not reasonable, a point of evidence rather than of law. Samuel Williston, "Liability for honest misrepresentation," 24 *Harvard Law Rev.* 415, 439 (1911).

15. The fraud rule therefore, said Herschell, was as follows: "Fraud is proved when it is shown that a false representation has been made (1) knowingly, or (2) without belief in its truth, or (3) recklessly, careless whether it be true or false. . . . The third is but an instance of the second, for one who makes a statement under such circumstances can have no real belief in the truth of what he states. To prevent a false statement being fraudulent, there must, I think, always be an honest belief in its truth. And this probably covers the whole ground, for one who knowingly alleges that which is false, has obviously no such belief."

16. Williston, "Liability for honest misrepresentation," 439.

17. Prosser and Keeton, *Torts*, 5th ed., 740.

18. Ibid., 740.

19. Ibid., §107.

20. Ibid., 745.

21. See chapter 4, note 23, and chapter 5, note 18.

22. See chapter 5, at note 48.

23. See chapter 5, following note 52.

24. Prosser and Keeton, *Torts*, 5th ed., chap. 17.

25. Or "strict responsibility." Ibid.

26. See chapter 7, note 30.

27. See detailed discussion in chapter 8.

28. Prosser and Keeton, *Torts*, 5th ed., 728.

Chapter 7. Opinion and Value Statements and Puffery

1. For warranty, see definitions in chapter 5, following note 18, and in note 23. For misrepresentation, see William L. Prosser and W. Page Keeton, *Prosser and Keeton on Torts*, 5th ed., 728, 755 (1984).

2. See discussions in chapters 2 and 3.

3. It did not begin with *Chandelor v. Lopus*; see chapter 4, note 33. Earl W. Kintner, as quoted although not cited in Frank Thayer, *Legal Control of the Press*, 4th ed., 647 (1962), has identified *Chandelor* as an exponent of the puffing privilege: "The court went on to say that the seller's simple declaration that the stone was a Bezor stone was mere legitimate puffing

of the article for sale." The court did not say that, although it did say that "every one in selling his wares will affirm that his wares are good." The affirmation about the stone, however, was treated by the court as one of fact rather than of value, although whether a thing was or wasn't a bezar-stone apparently was something on which people could differ. *Chandelor* was never cited as a precedent for opinion or puffery statements by any source prior to Kintner, who was FTC chairman from 1959 to 1961.

4. Yelv. 21, 80 Eng. Rep. 15 (1602).

5. Yelverton's report, dated Mich. 44 and 45 Eliz., was brief probably because it was merely a description by counsel of an earlier case, from Mich. 39 Eliz. That was noted by Justice Buller in *Pasley v. Freeman*; see note 10 below.

6. 3 Bulst. 94, 81 Eng. Rep. 81 (1615); Cro. Jac. 386, 79 Eng. Rep. 331 (1615).

7. Cro. Jac. 386, 387: "[I]t was a matter which lay in his own view and conusance; and if he doubted of the weight thereof, he might have weighed it; and was not bound to give credence to another's speech; and being his own negligence, he is without remedy: as where one buys an horse upon warranting him to have both his eyes, and he hath but one eye, he is remediless; . . . The whole Court was of that opinion: although it was said, that there was apparent fraud here in him who affirmed." The ruling was based on Brian's decision; see chapter 11, at note 2.

8. See chapter 6, at note 2.

9. This other report was labeled "*Leakins v. Clissel*," but is the same case: 1 Sid. 146, 82 Eng. Rep. 1022 (1663). "Land or jewels," the court explained further, "have more value to one man than to another, but otherwise is rent or other things certain, because the value is knowable and measurable to all."

10. 3 T.R. 51, 3 D. & E. 51, 100 Eng. Rep. 450 (1789). See chapter 5, at note 6, and chapter 6, at note 5.

11. Vol. 1, 101, pl. 16 (1668). The rule was discussed in chapter 8 of this book's first edition, omitted here; see last subsection of this chapter.

12. *Vernon v. Keys*, 12 East 632, 637, 104 Eng. Rep. 246, 249 (1810).

13. *Seixas* (see chapter 4, note 47). The portion prior to the parentheses referred to Buller's references to *Crosse v. Gardner* and *Medina v. Stoughton*, in which Lord Holt had helped establish the warranty concept; see chapter 5, at notes 2 and 4. The portion following the parentheses was drawn from Buller's reference to *Harvey v. Young*. *Harvey* and *Pasley* involved fraud, not warranty, and Buller had not discussed the exemption of opinion statements from warranty considerations. Kent's statement, nonetheless, appears to have brought the opinion exemption into warranty law in America.

14. *Cochrane v. Cummings*, 4 U.S. (Pa.) 250, 1 L.Ed. 820 (1802), tended to disavow the opinion rule by describing as facts what were usually called opinions.

In *Gimblin v. Harrison*, 2 Ky. 315 (1804), a buyer charged misrepresentation of land as "second-rate," the land actually being inferior to that description. However, the seller had reported what a third party had said, and thus was excused without discussion of the possible status of "second-rate" as an opinion statement. "Second-rate" is a "superlative" rarely encountered in American advertising, but once used successfully by Avis ("We're Number 2") to help capture business from the third, fourth, etc., car rental companies rather than from number one Hertz.

In *Sherwood v. Salmon*, 2 Day (Conn.) 128 (1805) (see chapter 11 at note 5). Sherwood's counsel argued that "the assertions of the defendant amount to no more than the expression of an opinion." He also claimed the defects were "discoverable by the exercise of due care," and therefore caveat emptor applied. The court decided for Sherwood on the second argument; thus the first was not discussed. Later review at chancery (equity) rather than at law, 5 Day (Conn.) 439 (1813), determined that the seller's misrepresentations were of material facts, citing *Cochrane v. Cummings*, but the earlier decision was not voided.

15. 5 Johns. (N.Y.) 354 (1810).

16. The decision stated: "Per Curiam. There was no express warranty or fraud proved in this case. The plaintiff below purchased the wagon, on sight, and the assertion of the defendant that it was worth more than its real value, furnishes no ground of action (1 Johns. Rep. 97. 274. 414. 4 Johns. Rep. 228. 4 Johns. Rep. 421). The judgment below must be reversed." The ruling appears to have been based on the authority of *Seixas* (see chapter 4. note 47), since three of the five cases cited found a basis in that case.

In 1827 Kent cited *Davis* along with *Harvey* and *Baily* in support of a similar rule: "A mere false assertion of value, when no warranty is intended, is no ground of relief to a purchaser, because the assertion is a matter of opinion, which does not imply knowledge, and in which men may differ. Every person reposes at his own peril in the opinion of others, when he has equal opportunity to form and exercise his own judgment." 2 *Commentaries on American Law*, 1st ed., 381 (1827). In his second edition, 2 *Commentaries* 485 (1832), Kent added to the above the following: "Simplex commendatio non obligat [mere recommendation does not bind]." No source was cited.

Kent apparently sided with Buller (from *Pasley*; see note 10 above) in feeling the opinion exemption should not apply when the opinion was stated falsely. His statement above is reminiscent of Buller, and the comment directly following it is even more so: "If the seller represents what he himself believes as to the qualities or value of an article, and leaves the determination to the judgment of the buyer, there is no fraud or warranty in the case." In support he cited *Jendwine v. Slade*, 2 Esp. Rep. 572, 170 Eng. Rep. 459 (1797).

17. 6 Metcalf (Mass.) 246 (1843).

18. This was dictum applying to statements between sellers and buyers; the actual decision went against the misrepresentor because he was a third party.

19. 3 Allen (Mass.) 380 (1862).

20. Walton H. Hamilton, "The ancient maxim caveat emptor," 40 *Yale Law Journal* 1133, 1186 (1931).

21. 11 Cush. (Mass.) 348 (1853). The decision continued, "And there are other cases, in which it is held that an action will not lie, when he who sustains damage from a false affirmation might, by ordinary vigilance and attention, have ascertained that the statement on which he acted was false. See Harvey v. Young, Yelv. 21; Baily v. Merrell. . . ."

22. 148 Mass. 504, 20 N.E. 107 (1889).

23. *Kimball v. Bangs*, 144 Mass. 321, 11 N.E. 113 (1887). See also *Gordon v. Parmelee*, 2 Allen (84 Mass.) 212 (1861); *Parker v. Moulton*, 114 Mass. 99 (1873); *Bishop v. Small*, 63 Me. 12 (1874). *Bishop* included this twist on the usual explanation as to why value statements should be exempt: "It is not so much that such representations are not enough to amount to fraud and imposition, but that they are, so to speak, too much for that purpose. Most of them are too preposterous to believe."

24. *Vulcan Metals v. Simmons*, 248 F. 853 (2d Cir., 1918).

25. *Gordon v. Butler*, 105 U.S. 553 (1881).

26. Another Supreme Court case, *Southern Development v. Silva*, 125 U.S. 247, 8 S.C. 881 (1888), was similar in topic and result.

27. *American School of Magnetic Healing v. McAnnulty*, 187 U.S. 94, 23 S.C. 33 (1902).

28. 241 U.S. 64 (1916).

29. *Uniform Commercial Code*, 10th ed., §2-313(2) (1987), hereafter cited as UCC. This result has been called "out of accord" with common law holdings that value statements under some conditions were held to be warranties: George Bogert, "Express warranties in sales of goods," 33 *Yale Law Journal* 14, 32 (1923).

30. It is possible in warranty law to obtain a ruling that an alleged opinion statement is in reality a factual statement, provided it makes a positive and unequivocal assertion of a fact. But warranty rulings favoring buyers are not made on the basis of what a statement implies (UCC, §2-313). This is one of the areas in which warranty law has not supplanted misrepresentation law in offering protection to the consumer in modern times.

31. *Stebbins v. Eddy*, 4 Mason 414, 22 Fed. Cas. 1192 (1827).

32. *Edgington v. Fitzmaurice*, L. R. 29 Ch. D. 459 (1885). Among American cases applying this rule, Samuel Williston, *The Law Governing Sales of Goods*, §628b (1948), gives strong credit to *Spead v. Tomlinson*, 73 N.H. 46, 59 A. 376 (1904).

33. "A representation of the state of mind . . . is a misrepresentation if the state of mind in question is otherwise than as represented. Thus, a statement that a particular person . . . is of a particular opinion or has a particular intention is a misrepresentation if the person in question does

not hold the opinion or have the intention asserted." *Restatement of the Law of Torts (Second)* §525, comment c (1977)

34. L. R. 28 Ch. D. 7, 51 L.T.N.S. 718, 49 J. P. 182 (1884).

35. See cases cited by *Restatement of the Law of Torts (Second)* as authority for section 539. One of them, *Andrews v. Jackson*, 168 Mass. 266, 47 N.E. 412 (1897), is noteworthy for being distinguished from *Deming v. Darling*. Both were decided in Massachusetts and dealt with vague claims about securities. In *Andrews* it was held that statements that certain notes were "as good as gold" could be intended to represent facts not knowable to the buyer, such as that the notes are known to be valid or that their maker is of known integrity and financial ability. The same holding would have been reasonable in *Deming*.

36. *Restatement of the Law of Torts (Second)*. The developments indicated by section 539 are due in part to the widening of the definition of fraud to include lack of knowledge of truth as well as knowledge of falsity, as discussed in chapter 6.

37. Ibid.

38. 11 Mich. 68 (1862).

39. *Picard* was based largely on summaries of the law by Joseph Story, *Equity Jurisprudence*, §198 (1836); William W. Story, *Sales*, §170 (1847); and Kent, 2 *Commentaries on American Law*, lst ed., 382, which suggest that the decision represents a natural development of Ellenborough's rule (see above, at note 12). In other words, while Ellenborough's rule was used at first to eliminate opinions from liability, the same principle was now being used to make them liable.

40. *Restatement of the Law of Torts (Second)*, §542, comment on clause (b). See also cases on which the clause is based,

41. Ibid., §542, comment on clause (c).

42. *Mattauch v. Walsh Bros.*, 136 Iowa 225, 113 N.W. 818 (1907).

43. *Restatement of the Law of Torts (Second)*, §542, comment on clause (d).

44. Ibid., §538A.

45. Little has been said about the buyer's role, but the assumption at law apparently is that the buyer will just as routinely make counterstatements which "blow down" the object that the seller is blowing up. No name has been given to this process of deflating.

46. See chapter 4, at note 51.

47. See chapter 4, at note 47.

48. Ivan L. Preston, "Why use false puffery?" *New York Times*, February 25, business section, 17 (1973).

49. H. Ross Ford, Jr., April 17, 1973. Mr. Ford pointed out that I had incorrectly implied that all the new personnel had moved from Philadelphia. Only some had done so.

50. The comments were, of course, freely offered only after they were solicited.

51. "ANA, 4 A's, hit FTC's proposed drug ad rules," *Advertising Age*, July 7, 1 (1969).

Chapter 8. The Federal Trade Commission

1. Federal Trade Commission Act, 38 Stat. 719 (1914), hereafter cited as FTC Act.

2. Ira M. Millstein, "The Federal Trade Commission and false advertising," 64 *Columbia Law Rev.* 439, 450 (1964).

3. FTC Act, section 5.

4. Millstein, "False advertising," 450ff.; Earl W. Kintner, *A Primer on the Law of Deceptive Practices*, 16–17 (1971); Milton Handler, "Jurisdiction of the Federal Trade Commission over false advertising," 31 *Columbia Law Rev.* 527, 539 (1931); FTC Annual Report 6 (1916).

5. *Sears, Roebuck v. FTC*, 258 F. 307 (7th Cir., 1919).

6. 253 U.S. 421, 40 S.C. 572 (1920).

7. *FTC v. Raladam*, 283 U.S. 643, 51 S.C. 587 (1931).

8. Rewriting of section 5: 52 Stat. 114, 115 (1938).

9. See detailed discussion in chapter 6.

10. *Sears, Roebuck v. FTC*. See note 5.

11. FTC Act, §5(b).

12. Even the violation of an order had no effective penalty apart from unattractive publicity until the Wheeler-Lea Amendments provided for a $5,000 fine; §14, 52 Stat. 115 (1938).

13. Edward F. Cox, Robert C. Fellmuth, and John E. Schulz, *Nader's Raiders: Report on the Federal Trade Commission* (1969); *Report of the American Bar Association Commission to Study the Federal Trade Commission* (1969).

14. *Printers' Ink*, November 23, 68 (1911), and several other 1911 issues beginning with November 16, 2; "Untrue advertising," 36 *Yale Law Journal* 1155 (1927); Milton Handler, "False and misleading advertising," 39 *Yale Law Journal* 22 (1929); "Developments in the law: deceptive advertising," 80 *Harvard Law Rev.* 1005, 1018 (1967).

15. A survey reported in 1956 showed that most states had never used the statute, and only a few had used it more than a handful of times. "Note: The regulation of advertising," 56 *Columbia Law Rev.* 1018, 1063 (1956).

16. "Deceptive advertising," 1123.

17. "Untrue advertising," 1157–60; Handler, "False and misleading advertising," 32.

18. *State v. Shaengold*, 13 Ohio Law Reporter 130 (1915).

19. It was also implied in *FTC v. Winsted*, 258 U.S. 483, 42 S.C. 384 (1922). See detailed discussion in chapter 13, at note 3.

20. 291 U.S. 67, 54 S.C. 315 (1934). See chapter 13, at note 5.

21. See chapter 6, at note 13.

22. 127 F.2d 792 (2d Cir., 1942).

23. The commissioners can be wrong, of course, and so are subject to appellate review. Review is limited, however, to matters of law and to interpretation of the facts upon which assessment of deceptiveness was based. Section 5(c) of the FTC Act provides that "the findings of the Commission as to the facts, if supported by evidence, shall be conclusive." The commission has been reversed at times when courts found no evidence for the stated findings of fact. But the courts have generally declined to interfere with the commission's interpretation that the potential to deceive exists.

The criterion of "capacity to deceive" was later replaced by "likeliness to mislead." *Cliffdale Associates*, 103 FTC 110 (1984), including a "Policy Statement on Deception," appendix at 174. The change made no difference in the general idea that the potential, i.e., deceptiveness, is the criterion, rather than actual deception. Other changes made in 1984 are discussed in chapter 9.

24. *Sears, Roebuck v. FTC*; see text at note 10 above.

25. See note 8.

26. 125 F.2d 679 (7th Cir., 1942).

27. Henry Bernstein, "New group asked rule on ads for 'identical' brands," *Advertising Age*, January 18, 1, and "We are what we are," January 25, 12 (1971).

28. Stanley Cohen, "Attack on nutrition-thwarting TV ads intensifies: food folk befuddled," *Advertising Age*, February 22, 10 (1971).

29. *ITT Continental Baking*, 83 FTC 865 (1973), modified, 90 FTC 181 (1977).

30. John Revett, "ITT strongly counters FTC charges, but execs split on Wonder ad claims," *Advertising Age*, July 17, 1 (1972). See also comments by Professor Yale Brozen in "Prof. Brozen, Pitofsky clash in Wonder case," ibid., May 22, 2 (1972).

31. *ITT Continental*. The commission soft-pedaled its charges against "uniqueness" in this final order. Still it ordered that Wonder Bread not be represented as an essential source of a nutritional value, where there were other sources of the same or similar values, unless the claim could be substantiated. For other cases that stopped uniqueness claims, see I. Preston, "The Federal Trade Commission's identification of implications as constituting deceptive advertising," 57 *Cincinnati Law Rev.* 1243, at 1284 (1989).

32. *Pfizer*, 81 FTC 23 (1972).

33. See I. Preston, *The Tangled Web They Weave* (1994). See also article cited in note 31.

34. FTC Act: "In determining whether any advertising is misleading, there shall be taken into account (among other things) not only representations made or suggested . . . but also the extent to which the advertisement fails to reveal facts material in the light of such representations or material with respect to consequences which may result. . . ."

35. 132 F.2d 165 (7th Cir., 1942).

36. 186 F.2d 52 (4th Cir., 1950). Similar cases included: *Charles of the Ritz v. FTC*, 143 F.2d 676 (2d Cir., 1944); and *Kalwajtys v. FTC*, 237 F.2d 654 (7th Cir., 1956).

37. 127 F.2d 765 (7th Cir., 1942).

38. *J. B. Williams*, 68 FTC 481 (1965), modified, *J. B. Williams v. FTC*, 381 F.2d 884 (6th Cir., 1967), modified, 72 FTC 865 (1967).

39. *American Brands et al.*, consent orders, 80 FTC 455 (1972).

40. Trade Regulation Rule for the Incandescent Lamp (Light Bulb) Industry, 2 TRR, ¶7972 (1970).

41. Trade Regulation Rule on Posting of Minimum Octane Numbers, 16 CFR 422, 4 TRR, ¶38,023 (1972) .

42. 36 FTC 563 (1943). Reversed by the Supreme Court, *Siegel v. FTC*, 327 U.S. 608, 66 S.C. 758 (1946), but not on this point.

43. *Gelb*, 33 FTC 1450 (1941), and *Gelb v. FTC*, 144 F.2d 580 (2d Cir., 1944). See chapter 9, at note 31.

44. *ITT Continental*, see notes 29–31; *Pfizer*, see note 32; *DuPont*, 81 FTC 169 (1971). Not all of the original allegations were dropped in these cases.

45. "Howard's research will draw debate until substantiated," *Advertising Age*, June 19, 16 (1972).

46. Ernest Gellhorn, "Proof of consumer deception before the Federal Trade Commission," 17 *Kansas Law Rev.* 559 (1969); "Does ad mislead consumers?" *Advertising Age*, November 13, 56 (1972). This topic has also been taken up at length by this author in the pieces cited in notes 31 and 33.

47. *Sun Oil*, 84 FTC 247 (1974).

48. 289 F. 985 (6th Cir., 1923), modifying *L. B. Silver*, 4 FTC 73 (1921).

49. The court cited the decision in *McAnnulty* (see chapter 7, note 27) as controlling, and also cited *Harrison v. U.S.*, 200 F. 662 (6th Cir., 1912), as determining that a scheme to defraud "can not be found in any mere expression of honest opinion."

50. *Raladam v. FTC*, 42 F.2d 430 (6th Cir., 1930), reversing *Raladam*, 12 FTC 363 (1929).

51. The case went to the Supreme Court, which did not reverse the ruling: *FTC v. Raladam*, note 7 above. The case is known primarily for its questioning of the FTC's jurisdiction over advertising, as discussed at note 7.

52. *Raladam*, 24 FTC 475 (1937).

53. *FTC v. Raladam*, 316 U.S. 149, 62 S.C. 966 (1942), following *Raladam v. FTC*, 123 F.2d 34 (6th Cir., 1941). A somewhat related case, *Scientific Manufacturing v. FTC*, 124 F.2d 640 (3d Cir., 1941), setting aside *Scientific Manufacturing*, 32 FTC 493 (1941), involved a person engaged not in trade but in voicing opinions about a matter of trade. For this reason alone the FTC's jurisdiction was voided, and the court stated, "Surely Congress did not intend to authorize the Federal Trade Commission to foreclose expression of honest opinion in the course of one's business of voicing opinion." The

opinions, describing harmful effects on food of cooking utensils made of aluminum, were found false but also honestly held.

54. *Justin Haynes v. FTC*, 105 F.2d 988 (2d Cir., 1939). For other cases see "Note: Proving the falsity of advertising: the McAnnulty rule and expert evidence," 32 *Indiana Law Journal* 350 (1957).

55. However, a case involving Standard Brands suggested that the commission may have mellowed sometimes to make decisions supported by the opinions of a minority of experts: "Margarine case reveals FTC shift in minority scientific opinion view," *Advertising Age*, January 8, 1 (1973).

56. Hearing before Administrative Law Judge Harry Hinkes, September 10 (1973). See note 47.

57. Actually one of the classes saw an alternate ad in which a car pulls two boxcars and a caboose along a railroad track. The claims made in that ad were virtually identical to those in the "Coliseum" version, so I discuss the project here as though it involved only one ad.

58. *Sun Oil* complaint; note 47 above. The alleged misrepresentations are paraphrased here for simplification. The "Coliseum" ad was only one of the ads alleged to contain these misrepresentations.

59. David Ogilvy, *Confessions of an Advertising Man*, 140 (1963).

60. The case resulted in an order against the claims: see note 47.

61. The hearings resulted in a new regulation: Price Comparison Advertising, chap. Ag 124, Department of Agriculture, State of Wisconsin, June 18 (1973).

Chapter 9. Reasonable Consumers or Other Consumers?

1. The law has traditionally called it the "reasonable man standard." While I used that phrase in this book's first edition of 1975, I now recognize compelling reasons to make it gender-free (whether the lawbooks change or not).

2. The FTC has given no specific name to this standard. The terms "credulous man standard" and "lowest standard of intelligence" have been used by other sources: *Truth in Advertising: A Symposium of the Toronto School of Theology*, 2–3, 30–34 (1972); Ira M. Millstein, "The Federal Trade Commission and false advertising," 64 *Columbia Law Rev.* 439, 458–62 (1964).

3. FTC Act, §5(b), see chapter 8, note 1; Ira M. Millstein, "The FTC and false advertising," 64 *Columbia Law Rev.* 483–87 (1964); "Developments in the law—deceptive advertising," 80 *Harvard Law Rev.* 1005, 1023–25 (1967).

4. See chapter 2, at note 10.

5. "Developments in the law: deceptive advertising," 80 *Harvard Law Rev.* 1082 (1967); Millstein, "False advertising," 494; Edward F. Cox, Robert C. Fellmuth, and John E. Schulz, *Nader's Raiders: Report on the Federal Trade Commission* (1969).

6. Millstein, "False advertising," 462–65; "Deceptive advertising," 1027–38.

7. *Restatement of the Law of Torts (Second)*, §283 (1977). Section 283A adds that a child must act as would a reasonable person of like age, intelligence, and experience under like circumstances.

8. *Vaughan v. Menlove*, 3 Bing. N.C. 468, 132 Eng. Rep. 490 (1837). For other cases and references see Reporter's Notes to §283 of *Restatement of the Law of Torts*.

9. See chapter 6, following note 11.

10. The term *contributory negligence* is not always used, but the idea is based on that concept. William L. Prosser and W. Page Keeton, *Prosser and Keeton on Torts*, 5th ed., §108 (1984).

11. Ibid.

12. See extended discussions in chapters 3, 7, and 10.

13. FTC Act, §5(b); see chapter 8, note 1.

14. *FTC v. Universal Battery*, 2 FTC 95 (1919).

15. See also *FTC v. A. A. Berry*, 2 FTC 427 (1920); *FTC v. Alben-Harley*, 4 FTC 31 (1921); *FTC v. Williams Soap*, 6 FTC 107 (1923); *Alfred Peats*, 8 FTC 366 (1925).

16. See discussion above at note 1ff.

17. *Restatement of the Law of Torts (Second)*, §283, comment c.

18. Francis H. Bohlen, "Mixed questions of law and fact," 72 *Univ. of Pennsylvania Law Rev.* 111, 113 (1923).

19. 8 FTC 177 (1924).

20. *John C. Winston v. FTC*, 3 F.2d 961 (3d Cir., 1925).

21. *Nugrape*, 9 FTC 20 (1925); *Ostermoor*, 10 FTC 45 (1926), but set aside in *Ostermoor v. FTC*, 16 F.2d 962 (2d Cir., 1927); *William F. Schied*, 10 FTC 85 (1926); *Good Grape*, 10 FTC 99 (1926); *Hobart Bradstreet*, 11 FTC 174 (1927); *Frank P. Snyder*, 11 FTC 390 (1927); *Dr. Eagan*, 11 FTC 436 (1927); *Berkey & Gay Furniture*, 12 FTC 227 (1928), but set aside in *Berkey & Gay Furniture v. FTC*, 42 F.2d 427 (6th Cir., 1930); *Northam-Warren*, 15 FTC 389 (1931), but set aside in *Northam-Warren v. FTC*, 59 F.2d 196 (2d Cir., 1932); *Fairyfoot Products*, 20 FTC 40 (1934), affirmed in *Fairyfoot v. FTC*, 80 F.2d 684 (7th Cir., 1935).

22. *Standard Education Society*, 16 FTC 1 (1931).

23. *FTC v. Standard Education Society*, 86 F.2d 692 (2d Cir., 1936).

24. 302 U.S. 112, 58 S.C. 113 (1937).

25. Ibid., 116: "It was clearly the practice of respondents through their agents, in accordance with a well matured plan, to mislead customers. . . ."

26. 114 F.2d 33 (2d Cir., 1940).

27. *Moretrench v. FTC*, 127 F.2d 792 (2d Cir., 1942). This was the same judge who once had rejected similar claims on the grounds that "there are some kinds of talk which no man takes seriously . . ."; *Vulcan Metals v. Simmons*; see chapter 7, note 24.

28. See notes 29 and 30 below.

29. *D.D.D. v. FTC* (1942), see chapter 8, note 26; *Aronberg v. FTC* (1942), see chapter 8, note 35; *Gulf Oil v. FTC*, 150 F.2d 106 (5th Cir., 1945); *Parker*

Pen v. FTC, 159 F.2d 509 (7th Cir., 1946). In the latter case the FTC's role was said to be to "protect the casual, one might say the negligent, reader, as well as the vigilant and more intelligent. . . ." A much-used quotation, cited in *Aronberg, Gulf Oil*, and *Gelb* (see note 31 below), stated, "The law is not made for the protection of experts, but for the public—that vast multitude which includes the ignorant, the unthinking, and the credulous, who, in making purchases, do not stop to analyze, but are governed by appearances and general impressions." *Florence v. Dowd*, 178 F. 73 (2d Cir., 1910). The latter was a pre-FTC case with evidence of deliberate deception.

30. *Charles of the Ritz v. FTC*, 143 F.2d 676 (2d Cir., 1944), following *Charles of the Ritz*, 34 FTC 1203 (1942).

31. *Gelb v. FTC*, 144 F.2d 580 (2d Cir., 1944), following *Gelb*, 33 FTC 1450 (1941).

32. 39 FTC 357 (1944).

33. *Carlay v. FTC*, 153 F.2d 493 (1946).

34. *Allen B. Wrisley v. FTC*, 113 F.2d 437 (7th Cir., 1940); also later in *Buchsbaum v. FTC*, 160 F.2d 121 (7th Cir., 1947).

35. See detailed discussion of such cases in chapter 7.

36. *Lorillard v. FTC* (1950), see chapter 8, note 36; *Independent Directory*, 47 FTC 13 (1950) (but see dissent by Commissioner Mason); *Goodman v. FTC*, 244 F.2d 584 (9th Cir., 1957); *FTC v. Sewell*, 353 U.S. 969, 77 S.Ct. 1055 (1957) (see chapter 10, at note 32); *Bantam Books v. FTC*, 275 F.2d 680 (2d Cir., 1960) (but see questions raised by Judge Moore); *Exposition Press v. FTC*, 295 F.2d 869 (2d Cir., 1961); *Giant Food v. FTC*, 322 F.2d 977 (D.C. Cir., 1963); *FTC v. Colgate*, 380 U.S. 374, 85 S.Ct. 1035 (1965) (see chapter 14, at notes 7–11).

37. 63 FTC 1282 (1963).

38. In *Papercraft*, 63 FTC 1965, 1997 (1963), Commissioner MacIntyre protested that the retreat from the extreme ignorant person position was unfortunate. The majority opinion had withdrawn from protecting the "foolish or feebleminded," and MacIntyre dissented that, "Should this observation be construed as a retreat from our long-held position that the public as a whole is entitled to protection, including even 'the ignorant, the unthinking, and the credulous,' then the result may well be confusion."

39. *Truth in Advertising*, 31.

40. "It might be said that the test of consumer competence generally employed by the Commission appears to approximate the least sophisticated level of understanding possessed by any substantial portion of the class of persons to whom the advertisement is addressed." Personal correspondence to Peter B. Turk from Gale T. Miller, law clerk, Bureau of Consumer Protection, Federal Trade Commission, December 6, 1971. The "class of persons" assumed generally consists of adults. Special consideration for representations made to children (see note 7) was recognized in *FTC v. Keppel*, 291 U.S. 304, 54 S.Ct. 423 (1934). As for other groups, Miller wrote: "It is the position of the staff that advertising geared towards other special audiences, such as

the ghetto dweller, the elderly, and the handicapped, might also be subjected to a more rigorous test than is applied to advertisements addressed to the public at large."

41. For extensive discussion and citations, see Preston, "The definition of deceptiveness in advertising and other commercial speech," 39 *Catholic Univ. Law Rev.* 1035 (1990).

42. Ibid.

Chapter 10. The FTC and Puffery

1. The ill-fated Printers' Ink statute (see chapter 8, at note 14) experienced the first two of these trends. Undoubtedly its authors wanted to control those opinion or value statements that might deceive. But the criminal sanctions made it unlikely that the courts would use the statute to prohibit anything but literally false facts. In *People v. Clarke*, 252 App. Div. (N.Y.) 122 (1937), the court said the statute prohibited "representations of fact," but found that some of the statements involved were only opinion. Conscious untruth was not found to exist in the case. Factual misrepresentations would have been liable even if not made with conscious knowledge of their untruth, but the court would not hold opinion statements liable unless that requirement were met.

2. *FTC v. Universal Battery*, see chapter 9, note 14.

3. See cases in chapter 9, note 15; also *Nugrape, Schied, Good Grape, Bradstreet, Snyder,* and *Eagan,* chapter 9, note 21. These decisions paralleled the type of analysis offered by §539, *Restatement of the Law of Torts (Second)* (1977). See chapter 7, at note 36.

4. *Electric Appliance*, 2 FTC 335 (1920).

5. *Vulcan Metals v. Simmons*, see chapter 7, at note 24, and chapter 9, at note 27.

6. *Ostermoor*, 10 FTC 45 (1926).

7. *Ostermoor v. FTC*, 16 F.2d 962 (2d Cir., 1927).

8. *Fairyfoot Products*, 20 FTC 40 (1934).

9. *Fairyfoot v. FTC*, 80 F.2d 684 (7th Cir., 1935).

10. *Kidder Oil*, 29 FTC 987 (1939).

11. *Kidder Oil v. FTC*, 117 F.2d 892 (7th Cir., 1941).

12. 52 Stat. 114, 115 (1938); see chapter 8, at note 8.

13. *Cong. Record*, 74th Cong., 2d sess., vol. 80, pt. 6, 6592, May 4 (1936).

14. *Moretrench*, 28 FTC 297 (1939).

15. *Moretrench v. FTC*, see chapter 9, note 27.

16. See chapter 9, at note 24.

17. See chapter 9, note 29. The court also provided this definition: "Puffing refers, generally, to an expression of opinion not made as a representation of fact."

18. Some other cases that attacked elements of puffery, though not labeling it as that: *David V. Bush*, 14 FTC 90 (1930); *Tarbell*, 14 FTC 442

(1931); *Howe v. FTC*, 148 F.2d 561 (9th Cir., 1945), affirming *Howe*, 36 FTC 685 (1943).

19. *Carlay v. FTC*, 153 F.2d 493 (7th Cir., 1946), setting aside *Carlay*, 39 FTC 357 (1944).

20. *Langendorf*, 43 FTC 132 (1946), may appear to contradict this point, since it involved FTC action against a company's claim to have "the bread that baking experts judged America's finest." What was called deceptive, however, was not the opinion claim about "finest" but a factual representation that experts had made such a judgment. The commission's findings stated, "No tests have been made by qualified experts."

21. 46 FTC 162 (1949). The record of the decision includes a report of the complaint, with date.

22. If the *Carlay* court reversal convinced the FTC, while the *Ostermoor* and *Kidder* reversals had not, the reason probably was that *Carlay* cited common law precedents favoring puffery while the others did not.

23. *Washington Mushroom*, 53 FTC 368 (1956).

24. *Postal Life and Casualty Insurance*, 54 FTC 494 (1957).

25. *Necchi*, 53 FTC 1040 (1957).

26. *Tanners Shoe*, 53 FTC 1137 (1957).

27. See chapter 7, note 28.

28. *Gulf Oil v. FTC*, discussed at note 17 above, said something similar, though without citing *New South Farm*. For similar cases see *Dobbs Truss*, 48 FTC 1090 (1952); *C. H. Stuart*, 53 FTC 1127 (1957); *Unicorn Press*, 47 FTC 258 (1950). But did the FTC temporarily disdain the *New South Farm* rule when it allowed as puffery the claim that Celanese was "different from any type of fiber ever made" although there was no evidence of difference between this fiber and other synthetics? *Celanese*, 50 FTC 170 (1953).

29. *Steelco*, 46 FTC 643 (1950), affirmed, *Steelco v. FTC*, 187 F.2d 693 (7th Cir., 1951).

30. *National Health Aids*, 49 FTC 1661 (1952), affirmed, *FTC v. National Health Aids*, 108 F.Supp. 340 (1952).

31. See note 26.

32. *Sewell*, 50 FTC 806 (1954), reversed, *Sewell v. FTC*, 240 F.2d 228 (9th Cir., 1956), but affirmed, *FTC v. Sewell*, 353 U.S. 969, 77 S.C. 1055 (1957), citing *Standard Education* and *Algoma*.

33. *Goodman*, 52 FTC 982 (1956), affirmed, *Goodman v. FTC*, 244 F.2d 584 (9th Cir., 1957).

34. See chapter 9, note 32.

35. 55 FTC 354 (1958).

36. The hearing examiner, now called administrative law judge, is the FTC official who conducts the preliminary hearing, hears the testimony of witnesses, oversees the introduction of other evidence, and renders a decision for the commissioners' consideration. The commissioners may agree or disagree with the judge in rendering the agency's final decision.

37. 59 FTC 1231 (1961).

38. 61 FTC 840 (1962).

39. 59 FTC 1452 (1961). The case has a history of appeals on matters other than puffery; see chapter 14, at notes 7–11.

40. As discussed at notes 6, 10, and 19 above.

41. *Western Radio*, 63 FTC 882 (1963), modified by *Western Radio v. FTC*, 339 F.2d 937 (7th Cir., 1964); *Wilmington Chemical*, 69 FTC 828 (1966); *Waltham Watch*, 60 FTC 1692 (1962); *Heinz W. Kirchner*, see chapter 9, note 37. In *Kirchner* the FTC refused to admit Swim-Ezy's "unsinkability" as puffery; the refusal was upheld on appeal in *Heinz W. Kirchner v. FTC*, 337 F.2d 751 (9th Cir., 1964). However, in accepting the term *invisible* the FTC appears to have treated it as puffery, although not calling it that. The commissioners compared it to "inconspicuousness," and invisibility is the maximum degree of that. Thus they were treating "invisible" perhaps overgenerously as an exaggeration of an actual quality. They passed up the chance to argue on the grounds of the *New South Farm* definition, at notes 27–28 above, that invisibility was a characteristic not literally present and thus not eligible to be called puffery. Also in *Kirchner* the FTC consented to regard two other matters as puffery.

42. *Carnation*, consent order, 77 FTC 1547 (1970). Stanley Cohen, "FTC hits loaded comparisons and 'deception' in food ads," *Advertising Age*, November 1, 21, 76 (1971).

43. Trade Regulation Rule; see chapter 8, note 40.

44. Speech before New York State Bar Association, food, drug, and cosmetics law section, January 1971; "Advertising needs 'fundamental attitude change': FTC's Jones," *Advertising Age*, February 1, 68 (1971). A similar comment had been made by Milton Handler: "The advertiser should be credited with sufficient business acumen not to waste valuable space on statements which serve no function"; *Trade Regulations*, 3d ed., 981 (1960). On such argument the FTC should find that puffery claims are material, i.e., they affect the buyers' purchasing decisions; see chapter 8, following note 25; chapter 3, at note 7. However, the FTC does not: *Thompson Medical*, 104 FTC 648, at note 45 (1984).

45. *Pfizer*, 81 FTC 23, 64 (1972).

46. 102 FTC 395, 752 (1983).

47. Published as appendix to *Cliffdale Associates*, 103 FTC 110 (1984), at 174, originally a letter dated Oct. 14, 1983, from FTC Chairman James C. Miller to Rep. John D. Dingell.

48. Firestone, 112 FTC 591 (1989).

49. C & H Sugar (1995). For eventual publication in FTC Decisions; until then, copies available from Public Reference Branch, FTC, Washington, DC 20580.

50. I. Preston, "The definition of deceptiveness in advertising and other commercial speech," 39 *Catholic Univ. Law Review* 1035 (1990).

51. I. Preston, "False or deceptive advertising under the Lanham Act: analysis of factual findings and types of evidence," 79 *Trademark Reporter* 508 (1989).

Chapter 11. Additional Kinds of Puffery, Beginning with Obvious Falsity

1. See chapter 2, at note 10.
2. Y.B. 11 Edw. IV, 6, 10 (1471). Note that warranty and misrepresentation (deceit) are combined in a confusing way. That was typical in early times, before the two concepts were established as separate legal actions; William L. Prosser and W. Page Keeton, *Prosser and Keeton on Torts*, 5th ed., 728 (1984). Establishment of Brian's rule was aided considerably by its mention in *Ekins v. Tresham*; see chapter 6, note 2.
3. See chapter 7, notes 6–7.
4. Brian's rule was stated in *Baily*, Cro. Jac. 387, and it was cited in *Baily*, 3 Bulst. 94, 95, as "11 E. 4."
5. 2 Day (Conn.) 128 (1805). See chapter 7, note 14.
6. See chapter 7, note 23.
7. 80 U.S. 379 (1871).
8. 153 Mass. 60, 26 N.E. 416 (1891).
9. 215 Mo. 312, 114 S.W. 979 (1908).
10. But for a strong opposing view just one year later, see *Mabardy v. McHugh*, 202 Mass. 148, 88 N.E. 894 (1909).
11. See chapter 9. at note 24.
12. *Uniform Commercial Code*, 10th ed., §2-313 (1987) (hereafter cited as UCC).
13. Samuel Williston, *The Law Governing Sales of Goods*, §207 (1948). The same source notes, however, that a general warranty of soundness is not intended to cover any obvious defects. To warrant a blind horse as "sound" is to mean "sound except as to his eyes." Thus the obvious falsity rule remains but reduced to matters that are truly obvious.
14. *Restatement of the Law of Torts (Second)* (1977). Curiously, the attached comment refers to the horse example in note 13, causing one to wonder whether section 541 means precisely what it says.
15. *Restatement of the Law of Torts.* An attempt to redraft in 1964 was rejected; see note 16.
16. Francis Bohlen, 13 *American Law Institute Proceedings* 342 (1936). This historical trend was emphasized in 1964 when William Prosser proposed a new version of section 540, to read: "The recipient of a fraudulent misrepresentation is justified in relying upon its truth without investigation, unless he knows or has reason to know of facts which make his reliance unreasonable." Certain ALI members thought this was a return to the notion that the buyer's contributory negligence would negate an action for fraudulent misrepresentation. Prosser said it concerned the issue of "notice," not

negligence. Professor R. E. Keeton observed that the developments since the first drafting of the *Restatement* "have all been in the line of giving the fool somewhat greater protection against the defrauder than he had in those days." 4 *ALI* 509 (1964). In a heated discussion adjourned for one year and renewed, ALI members voted 67–39 to retain the original wording of section 540, which thoroughly negated the buyer's obligation to inspect. 42 *ALI* 322 (1965).

17. Remaining are rulings, regarding both warranties and misrepresentations, covering the situation where buyers choose to inspect and their inspection successfully detects the truth about a defect. UCC, §§2-313, 2-316; *Restatement of the Law of Torts (Second)*, §541. If buyers buy the object anyway, they must rely upon anything they happen to know. Similarly, if they happen to indicate that they will rely on their own inspection, then it, whether successful or not, supersedes sellers' liability. But those are not serious impediments to consumerism because they are matters of volunteering to inspect rather than being obligated to inspect.

18. *Williams v. Rank & Son Buick*; see chapter 2, note 10.

19. The dissenting opinion in the 4–3 decision, ibid., stated: "At a time when there is so much emphasis on consumer protection the majority, in effect, revitalizes the old caveat emptor doctrine without specifically mentioning it."

20. *Marriott et al. v. Ramada*, 826 F. Supp. 726 (SDNY 1993).

21. For FTC, see text of chapter 8, at note 25; for common law, see *Restatement of the Law of Torts (Second)*, §§525, 538.

22. *Lever Bros.*, affadavit of voluntary compliance, TRR 1967–70, Transfer Binder, ¶18,711 (1969). The company claimed it was a spoof; "Case talks to FTC," *Advertising Age*, November 8, 148 (1971).

23. "Case talks to FTC," 148.

Chapter 12. Puffing with Social and Psychological Claims

1. See chapter 3, at note 7ff.

2. See chapter 3, at note 1.

3. The analysis that follows owes much to David Potter, "The institution of abundance: advertising," chap. 8 of his *People of Plenty* (1954).

4. See chapter 8, at notes 29–31.

5. "Leigh R. Isaacs, "Psychological advertising: a new area of FTC regulation," 1972 *Wisconsin Law Rev.* 1097 (1972).

6. *J. B. Williams*, consent order, 81 FTC 238 (1972). The advertising agency, Della Femina, Travisano, and Partners, was also a party to the order.

Chapter 13. Puffing with Literally Misdescriptive Names

1. These decisions have been made not by specific regulatory actions, but merely by the lack of such actions. To suggest that such lack of action amounts to deliberate decisions seems reasonable in the light of other cases we will see in which action was taken.

2. Stone China: *Harker China*, consent order, 62 FTC 1382 (1963); Plyhide: *Sales Development Corp.*, consent order, 62 FTC 1461 (1963); Six Month Floor Wax: *Continental Wax v. FTC*, 330 F.2d 475 (2d Cir., 1964); Made in USA: I swear I saw a citation to this once, but I can't find it now, so caveat reader. There's no question, though, that goods made in Japan have been so mislabeled: *Giant Plastics*, consent order, 61 FTC 179 (1962), among others; *National Laboratories of St. Louis*, 63 FTC 948 (1963).

3. 258 U.S. 483, 42 S.C. 384 (1922).

4. 288 U.S. 212, 53 S.C. 335 (1933).

5. 291 U.S. 67, 54 S.C. 315 (1934). See chapter 8, at note 20.

6. An exception occurred when American producers of Danish pastry used labels such as "Genuine Danish pastry." The FTC recognized that as an attempt to falsely reinstate the original meaning in the consumer's mind, and prohibited such labels when not literally true. Earl W. Kintner, *A Primer on the Law of Deceptive Practices*, 118 (1971).

7. *Institute of Hydraulic Jack Repair*, 63 FTC 127 (1963).

8. *Ship 'n Shore*, consent order, 58 FTC 757 (1961); modified order, 70 FTC 631 (1966). FTC statement on use of the term *Madras: FTC Advertising Alert*, No. 6. June 30 (1965).

9. *United Garment*, 66 FTC 711 (1964).

10. *Pan American Cigar*, consent order, 72 FTC 752 (1967).

11. *Carter Products v. FTC*, 268 F.2d 461 (9th Cir., 1959).

12. *Grand Rapids Furniture v. FTC*, 134 F.2d 332 (3d Cir., 1943).

13. *Virginia Products*, 29 FTC 451 (1939).

14. *United States Testing Co.*, consent order, 61 FTC 1312 (1962).

15. *National Commission on Egg Nutrition*, 92 FTC 848 (1978). For additional cases, see Ivan L. Preston, "The FTC's identification of implications as constituting deceptive advertising," 57 *Cincinnati Law Rev.* 1243, §14 (1989).

16. Fed. Alcohol Admin. Act, §5.22, 27 CFR 12 (1973); "Brandies," *Consumer Reports*, November, 603 (1967).

17. FAAA, §5.22, 27 CFR 34 (1973); "Scotch whiskies,' *Consumer Reports*, November, 622 (1968).

18. FAAA, §4, 27 CFR 12 (1973); "Champagne," *Consumer Reports*, November, 638 (1969).

19. Felix Kessler, "A territorial question brings strife to home of Roquefort cheese," *Wall Street Journal*, November 13, 1 (1972).

20. It backfired because the FTC Act entitled the commission to go beyond common law without attention to past limitations, meaning its decisions on misdescription could involve setting precedent rather than just following it. No precedent existed that misdescription was unfair to the public, but none said it was fair, either. For *Winsted*, see note 3 above.

21. 311 F.2d 358 (1st Cir.), following *Korber Hats*, 60 FTC 642 (1962).

22. See discussion of those earlier times in chapter 4, at note 7ff.

23. "Some McDonald's patties cited for short weight," *New York Times*, July 25, 46 (1973). Perhaps McDonald's should have said "approximately."

The FTC once stopped the selling of rugs by the description "9 x 12" when they were actually 103" x 139". The statement "All sizes approximate" had been used, but was adjudged impermissible for describing such a difference. The commission said, however, "The word approximate will perhaps cover an inch or two departure from the norm." *Gimbel Bros.*, 61 FTC 1051 (1962). Re the issue of where one draws the line, see the discussion of permissible puffing versus impermissible exaggeration in chapter 7, following note 45.

24. Charlotte Montgomery, "Consumerism today: where it's at," *Context*, DuPont Company, No. 1 (1973).

Chapter 14. Puffing with Mock-Ups

1. See details below, particularly following note 11, on the legality of such actions.

2. *Aluminum Company of America*, 58 FTC 265 (1961).

3. Colgate, 58 FTC 422 (1961).

4. *Standard Brands*, 56 FTC 1491 (1960).

5. *Libby-Owens-Ford*, 63 FTC 746 (1963), affirmed, *Libby-Owens-Ford v. FTC*, 352 F.2d 415 (6th Cir., 1965).

6. *Carter Products*, 63 FTC 1651 (1963).

7. *Colgate*, 59 FTC 1452 (1961); see also chapter 10, at note 39, and Daniel Seligman, "The great sandpaper shave: a real-life story of truth in advertising," *Fortune*, December, 131 (1964).

8. 310 F.2d 89 (1st Cir., 1962).

9. *Colgate*, 62 FTC 1269 (1963).

10. *Colgate v. FTC*, 326 F.2d 517 (1st Cir., 1963).

11. *FTC v. Colgate*, 380 U.S. 374, 85 S.C. 1035 (1965).

12. "Johnny Carson hits 'dishonest' ads on his show," *Advertising Age*, October 31, 167 (1966).

13. Maurine Christopher, "Creative folk say they don't dig FTC rules," *Advertising Age*, 253 March 16, 3 (1970).

14. *Philadelphia Inquirer*, July 10, 1-B (1973).

15. *Campbell Soup*, consent order, 77 FTC 664 (1970). Another result of the case was the development of Students Opposing Unfair Practices (SOUP), a law students' organization that participated in the case and urged the FTC to make Campbell's not only stop using marbles but admit in future ads that it had practiced deception in doing so. The latter request was denied on a 3–2 vote of the commissioners in which one dissenter noted that Campbell's violation was particularly flagrant since it was committed in the face of the Supreme Court's decision about mock-ups in *Colgate*. The remedy requested caught on later, however, under the name of "corrective advertising."

16. *Borden*, consent order, 78 FTC 686 (1971).

17. *DuPont*, 81 FTC 169 (1972). For withdrawal of mock-up charges see: TRR 1970–73 Transfer Binder, ¶19,849 (1971).

18. A demonstration showing Black Flag bug killer superior to Raid used roaches immune to one of Raid's critical ingredients. Typical American household roaches had no such immunity. *American Home Products*, consent order, 81 FTC 579 (1972). When Easy-On starch and a competitor were sprinkled on white shirts and ironed, the other starch scorched and Easy-On did not. The iron was superheated. Ibid. Easy Off's superiority over another window cleaner was "shown," but the other brand's directions for use were not followed. Ibid. Sudden Change facial lotion was shown to conceal lines, wrinkles, and puffs, but in the "after" picture the woman was wearing not only Sudden Change but also eyeliner, eye shadow, lipstick, cream and powder, complexion base, and compact powder. *Bishop Industries*, consent order, 77 FTC 380 (1970). Toy racers were "shown" traveling at swift speeds by the use of camera angles greatly exaggerating actual performance. See chapter 2, note 2. Dancerina doll appeared to walk and dance on its own; but in reality could stay up only with human assistance. Ibid. Mickey Spillane took a shower with Dove in a Lifebuoy commercial when he couldn't get the Lifebuoy to lather enough. "Did Lever use bootlegged lather in '64 for Lifebuoy tv commercial?" *Advertising Age*, August 16, 6 (1971).

19. Ivan L. Preston, *The Tangled Web They Weave*, chap. 8 (1994).

20. See cases, all 1993, involving Michael S. Levey and Positive Response Marketing, National Media Corp., Hasbro Inc., and ad agency Griffin Bacal. To be published in *FTC Decisions*; available before then from Public Reference Branch, FTC, Washington, DC 20580.

Chapter 15. Puffery's Immunity Should Be Eliminated

1. Many more examples of puffery could have been included. While it is essential to demonstrate that a large number exist, I stopped at an arbitrary point to reflect space considerations and avoid reader burnout.

2. See chapter 3, note 1.

3. See chapter 7, note 24.

4. *Standard Education Society*; see chapter 9 at note 24ff., and Chapter 10 at notes 14–18.

5. Chapter 10, at note 19ff.

6. *The Bruskin Report*, no. 40, New Brunswick, N.J. (1971).

7. A later Bruskin survey found even higher belief levels. Hallmark's "When you care enough to send the very best" was rated completely true by 62 percent of those surveyed, "Kodak makes your pictures count" by 60 percent, and Zenith's "The quality goes in before the name goes on" by 49 percent. "Adbeat," *Advertising Age*, Oct. 24, 94 (1977).

8. Herbert J. Rotfeld and Kim B. Rotzoll, 10 *Journal of Advertising*, 16–20, (1980). Another report of the study with additional information appeared in Rotfeld and Rotzoll, "Puffery vs. fact claims—really different?" *Current Issues and Research in Advertising* (James H. Leigh and Claude R. Martin, eds.), 85–103 (1981).

9. Terence A. Shimp, "Do incomplete comparisons mislead?" 18 *Journal of Advertising Research* 21–27 (1978).

10. Morris B. Holbrook, "Beyond attitude structure: toward the informational determinants of attitude," 15 *Journal of Marketing Research*, 545–56 (1978).

11. Jerry C. Olson and Philip A. Dover, "Cognitive effects of deceptive advertising," 15 *Journal of Marketing Research* 29–38 (1978).

12. Bruce G. Vanden Bergh and Leonard N. Reid, "Effects of product puffery on response to print advertisements," *Current Issues and Research in Advertising 1980* (James H. Leigh and Claude R. Martin, eds.), 123–34 (1980).

13. Bruce G. Vanden Bergh and Leonard N. Reid, "Puffery and magazine ad readership," 44 *Journal of Marketing* 78–81 (1980).

14. Herbert Rotfeld and Ivan L. Preston, "The potential impact of research on advertising law," 21 *Journal of Advertising Research*, April, 9–18 (1981).

15. Terence A. Shimp and J. Thomas Yocum, "Advertising inputs and psychophysical judgments in vending-machine retailing," 58 *Journal of Retailing*, Spring, 95–113 (1982).

16. Bruce G. Vanden Bergh and Nancy Fink, "Is believability of puffery affected by brand credibility?" 60 *Journalism Quarterly*, Summer, 344–48 (1983).

17. Bruce G. Vanden Bergh and Nan Bartlett, "Puffery and magazine ads," 59 *Journalism Quarterly*, 645–48 (1982).

18. Gary Kurzbard and Lawrence C. Soley, "Puffery and industrial advertising readership and evaluation," *Proceedings, American Academy of Advertising*, 104–7 (1984).

19. Robert G. Wyckham, "Implied superiority claims," 27 *Journal of Advertising Research*, February–March, 54–63 (1987).

20. Gregory S. Carpenter, Rashi Glazer, and Kent Nakamoto, "Meaningful brands from meaningless differentiation: the dependence on irrelevant attributes," 31 *Journal of Marketing Research*, August, 339–50 (1991).

21. See index references to "Federal Trade Commission" and "Evidence" in Ivan L. Preston, *The Tangled Web They Weave* (1994). See also citations at that book's pp. 213–14 to articles on these topics.

22. Fara Warner, "Code revisions would limit 'puffery,'" *Wall Street Journal*, May 17, B8 (1995); Alicia Mundy, "Alicia Mundy," *Adweek*, July 17, 21 (1995); Thom Weidlich, "The UCC takes aim at slogans," *National Law Journal*, June 12, 1 (1995). These articles are based on proposed revisions to the Uniform Commercial Code, as discussed later in this chapter.

23. I first identified the Puffery Implication in my article "The FTC's identification of implications as constituting deceptive advertising." 57 *Univ. of Cincinnati Law Rev.* 1243–1310 (1989). It is further discussed in my book, *The Tangled Web They Weave*.

24. Letter from Douglas K. Ritter, Division Manager, Marketing Communications, AT&T, June 29, 1994.

25. Letter from Frank L. Policano, Trademark and Copyight Counsel, AT&T, July 27, 1944. He added, "AT&T has ceased using the expression for some time and we have withdrawn our service mark application."

26. See chapter 10, at note 46.

27. Mentioned as an illustrative example in a commission opinion on another matter: *Bristol-Myers*, 102 FTC 21, 321 (1983).

28. See chapter 3, note 1; chapter 5, passim; chapter 7, at note 29.

29. *Uniform Commercial Code*, Revised Article 2, Sales, National Conference of Commissioners on Uniform State Laws, Draft, October 1 (1995). Available in typed form only, NCCUSL, Chicago.

30. David Ogilvy, *Confessions of an Advertising Man*, 84 (1963).

31. Sid Bernstein, " 'The public is not a moron' . . . but??" *Advertising Age*, July 16, 14 (1973).

32. Sissela Bok, *Lying* (1978).

Table of Cases

To find full cases citations see page references set in italics.

Alfred Peats (1925), *216*
Allen B. Wrisley v. FTC (1940), *217*
Aluminum Company of America (1961), 168, *224*
American Brands et al (1972), *214*
American Home Products (1972), *225*
American School of Magnetic Healing v. McAnnulty (1902), 79, *210*, 214
Andrews v. Jackson (1897), *211*
Aronberg v. FTC (1942), *99*, 216–17

Bailey v. Merrell (1615), *70*, 72–73, 140–41, 143, 147, 177, 209, 210, 221
Bantam Books v. FTC (1960), *217*
Barnard v. Kellogg (1870), *201*, 202
Baxter v. Ford Motor (1932), *58*
Berkey & Gay Furniture (1928), reversed, Berkey & Gay Furniture v. FTC (1930), *216*
Bishop v. Small (1874), *210*
Bishop Industries (1970), *225*
Bluett v. Osborne (1816), *205*
Borden (1971), 174, *224*
Borrekins v. Bevan (1831), *203*
Bradford v. Manly (1816), *49*, 49–51
Bree v. Holbech (1781), *206*
Brian's rule, *140*, 208, 221
Bristol-Myers (1949), *128*, 128–30
Bristol-Myers (1983), *227*
Brown v. Castles (1853), *76*, 77, 78, 178, 180, 198
Buchsbaum v. FTC (1947), *217*
Budd v. Fairmaner (1831), 50, *203*
Burns v. Lane (1885), *202*

C & H Sugar (1995), 137, *220*

Campbell Soup (marbles) (1970), 173–74, *224*

Campbell Soup (1992), 7, *198*

Carlay (Ayds) (1944), reversed, Carlay v. FTC (1946), *121*, 131, 128–29, 133, 180, *217, 219*

Carnation (1970), 133, *220*

Carter Products v. FTC (Liver Pills) (1959), *223*

Carter Products (Rise) (1963), Carter Products v. FTC (1963), 169, *224*

Celanese (1953), *219*

Chandelor v. Lopus, (1603), 34, *35*, 35–40, 45, 47–51, 54, 59, 62, 82, 202, 207–8

Charles of the Ritz (1942), affirmed, Charles of the Ritz v. FTC (1944), *120, 214, 217*

C. H. Stuart (1957), *219*

Cliffdale (1984), *199, 213, 220*

Cochrane v. Cummings (1802), *208*, 209

Colgate (Dental Cream) (1961), 168, *224*

Colgate (Rapid Shave) (1961), remanded, Colgate v. FTC (1962), modified, Colgate (1963), remanded, Colgate v. FTC (1963), reversed, FTC v. Colgate (1965), 132–33, 169–71, 172, *199*, *217, 224*

Continental Wax v. FTC (1964), *223*

CPC International (1990), *198*

Cross v. Garnet (1689), *203*

Crosse v. Gardner (1689), 47–48, 53, 62, *203*, 208

Dale's Case (1585), *34*, 48, 51, 53, 202

Dannon (1962), *132*

David V. Bush (1930), *218*

Davis v. Meeker (1810), *74*, 209

D.D.D. v. FTC (1942), *97*, 97–98, 216

Deming v. Darling (1889), 76, *198*, 211

Derry v. Peek, (1889), *64*, 64–66, 96

Dobbs Truss (1952), *219*

Dr. Eagan (1927), *216*, 218

DuPont (1972), *214, 224*

Edgington v. Fitzmaurice (1885), *210*

Eichholz v. Bannister (1864), *204*

Ekins v. Tresham (1663), *62*, 70, 71, 72, 73, 177, 221

Electric Appliance (1920), *216*, 218

Exposition Press v. FTC (1961), *217*

Fairyfoot Products (1934), affirmed, Fairyfoot Products v. FTC (1935), 126, *216, 218*

Firestone (1989), 136–37, *220*

First Brands (1992), *198*
Florence v. Dowd (1910), *217*
Frank P. Snyder (1927), *216*, 218
FTC v. A. A. Berry (1920), *216*
FTC v. Alben-Harley (1921), *216*
FTC v. Algoma (1934), *96*, *160–61*, 219
FTC v. Colgate (1965). *See* Colgate (Rapid Shave)
FTC v. Gratz (1920), *91*
FTC v. Keppel (1934), *217*
FTC v. National Health Aids (1952), affirmed (1952), *219*
FTC v. Raladam (1931). *See* Raladam
FTC v. Raladam (1942). *See* Raladam
FTC v. Royal Milling Co. (1933), *160*
FTC v. Sewell (1957). *See* Sewell
FTC v. Standard Education Society (1936, 1937). *See* Standard Education Society
FTC v. Sterling Drug (1963), *203*
FTC v. Universal Battery (1919), *216*, 218
FTC v. Williams Soap (1923), *216*
FTC v. Winsted Hosiery (1922), *159*, 159–60, 162, *212*, 223

Gardiner v. Gray (1815), 55–56, *205*
Gelb (1941), affirmed, Gelb v. FTC (1944), *214*, *217*
General Electric (1993), 7, *198*
General Motors v. FTC (1940), *119*
Giant Food v. FTC (1963), *217*
Giant Plastics (1962), *223*
Gimbel Bros. (1962), *224*
Gimblin v. Harrison (1804), *208*
Good Grape (1926), *216*, 218
Goodman (1956), affirmed, Goodman v. FTC (1957), *203*, 217, *219*
Gordon v. Butler (1881), *210*
Gordon v. Parmelee (1861), 143, 144, *210*
Grand Rapids Furniture v. FTC (1943), 161, *223*
Gulf Oil v. FTC (1945), 128, *199*, *216*, 217, 219

Häagen Dazs (1994), 7, *198*
Harker China (1963), *223*
Harrison v. U.S. (1912), *214*
Harvey v. Young (1602), *69*, 70, 71, 72, 73, 75, 177, 208, 209, 210
Hasbro (and its ad agency, Griffin Bacal) (1993), 7, *198*, 225
Haskelite v. FTC (1942), *101*
Hawkins v. Pemberton (1872), *51*
Haycraft v. Creasey (1801), 63, *206*
Heilbut v. Buckleton (1913), 52, *203*

Heinz W. Kirchner (1963), modified, Heinz W. Kirchner v. FTC (1964), *122*, 220
Henningsen v. Bloomfield Motors (1960), *58*, 58–59, 60
Hobart Bradstreet (1927), *216*, 218
Hoe v. Sanborn (1860), *205*
Howe (1943), affirmed, Howe v. FTC (1945), *219*

Independent Directory (1950), *217*
Institute of Hydraulic Jack Repair (1963), 161, *223*
ITT-Continental (1973), modified (1977), 98, 155, *213*, 214

J. B. Williams (Geritol) (1965), modified, J. B. Williams v. FTC (1967), modified (1967), *214*
J. B. Williams (Vivarin) (1972), *222*
Jendwine v. Slade (1797), *209*
Jenny Craig (1995), 7, *198*
John C. Winston (1924), reversed, John C. Winston v. FTC (1925), *117*, 117–18, 216
Jones v. Bright (1829), *205*
Judd v. Walker (1908), *144*, 144–45
Justin Haynes v. FTC (1939), *215*

Kalwajtys v. FTC (1956), *214*
Kell v. Trenchard (1905), *201*
Kellogg Bridge v. Hamilton (1884), *56*, 56–57
Kidder Oil (1939), reversed, Kidder Oil v. FTC (1941), 126–27, 133, *218*, 219
Kimball v. Bangs (1887), *210*
Korber Hats (1962), affirmed, Korber Hats v. FTC (1962), *163*, 163–64, *223*
Kraft (1991), affirmed (1992), 7, *198*

Langendorf (1946), *219*
L. B. Silver (1921), modified, L. B. Silver v. FTC (1923), *103*, 104, *214*
Leakins v. Clissel (1663), 71, *208*
Lever Bros. (1969), *222*
Libby-Owens-Ford (1963), affirmed, Libby-Owens-Ford v. FTC (1965), 169, *224*
Lifetime (1961), *132*
Liggett & Myers (1958), *131*, 131–32
Lorillard v. FTC (1950), *100*, 217

Mabardy v. McHugh (1909), *221*
MacPherson v. Buick (1916), *206*
Marriott et al v. Ramada (1993), 148, *222*
Mattauch v. Walsh Bros. (1907), 83, *211*
Mattel (1971), 6, *198*

McFarland v. Newman (1839), *50,* 52, 54
Medbury v. Watson (1843), *74,* 75, 178
Medina v. Stoughton (1700), *203,* 208
Michael S. Levey and Positive Response Marketing (1993), *225*
Michelin Tire v. Schulz (1929), *203*
Mr. Coffee, FTC (1993), 7, *198*
Mobil Oil, FTC (1992), *198*
Monstrauns de Faits (no title given) (1577), 35, *202*
Moretrench (1939), affirmed, Moretrench v. FTC (1942), *96,* 119, 121, 127–28,
    129, 179, *216,* 218
Morley v. Attenborough (1849), *204*

National Commission on Egg Nutrition (1978), 162, *223*
National Health Aids (1952), affirmed, FTC v. National Health Aids (seeking
    enforcement) (1952), 130–31, *219*
National Laboratories of St. Louis (1963), 159, *223*
National Media Corp. (1993), *225*
Necchi (1957), *219*
Nissan (1994), *198*
Northam-Warren (1931), reversed, Northam-Warren v. FTC (1932), *216*
Nugrape (1925), *216,* 218

Orkin Exterminating (1992), 7, *198*
Ostermoor (1926), reversed, Ostermoor v. FTC (1927), 125–26, 133, *216, 218,*
    219

Pan American Cigar (1967), *223*
Papercraft (1963), *217*
Parker v. Moulton (1873), *210*
Parker Pen v. FTC (1946), *216–17*
Parkinson v. Lee (1802), *54,* 54–56, 59
Pasley v. Freeman (1789), *48,* 63, *70,* 70–71, 72–73, *74–75,* 178, 208, 209
People v. Clarke (1937), *218*
Pfizer (1972), 98–99, 134, *213,* 214, *220*
Picard v. McCormick (1862), *81,* 81–82, 85
Postal Life and Casualty Insurance (1957), *219*
Pritchard v. Liggett & Myers (1965), *203,* 204

Raladam (1929), reversed, Raladam v. FTC (1930), affirmed on this point,
    Raladam v. FTC (1931), *212, 214*
Raladam (1937), reversed, Raladam v. FTC (1941), reversed, FTC v. Raladam
    (1942), 104, *214*
Revlon (1993), 7, *198*
Roberts v. French (1891), *144*

Sales Development Corp. (1963), *223*

Scientific Manufacturing (1941), reversed, Scientific Manufacturing v. FTC (1941), *214–15*

Sears, Roebuck v. FTC (1919), 91, 93–94, 96, *212*, 213

Seixas and Seixas v. Woods (1804), *42*, 42–44, 48–51, 54, 59, 63, 74, 87, 202, 206, 208, 209

Sewell (1954), reversed, Sewell v. FTC (1956), reversed, FTC v. Sewell (1957), 217, *219*

Sherwood v. Salmon (1805), reviewed, Sherwood v. Salmon (1813), *141*, 141–43, 209

Ship 'n Shore (1961), modified, Ship 'n Shore (1966), *223*

Siegel (1943), reversed, Siegel v. FTC (1946), 101–02, *214*

Slaughter's Administrator v. Gerson (1871), *143*, 143–44

Smith v. Land and House (1884), *80*, 80–81, 86

Southern v. Howard (1618), 40, *202*

Southern Development v. Silva (1888), *210*

Spead v. Tomlinson (1904), *210*

Standard Brands (Blue Bonnet) (1960), 168, *224*

Standard Education Society (1931), modified, FTC v. Standard Education Society (seeking enforcement) (1936), modified, FTC v. Standard Education Society (1937), *118*, 118–19, 121, 127, 129, 146, *203*, 216, 219, 225

State v. Shaengold (1915), *212*

Stebbins v. Eddy (1827), *210*

Steelco (1950), affirmed, Steelco v. FTC (1951), 130, *219*

Sterling Drug (Bayer), 102 FTC 395 (1983), *134*

Stouffer Foods (1994), 7, *198*

Stuart v. Wilkins (1778), *205*

Sun Oil (1974), 102–110, *214*, 215

Tanners Shoe (1957), 130, 131, *219*

Tarbell (1931), *218*

Taylor v. Ashton (1843), *63*

Thompson Medical (1984), *220*

Topper (1971), *198*

Unicorn Press (1950), *219*

United Garment (1964), *223*

United States Testing Co. (1962), 162, *223*

Unocal (1994), 7, *198*

U.S. v. New South Farm (1916), *79*, 130, *199*, 219, 220

Vaughan v. Menlove (1837), *216*

Veasey v. Doton (1862), *75*

Vernon v. Keys (1810), *208*

Virginia Products (1939), 161–62, *223*
Volvo (1991), 7, *198*
Vulcan Metals v. Simmons (1918), *210*, 216, 218

Walker v. Kirk (1919), *203*
Waltham Watch (1962), *220*
Washington Mushroom (1956), 130, *219*
Way v. Ryther (1896), *201*
Western Bank of Scotland v. Addie (1867), *64*, 64–65
Western Radio (1963), modified, Western Radio v. FTC (1964), *220*
White v. Miller (1877), *203*
William F. Schied (1926), *216*, 218
Williams v. Rank & Son Buick (1969), 9–10, 139, 147, *198*, 222
Wilmington Chemical (1966), *135*, *220*

Y.B. 42 Ass. 259 (no name given) (1367), *202*

Index

Accidental events: as cause of legal decisions, 38–40, 47, 72–76
Administrative law judge, 215, 219. SEE ALSO Hearing Examiner
Advertising: credibility of, 94, 169, 188
Advertising Age, 24, 102, 200, 201, 206, 212, 213, 214, 215, 220, 222, 224, 225, 227
Advil claim, 188
Affirmative disclosure, 101, 133, 171
Air-conditioner claims, 9–10, 24, 115, 139, 140, 147
Alcoa claims, 168, 181
Alexander, George J., 203
Alka Seltzer claim, 150
All detergent claim, 149
Alpacuna claim, 101–2
American Advertising Federation, 193
American Bar Association: report on FTC, 212
American Dental Association, 23
American law, as derived from English law. SEE English law
American Law Institute, 81, 190, 221
Anderson, Justice, 34, 40, 48, 53
Aquinas, St. Thomas, 30, 33, 35
Atlanta Journal claim, 200
AT&T claim, 189

Aunt Jemima, 173
Avis claim, 17, 209
Ayds claim (Carlay case), 121, 128–29, 131

Baker's dozen, 164
Bare assertions, 69–74, 177
Barnum, P. T.: puffery claim, 13, 21
Bathtub ring claim, 173
Battery claims, 116, 124–25
Bayer claims, 98, 134, 136, 189
Beer claims, 114–15, 121, 122, 147, 148, 154, 167
Bernstein, Sid: articles of, 200, 227
"Best"; and "best possible," claims of. SEE Puffery, categories of
Bezar-stone claim. SEE *Chandelor v. Lopus* (Table of Cases)
Bird, Larry, 147
Black, Hugo, Justice, 118, 121, 146
Black Flag claim, 225
Blackstone, Sir William: *Commentaries,* 53
Blue Bonnet claim, 168
Blue vitriol claim, 51
Boat draught claim, 143–44
Bohlen, Francis, 146, 216
Bok, Sissela, 193
Borden claim, 174
Bounty claim, 149
Bowen, Lord, 80–81

Brandeis, Judge Louis, 91
Brazilletto claim. SEE *Seixas & Seixas v. Woods* (Table of Cases)
Breeder's claim. SEE *L. B. Silver v. FTC* (Table of Cases)
Brian, Judge, 140, 141, 208, 221
Bruskin, R. H., Associates: survey, 180, 181, 225
Budd, Mr., 50
Buller, Justice, 48, 52, 63, 71, 73–75, 178, 208, 209
Bunion plaster claim, 126
Buyers: trust and distrust by, 4, 29, 31, 36–37, 45, 49, 63, 69, 76–78, 83, 87, 118, 121, 136–37, 140, 145–46, 147, 201; responsibility of, for deception, 9–10; obligation and opportunity of, to determine truth independently of sellers' claims, 9–10, 29–32, 35, 41–45, 47–49, 52–53, 54–57, 70–78, 82–87, 140–47; equality of, with sellers, questioned, 41–43, 73–74, 87. SEE ALSO Caveat Emptor; Consumerism; Sellerism

C & H Sugar claims, 137
Campbell's Soup claim, 189
Canada's control of puffery, 200–201
Carnation instant breakfast claim, 133
Carpenter, Gregory S., 184
Carraccas cocoa claim, 49
Carson, Johnny, 171–72
Carter's Little Liver Pills claim, 161
Case, Eugene, 150, 222
"Catch 22" for advertisers, 193
Cattle claims, 33, 53
Caveat emptor: definition, development, and application, 29–33, 35–37, 39–46, 47–48, 52–55, 61, 68–69, 75, 84, 86, 87, 118, 140, 141–44, 146, 162–63, 164–65, 176–77, 192, 202–3, 209,

222; as foundation of sellerism, 29; contrasted to rules outside marketplace, 44–45, 84, 87; modern rejection of, 45, 52–54, 61, 118, 192, 202–3; persistence of, in today's law, though called "dead," 46, 68, 84, 86, 162, 176, 222; leading case of, in America, 48; most unfair aspect of, 55; most absolute form of, 143–44, 146. SEE ALSO Accidental events; Legalized lying; Sellerism
Caveat reader, 223
Caveat venditor, 41, 43
Chandelor. SEE *Chandelor v. Lopus* (Table of Cases)
Chesterfield claim, 131
Chicago Tribune claim, 199
Children, claims made to, 6, 148, 155, 217
Church. SEE Roman Catholic Church
Cigar claim, 161
Cigarettes: claims of; 100, 131; warning message on, 101
Civil law (Roman), 31, 33, 43
Civil law (modern). SEE Criminal law
Clairol claim, 102, 120–21
Clark, Judge, 120
Clorox claim, 188
Cloves claim, 49
Coffee claim (nonbitterness), 183
Coke, Lord, 43, 202, 204
Colgate claims. SEE Colgate, *Colgate v. FTC, FTC v. Colgate* (Table of Cases)
"Coliseum" commercial, 105–10, 215
Colt, four-year-old, claim, 50
Common law: of early English kings, 33–35, 43, 53; of cases (not statutes), 44, 51, 67, 69, 79, 80,

Common law (*continued*)
91–97, 115–16, 119, 124–25,
131, 134, 135, 180, 197, 198, 204,
210, 219, 222, 223
Consumers. SEE Buyers
Consumerism: trend toward, and
impact of, 4, 8, 27–28, 31, 38–39,
45–46, 47–48, 52, 57–58, 59, 60–61,
64, 66–67, 80, 92, 93, 97, 112,
113, 144–47, 163, 176, 192, 222;
defined, 27. SEE ALSO Sellerism
Consumer Reports, 223
Consumer research on effects of
puffery. SEE Puffery
Copeland, Senator, 127
Corrective advertising, 224
Courts of Appeal, U.S.: inconsistent
rulings by, 121–22, 180
Craft guilds, 30, 31, 164
Credit claims, 63, 71
Crest toothpaste claim, 24
Criminal law, distinguished from
civil law, 95
Crocker, Betty, 173

Dancerina doll claim, 225
Danish pastry, 158–59, 161, 223
Davis, Justice, 44
D.D.D. Prescription claim, 97
Dealer's talk. SEE Puffery
Deceit. SEE Misrepresentation,
fraudulent
Deception (deceit, misrepresentation), deceptive claims: not
found in puffery, but should
be, 3–4, 6–7, 11, 12–13, 24, 26,
46, 124–37, 139–40, 151, 176–94;
legal in earlier era, 4, 29; not
always present when falsity
present, 4, 5–11, 28–29; found
illegal by law today, 5, 8, 90–112;
sometimes subjectively present
when falsity not present, 5–11,
21, 97–99; difficult to identify,

6–8, 11, 102–4, 112, 174; proper
standard for identifying harm,
8–9; responsible party difficult
to identify, 9–10; actions of
FTC toward, 60, 67, 90–112,
134–37, 147–50, 155–56, 159–64,
168–74, 179–80; identified at
FTC by mere potential, 93,
96–98, 101; identified in Printers'
Ink statute, 95–96; based on
overall impression, 99–100;
occurring through omission,
99–101; determined by surveying
consumers, 104–10; determined
by choice of reasonable person
standard or ignorant person
standard, 113–23. SEE ALSO Falsity,
Federal Trade Commission;
Material nature of claims;
Misrepresentation; Puffery,
effects of
DeCoux, John, 114
Dingell, John D., Rep., 220
Distrust. SEE Buyers, trust and
distrust by
Dove soap, 225
Dr. Scholl's claim, 148
Drug advertisers' claims, 88, 97–99

Easy-Off and Easy-On claims, 225
Electric belts and insoles claim, 124
Eli Lilly claim, 25
Ellenborough, Lord, 55, 73–74, 178,
205, 211
Encyclopedia claims, 117–19
English law: as source of American
law, 29, 43, 47, 54, 56, 64, 65–66,
69, 70–71, 81, 115
Equality of buyers and sellers. SEE
Buyers, equality of with sellers

Face cream claim, 120
Factual puffery. SEE Puffery

Falsity, false claims, 3–4, 5–11, 12, 24, 26, 28–30, 32–36, 42–46, 49, 58, 62–65, 67, 68–83, 86–88, 91–93, 95, 97–100, 104, 108, 110, 112, 115–16, 118, 121–22, 125, 128–34, 136, 151–53, 155–56, 158, 161, 163–65, 167–69, 171, 175, 178–79, 186, 188–89, 193–94, 197, 198, 199, 206, 207, 209, 210, 211, 215, 218, 223; easier than deception to identify, 8; obvious falsity, 8, 9–10, 12, 24, 45, 64, 118, 139–50, 151, 153, 156, 159, 162, 175, 176, 186, 221; technically-required falsity, 167, 171. See also Deception; Misrepresentation; Material nature of claims
Federal Trade Commission, 6, 8, 25, 46, 88, 192, 197, 214; relationship to warranty law of, 59, 60; relationship to misrepresentation law of, 67; general procedures of, regarding deceptive claims, 90–123, 202, 213; and puffery, 79, 124–38, 179–80, 185, 189, 199, 200, 208, 219, 220; use of reasonable person and ignorant person standards, 113–23, 215, 217; and 1983 Policy Statement on Deception, 122–23, 134–35; and obvious falsity, 147–50; and social-psychological misrepresentations, 155–56; and literally misdescriptive names, 159–62, 163, 223, 224; and mock-ups, 168–71, 173–75, 224
Firestone claims, 136–37
Fitzherbert, Anthony, 29, 31, 32, 35, 40, 202
Fonblanque, 43
Ford, H. Ross, Jr., 211
Ford claims, 58, 187
Fraud. See Misrepresentation, fraudulent

Galbreath, John, & Co.: claim, 88
Gasoline octane disclosure, 101
Geer, Peter, 25
General Mills claim, 173
George Washington University students' petition to FTC, 98
Geritol claim, 101
Germany's control of puffery, 127, 201
Gibson, Chief Justice, 50, 52, 54
Gilmore, Grant, 37–38, 202
Goodyear: claim, 21; blimp, 147
Grain claim, 54–55
Grolier claim, 29
Grose, Justice, 71–73, 75, 178

Hamilton, Walton H., 29, 30, 31, 41, 42, 75
Hand, Augustus, Judge, 119, 120
Hand, Learned, Judge, 77, 118, 119, 125, 127–28, 179–80
Handler, Milton, 220
Havana Florida Co. claim, 161
Hearing examiner, 131–32, 219. See also Administrative Law Judge
Herschell, Lord, 65, 207
Hidden defects. See Latent detects
Hinkes, Harry R., administrative law judge, 215
Holmes, Oliver W., Justice, 44–45, 76, 87, 89, 198
Holt, Lord, 47–48, 52, 62, 203, 204, 208
Honda claim, 152–53
Hops claim, 55–56
Horses, matters involving, 29, 31, 35, 38, 50, 70, 140, 141, 208, 221
Hot Wheels claim, 198
House of Lords, 52
Hubbard, Justice, 74–75
Humphreys, William E., FTC commissioner, 125
Hyatt hotels. See Ramada claims

Ignorant person standard. SEE Federal Trade Commission

Images in advertising. SEE Social-psychological misrepresentations

Implications (implied meanings) of ad messages, 8, 13, 18, 21–23, 24, 36, 51, 55, 67, 69, 70, 71, 73, 80–81, 86–87, 93, 97, 98, 99, 105–6, 108, 110, 125, 127, 128–29, 130, 133, 134–35, 136, 149, 150, 152, 155, 162, 167, 168, 170, 171, 174, 176–77, 178, 181–83, 185, 186, 187–90. SEE ALSO Opinion; Puffery; Warranties, implied

"Implied superiority" claims, 183

Individualism: philosophy of, 41

Innocent misrepresentation. SEE Misrepresentanon

Inspection of advertised goods: opportunity and obligation of buyers. SEE Buyers

Ipana claim, 128–29

"Irrelevant" claims, 184

ITT-Continental Baking Co., 98, 213

Jewelers' claims, 35, 82, 84–85, 86, 208

Johnny Lightning claim, 198

Joke claims. SEE Spoof claims

Jones, Mary Gardiner (FTC Commissioner), 25, 134, 150

Jordan, Michael, 147

Kava coffee claim, 174

Keeton, W. Page. SEE Prosser, William L.

Kellogg claim, 24

Kent, James, Justice, 43, 48, 50–51, 74, 178, 202, 208, 209

King's common law. SEE Common law

Kintner, Earl W., 207

Kirkpatrick, Clayton, 199

Kleenex, 154

Kodak claim, 23

Kraft claims, 8, 198

Laches. SEE Misrepresentation, negligent

Lamm, Judge, 145–46

Lanham Trademark Act, 137–38

Latent (hidden) defects, 30–34, 36, 43, 54–57, 142, 145

Lawless traders, 31–32

Law merchant, 31, 33

Legalized lying. SEE Puffery

Lifebuoy claim, 225

Light bulb disclosures, 101, 133

Lilly, Eli, claim, 25

Liquor names protected, 162

Literally misdescriptive names, 12, 158–66, 169, 175, 176, 223

Lopus. SEE *Chandelor v. Lopus* (Table of Cases)

Lottery tickets claim, 203

"Lumberyard explanation," 164–65

McDonald's claim, 165, 223

McMahon, Ed, 171

"Made in USA" claim, 159

Madras claim, 161

Mail fraud statute, 79

Marmola claims, 104

Marriott hotels. SEE Ramada claims

Mason, Commissioner, 217

Material nature of claims, 77, 81, 82, 97, 132, 145, 148, 149, 150, 199, 209, 213, 220

Mattress claim, 125–26

Meat, mock-up of, 172

Mennen deodorant claims, 182

Middle Ages, 29–31, 33, 41, 53

Milan hats claim, 163–64

Miller, Gale T., 217

Miller, James C., 220

Milwaukee Journal, 10

"Miracle ingredient" claim, 88

Misrepresentation, 10, 12, 32, 38, 45, 48, 52, 61, 62–67, 70, 87, 115, 118, 179, 197, 208, 210, 221, 222; social-psychological, 12, 151–57, 159, 163, 175, 176; relation of, to warranty law and FTC actions, 67, 92–96, 102, 104, 109, 111, 126, 130, 131, 132, 210; limitations of, for opinion and puffery statements, 68, 80, 86–87, 121, 125, 126, 134–35, 199, 207, 218; relation of, to obvious falsity, 140–48, 150; of names, 158–66; through mock-ups, 167–75. SEE ALSO Deception; Falsity

Misrepresentation, fraudulent (also called fraud), 10, 33–35, 39–40, 42–43, 45, 52, 62–66, 69–72, 78–79, 116, 118, 201, 203, 208, 209, 221; known in early law as deceit, 4, 33, 39, 64, 70, 73–74, 77, 82, 140, 201, 221; defined, 32, 34, 63–64, 73–74, 93, 206, 207, 211; relationship to opinion claims, 73–76, 81–83, 85, 86, 177–79, 210, 214

Misrepresentation, innocent (strict liability), 34, 62, 66, 93; relation of, to warranty law, 66

Misrepresentation, negligent, 64–66, 93, 115; called "Laches" in early law, 71

Mock-ups, 12, 132, 167–75, 176, 224

Model statutes, 51, 95, 190

"Multa fidem promissa levant," 76

Mushroom-growing claim, 130

Nader, Ralph, 98

Naked, or nude assertions. SEE Bare assertions

Names. SEE Literally misdescriptive names

National Commmission on Egg Nutrition claim, 162

National Conference of Commissioners on Uniform State Laws, 190

Negligence, 43–44, 56, 64, 65, 69, 70, 71, 82, 94, 115, 117, 145, 177, 208, 217; contributory, 115, 216, 221; in manufacturing, 206

Negligent misrepresentation. SEE Misrepresentation

Nestle's claim, 21–22, 136

N.H.A. complex claim, 130

Obvious falsity. SEE Falsity

Octane ratings disclosure, 101

Ogilvy, David, 193

Olde Frothingslosh beer claims, 114–15, 121, 122, 147

Old Golds claim, 100

Opinion or value claims. SEE Puffery

Opportunity of buyers to inspect goods. SEE Buyers

Origin of goods, claim of, 137, 158, 160, 162

Ownership. SEE Title

Oxen claim, 47–48

Parker, Chief Judge, 100

Parker, Chief Justice, 49

Peachum wood, 42, 54

Pennsylvania, unusual interpretation of warranty law, 50, 51, 52

Pfizer claim, 99

Pie size claim, 165

Pine, California white, claim, 161

Pirenne, Henri: *Economic and Social History of Medieval Europe*, 201

Pittsburgh Brewing Co., 114

Placebos, 37, 124

Playboy claim, 152

Plyhide claim, 158–59

Polaroid claim, 22–23

Potter, David, 222

Preston, Ivan L.: criticism of realtor ad, 87–88; FTC witness, 102–10; Wisconsin hearing witness, 110–12; experience with literally misdescriptive name, 164, 166; correspondence with AT&T, 189

Price comparison claim, 110–12

Printers' Ink model statute, 95–96, 218

Procter and Gamble, 23

Prosser, William L., 38, 65, 179, 221

Puerto Rico rums claim, 24

Puffery: identification of, defined, 3, 12, 21, 198–99, 218; examples of, 3–4 13–20, 176, 177, 185–90; defined in expanded way to include related claim categories, 12, 139; quintessential form, 13; categories of, and their significance for assessment, 13–21, 185–90; called "dealer's talk" (also sales talk, seller's talk), 76, 85; earliest occurrence of term "puffery," 81; contrasted to opinions-as-to-fact, 84, 103; extinct category called "factual puffery," 89; called hyperbole, 134; categories of claims that are not puffery, 186; contrasted to "counter-puffery" by buyers, 221

Puffery, legal treatment of: treated separately from facts because explicitly nonfactual, 4, 11, 12, 21–22, 68–79, 127, 134–37, 177, 190–91; called nondeceptive and harmless even when spoken in bad faith because buyers know to distrust and not rely on it, 4, 24–26, 69–79, 84–87, 135, 177–79; . . . and because buyers distrust and do not rely on it, 4, 76–79, 85, 135, 147, 179; reflective of sellerism and caveat emptor, 27, 29, 46, 87, 147, 176–77, 192;

originated in early English law of opinion and value claims (including bare [naked, nude] assertions), 68–74, 177, 207; further developed in U.S. law, 74–79; treatment by contemporary warranty law (as opinion and value claims), 67, 79, 190–93; treatment by contemporary misrepresentation law, 67, 81–87; later separated from rules covering opinion and value claims, 78, 80–87; treatment by FTC, 79, 120–22, 123, 124–37, 150, 179–80, 200, 219, 220; relationship to reasonable and ignorant standards, 116, 120–22, 123, 127–30; treatment by other countries, 200–201; treatment by Lanham Act, 137–38

Puffery, criticism of current legal treatment of: as usually being implicitly factual, false, deceptive, and harmful, 3–4, 7, 16, 21–26, 69, 87–89, 136, 153, 176–94; as soft-core deception, 4; as legalized lying, 4, 24, 29, 62, 73, 76; as not deserving legal immunity, 4, 87, 136, 176–94; as interfering with consumerism trend, 4, 147, 176; as supported by consumer research, 180–85; as producing "Puffery Implication," 189

Raid roach killer claim, 225

Railroad bond claim, 76

Ramada hotel claims, 148–49

Rank & Son Buick claim, 9

Rapid Shave claim, 132, 169–71, 172

Reader's Digest cigarette story, 100

Reasonable person standard. SEE Federal Trade Commission

Reebok claim, 152

Rejuvenescence claim, 120
Rent claims, 62–63, 70–71, 80
Research in support of removing
   of puffery's legal immunity. SEE
   Puffery
Restatement of the Law of Torts, 81, 84,
   85, 86, 134, 146, 222
Reweaving claim, 131
Robertson, Miss, 63
Rolle's Abridgement rule, 73
Roman Catholic Church, 30, 31, 41;
   canon law of, 31
Romans, 29–30, 31, 43, 201
Roquefort cheese claim, 162
Rotfeld, Herbert J., and Kim B.
   Rotzoll research, 181

Sale of Goods Act. SEE Warranties
Sales talk, seller's talk. SEE Puffery
Sandpaper claim. SEE shaving and
   shaving cream claims
Schlitz claims, 154
"Scout" sleeping bags claim, 161
Secret deodorant claim, 129
Sellerism, 27–46, 47, 53, 57, 75,
   80, 112, 145, 147; contrasted to
   consumerism, 27, 28; defined,
   27, 29, elements remaining
   today, including as support for
   puffery, 28, 29, 38, 39, 46, 68ff,
   147, 192. SEE ALSO Caveat emptor;
   Consumerism
Seller's talk, seller's statements,
   sales talk. SEE Puffery
Semantics, 22, 192, 200
Sewing machine claims, 130
Shaving or shaving cream claims,
   132–33, 169–71, 172
Shoe insert and innersole claims,
   130, 131
"Simplex commendatio non
   obligat," 209
Six Month Floor Wax claim, 159
Smucker's ice cream mock-up, 171

Smithsonian, 23
Social-psychological misrepresenta-
   tions. SEE Misrepresentation
Speidel, Richard E., 192
Spillane, Mickey, 225
Spoof or joke claims, 147–50, 186
State Farm claim, 3, 181
Stone China claim, 158–59, 163
Strawberries claim, 111–12
Strenio, Andrew (FTC
   commissioner), 136–37
Strict liability. SEE Misrepresentation
Students Against Misleading
   Enterprises (SAME), 98
Students Opposed to Unfair
   Practices (SOUP), 224
Substantiation requirement for
   claims, 99, 136–37, 189, 213
Sudden Change facial lotion claim,
   225
Sunoco (Sun Oil) claims, 102–3,
   104–10
Swan, Judge, 120
Sweden's control of puffery, 201
Swim-Ezy swimming claim, 122,
   220

Technically-required falsity. SEE
   Falsity
Tenant claims. SEE Rent claims
Term for years, claim, 69
Title (ownership), claims of, 47,
   53–54
Toothpaste claims, 6, 23, 128–29, 168
Tranway claim, 64
Trust. SEE Buyers, trust and distrust
   by

Un-Burn claim, 98–99
Underwear (Winsted) claims,
   159–60
Uniform Commercial Code. SEE
   Warranties
Uniform Sales Act. SEE Warranties

Uniqueness claims, 98, 185, 213
U. S. Steel Building claim, 87–88
University of Wisconsin, 105

Vacuum cleaner claim, 125
Value claims. See Puffery
Virginia hams claim, 161–62
Vivarin claim, 155–56
Volvo claim, 198

Wagon claims, 70, 74, 141, 174–5
Warranties: 32–33, 34–38, 40, 42–43,
   45, 47–61, 62, 69, 142, 179, 208,
   209; definitions, rules, and types
   of, 32, 35, 36, 43, 48–51, 52, 57–60,
   66–67, 69, 74, 79, 199, 204; implied,
   52–57; limitations of, for opinion
   and puffery, 68, 74, 79, 80, 209,
   210; in Uniform Sales Act, 51–52,
   56, 57, 60, 66, 204; in Sale of Goods
   Act, 52; in Uniform Commercial
   Code, 52, 56, 57, 59, 60, 66,
   190–93, 199, 204–5, 210; related
   to FTC proceedings, 59, 60, 93;

relation of, to misrepresentation,
   61, 66–67, 221; relation of,
   to obvious falsity, 140, 143,
   146–47, 208, 221, 222; relation
   of, to social-psychological
   misrepresentations, 152;
   proposed change in limitations
   of, for puffery, 190–93
Waste silk claim, 55, 205
"Weasel" claim, 110
Wheeler, Senator Burton K., 127
Williams, Herbert A., 9–10, 24, 43,
   115, 139, 140, 147
Williston, Samuel, 50, 65, 204
Wine names, protected, 162
Wisconsin, State of: hearings on
   price claims 110–11
Wisconsin Supreme Court, 9–10
Wonder Bread claims, 98–99, 155–56
Wood, load of, claim, 70, 72–73,
   140–41, 143, 147
Wool claims, 159–60

Zerex claim, 174